WHEN THE WORLD
DIDN'T END

WHEN THE WORLD DIDN'T END

A MEMOIR

GUINEVERE TURNER

CROWN

NEW YORK

Copyright © 2023 by Guinevere Turner

Published in the United States by Crown,
an imprint of Random House, a division of
Penguin Random House LLC, New York.

CROWN and the Crown colophon are registered
trademarks of Penguin Random House LLC.

LIBRARY OF CONGRESS CATALOGING-IN-PUBLICATION DATA
Names: Turner, Guinevere, author.
Title: When the world didn't end / by Guinevere Turner.
Description: New York : Crown, [2023] |
Identifiers: LCCN 2022057073 (print) | LCCN 2022057074 (ebook) |
ISBN 9780593237595 (hardcover) | ISBN 9780593237601 (ebook)
Subjects: LCSH: Turner, Guinevere. | Fort Hill Community (Organization)—
Biography. | Ex-cultists—United States—Biography.
Classification: LCC BP605.F67 T8 2023 (print) | LCC BP605.F67 (ebook) |
DDC 209.0973—dc23/eng/20230213
LC record available at https://lccn.loc.gov/2022057073
LC ebook record available at https://lccn.loc.gov/2022057074

Printed in the United States of America on acid-free paper

crownpublishing.com

9 8 7 6 5 4 3 2 1

FIRST EDITION

Book design by Barbara M. Bachman

For Annalee,
    and for all my sisters

WHEN SOMETHING WE LOVE IS TAKEN FROM US, WE LOVE it more. So it was for me when I was cut off from one world and forced into another that felt strange and dangerous. My way of coping with the loss was to preserve with a passion every detail of where I came from, to recite over and over to myself a list of the people I missed, to tell myself the stories of the world I left behind with a ferocious will to savor and protect my memories. I did this through writing, and through reading and rereading the diaries I'd already written, desperate to keep it all alive, sure that I would go back to it someday, and hell-bent on being worthy of a return.

With my childhood diaries as an anchor, I have written this book from the perspective of my six- to eighteen-year-old self—only what I saw and knew and felt at the time, resisting the urge to let my adult hindsight interfere or comment. I don't write for any reason except that writing is what I do. It is my response to everything, and I'm grateful to the people who first put a diary and pen into my hands. There have been points in my life when keeping a record of what was happening to me felt like the only power I had.

WHEN THE WORLD
DIDN'T END

CHAPTER 1

*"We have not gathered here to isolate ourselves from the rest
of the world but rather to establish a greater order within that
order, an order born of willing cooperation and necessary
discipline."*

— MELVIN LYMAN, 1969

ON JANUARY 5, 1975, THE WORLD WAS GOING TO END. ALL the World People were going to be wiped off the face of the earth, but not us, because a spaceship was going to come and take us to Venus, where we would live. This seemed completely plausible to my six-year-old self—exciting, even. We were going to live on the planet of love!

I spent the day dreamily wandering the grounds of our Los Angeles property, knowing I would never see this place again. I was feeling sentimental and melancholy, but not really. Really I was humming Billie Holiday's "Sentimental and Melancholy" to myself and enjoying the idea of feeling the "sugar coated misery" she sang about. I started upstairs in the Big House, where most of the adults stayed, and where our Lord, Melvin, lived sequestered away. The house was full of people; I could hear murmurs and muted footsteps from its corners, but it was always in a hush during the day—Melvin slept from sunrise to sundown and was rarely seen by anyone but Jessie. Jessie, our Queen, had her own elegant bedroom on that floor, with a four-poster bed and windows that looked out onto the giant lawn. Upstairs from this was the Studio, where kids weren't allowed unless we were listening to a "tape," which is what we called the semiannual curated recordings Melvin released to us—the communities—complete with liner notes for each compilation.

Passing a framed photograph of Melvin looking intensely into the camera, his eyes kind, wise, and a little haunted, I tiptoed down the stairs and felt happy that I would never have to vacuum them again. The smell of coffee and cigarettes wafted from the kitchen, and the twelve-seat dining room table gleamed, reflecting the sparkling chandelier that hung above it. Everything was, as always, perfectly in its place and very still.

Outside, I wandered to the swimming pool, crouching to run my fingers through the turquoise water, the smell of chlorine mixing with the fragrance of the jasmine vines that clung to the twelve-foot fence surrounding our property. To my left, the tennis court, where I'd first learned to ride a bike. Behind me, Melvin's pyramid, high on stilts and looming against the sky, the ladder leading up to its entrance three times as tall as me. I'd never been inside, but I knew it was where he went to meditate for hours on end. If you stood underneath it and looked up, you could see the slats that formed its floor and, through them, the deep-blue velvet cushions that were made for him to sit on.

On the way to the Kids' House, I passed the koi pond and stopped to watch their white-and-orange bodies glide around under the water. I wondered if animals were going to be taken to Venus too or if these fish would just boil inside their little habitat. But I didn't dwell—we'd all been looking forward to this day for weeks, and there was much to do before sundown.

Now I hurried down the narrow path, past our own pyramid—a much bigger one than Melvin's, and only a few feet off the ground—and into the Kids' House, where Carolee hovered over a counter covered with twenty thick slices of homemade bread, slathering each with peanut butter. Frida was at another counter, spreading jelly on slices and handing them to Jackie, who wielded a bread knife, putting the two sides together and cutting each in half. They were singing "Going Home," Jackie and Frida harmonizing beautifully, with Carolee humming along, distracted. "Going home . . . I'm just going home . . . It's not far, just close by, through an open door."

Over our heads was the soft thud of kids' feet running down the hall. Someone was playing the harmonica in the living room, and I could faintly hear an eruption of girls' laughter trickling down from one of the upstairs bedrooms. I stood there in the kitchen—I loved "Going Home," and it was the perfect song for the moment. I joined in for the end. "All the friends we knew . . ." imitating an emotional Olivia de Havilland at the end of the film *The Snake Pit*.

Carolee pushed her long brown hair out of her face with the side of her arm, her hands otherwise occupied, and noticed me for the first time.

"Where have you been, you little space cadet?" she asked affectionately. "Go round up the kids and tell them it's lunchtime and after that it's baths and get your spaceship clothes on." I loved Carolee. She was the only adult who slept here in the Kids' House with us and one of the only adults who rarely raised her voice and was generous with hugs and lenient with rules. "And take that laundry basket upstairs—you girls get it all folded up before we eat."

I could barely carry the basket overflowing with clean clothes, but I hoisted it onto my hip and made my way up the curved staircase. The strip of carpet that ran along the middle of the terra-cotta steps was worn in a way that only twenty-five kids running up and down it daily could do, and the curved wall bore the smudges of our grubby hands. Samantha and Corrina hurried past me down the stairs, each holding several dolls, in deep conversation about which they would choose to bring to Venus.

I stopped on the second-floor landing to rest, putting the laundry basket down, and decided I wanted to spend one last moment in the beloved room on the third floor, which was a turret—a circular single room—and a place where mostly just the girls hung out. Up its skinny staircase with the basket once again, I dumped all the clothes on the floor and sat on top of the pile, contemplating my favorite thing in the house: a dollhouse we'd made out of three tiers of curved shelves, which took up most of one wall. We'd created an elaborate tiny world, spending hours on the most minute of details—a bedspread made of a fabric scrap but finished around the edges with intricate stitches; a dining room rug made from yarn, braided and carefully looped into an oval that could rest perfectly in the palm of your hand. I was especially proud of the toilet-paper roll I'd made, no bigger than my pinky nail, crafted by slicing ever so cautiously up the side of a regular roll of toilet paper and rolling it around a toothpick; I'd turned the three-ply into one-ply, realizing that the life-sized thickness just wouldn't do. I stood up and began to fold the laundry into two piles—girls' clothes and boys' clothes—vaguely wondering why this task was necessary, given that the world was ending.

All of us had been told to choose our favorite toy and put on our favorite clothes and then wait for the spaceship to come. I decided on my party dress, light blue with red flowers, and a black-and-white stuffed dog that was made of rabbit fur. After dinner, we all sat in the living room and waited.

I of course did not know that Venus is a place with no water and that its surface temperature is hot enough to melt lead, but the adults around me, many of them college-educated, must have known this. Years later I asked my mother, "Mom—you must have known humans can't live on Venus. How did you reconcile that in your head?"

She took a deep breath and let out an epic sigh. "It's complicated," she said, and walked out of the room.

I don't know what it was like for her in the San Francisco community, where she lived at the time, but here in L.A. we were giddy, barely able to sit still in our seats. This lasted for the first few hours, and then the kids got so squirrelly that we decided to go into the backyard and sit in the pyramid for a while. The smell of blooming jasmine surrounded us as we crouched through the small doorway of the pyramid one by one, sat cross-legged in a circle, and sang one note all together. We had practiced calling spaceships before, for hours on end, but tonight we really needed them to hear us. Our faces were pointed upward to the skylights where the four walls of the pyramid came to a point, and we stared at the stars as we sang. We would each hold on to the note until it felt like our lungs would burst, then take a deep breath and start again. The note we were singing would morph and mutate into a different note, but the sound never stopped. We took this very seriously, a solemn duty. There was no laughter and no joking around, but the sound was beautiful to me, like we could be one person. I wondered if Faedra, the only spirit us kids were allowed to talk to on the Ouija board, could hear us.

Once our voices became hoarse, we went back into the Kids' House and waited some more and, as the hours wore on, struggled to keep our eyes open. We weren't allowed to fall asleep—the spaceship would come at any minute, and the adults didn't want to have to waste time waking us up. Who knew how long it would wait for us after it landed? I was tucked into the corner of a giant green velvet couch, and I drew stars in the fabric with my index finger and then smoothed them away. I brushed the fur on my stuffed dog so that it stood up, then brushed it back down again. I made his floppy ears cover his eyes, then sleepily wondered, "How can a dog have the fur of a rabbit?" Normalynn, the oldest of us at fifteen, was sitting next to me, wearing a thin blouse with butterflies she'd embroidered up one sleeve. I leaned my head on her shoulder, drifting off, until she gently pinched me and I sat up straight again, opening my eyes wide in an attempt to make the lids feel less heavy. I dug my nails into my palms to stay awake. I started to doubt this choice of clothing I'd made, pulling the flowery fabric over my knees. I really liked to climb trees, and a dress wouldn't be very good for that. You needed something covering your legs so the bark didn't scratch you. You needed pants so everyone couldn't see your underwear once you were very high up. Were there trees on Venus?

The adults were also dressed nicely, the ladies all with a purse or bag of some kind sitting next to them, ready to go. They had started out the evening quite serious, shushing us, telling us to stay focused on the spaceship so it could find us, but with a buzz of expectation in the air. Now, as the first light of dawn started to show, the mood turned very tense, and they were speaking in low tones to each other, off in a corner so we couldn't hear. Some of the kids had fallen into deep sleep, and by this time no one bothered to wake them. The phone rang—well, not the phone but the intercom phone we used between houses on the property; we called it the buzzer—and now everyone was very awake. Maybe this was news from Melvin. He was, after all, the one who told us the spaceships were coming in the first place. I'd never thought to ask who told *him*. I wasn't clear, I realized, who would be flying these spaceships, but maybe whoever it was got sick or lost?

The most powerful adults in the Family were in the Big House, no doubt surrounding Melvin as they waited; here, there were only a few, mostly the women who took care of the kids. Marilyn, who had been conferring with some of the ladies, darted into the other room to answer the buzzer. We all waited, straining to hear what she was saying, but she was speaking softly and mostly listening.

About five minutes later she came into the room, and she looked like she'd been crying. "Melvin says . . ." she began, and then choked up a little. "Melvin says the spaceships aren't coming and the world isn't ending, because some of our souls aren't ready. We ruined it for him. He was ready, but now he's stuck here because some of us still have work to do."

I was certain it was me. We'd all been taught that Planet Earth was a school and that you were reincarnated back to it over and over until you learned your lesson. I personally had been told that I'd been here too many times, that I just hadn't learned whatever it was I was supposed to learn, and that I would have to keep coming back until I did. I can't remember not knowing this about myself and not living with the shame of it, and the mystery. "What *is* it?" I would hound myself. "I'm going to have to live this whole life and die and then have to come back *again* if I don't figure it out, and I'll come back and be surrounded by strangers." (This logic made sense to me at the time.) And now Melvin had said our souls weren't ready. Maybe it was just *my* soul that was dragging everyone else down. I looked around the room and some of the kids were crying, but some of the crying seemed forced and some of it seemed like they were just tired. Maybe they felt like their souls were perfectly ready and it wasn't fair they had to stay.

"Let's all just go to sleep," said Marilyn. "Come on, kids, get upstairs." We shuffled up the staircase to the bedrooms. I was in a room full of bunk beds, where most of the other girls slept too. It was a strange sensation walking into that room, because when I'd walked out of it last night, I imagined it would soon be in flames, as would the house, the city, and the world. But there was the bottom bunk where I slept, just as I had left it, neatly made, my nightgown folded and sitting on my pillow.

In the days that followed, we learned there would be some new rules. To honor the year the world was supposed to end, we would reset the date: 1975 was now the year 00. And we would stop using Daylight Savings Time—we would live with World Time and Our Time. This didn't have a huge impact on the kids, since we never left the properties, so there was no World Time to navigate. I'd never been to a doctor or to the movies, and adults went on their own to buy massive amounts of groceries once a week. They'd sent us to public school once, but we clung to each other in a cluster on the playground and were made fun of, and so that lasted only a few weeks.

The only real impact the new rules about time had on us was in the form of the *TV Guide*, which now had notes in the columns for things we were going to watch that looked like this: "10:00 O.T.," as if doing the math of one hour ahead or behind was too challenging, or no one could risk getting it wrong because it was now the law of the land.

Not that we were allowed to simply turn on the television. Quite the opposite. No kids were allowed to turn it on at all. There was no casual watching of TV shows, and definitely not the news. Melvin was a Red Sox fan and a Lakers fan, so the adults would sometimes watch those games. We watched some of the Olympics. Once in a while, the kids were permitted to watch *Sesame Street*, but it was an unpredictable exception. The *TV Guide* was important—essential, really—because of the Lord's List, which was a list of one hundred films compiled by Melvin. If any of those films were on TV, we had to watch them. To say that they were his "favorites" is not really accurate—it was more like these were the only movies he deemed worthy of watching at all. We weren't allowed to watch any others, and we didn't want to. The listings for these films were carefully marked in the *TV Guide*, and no matter what time they were showing, we were all required to watch.

This meant that, for example, we were once all woken at 2:00 A.M. to watch Bette Davis in the 1939 film *Dark Victory*. We were allowed to stay in our pajamas, but woe to the person who fell asleep during the movie. I was grumpy and disoriented when we shuffled into the living room to watch, but I was soon swept away by the character of Judith Traherne, with her impetuous attitude and glamorous hats, and had no trouble staying awake. This was not the first time I'd seen it, and I wept openly from the moment Judith starts to go blind until she lays her head down on her silky pillow to die, her best friend having run down the street in tears. I thought it was the saddest thing I'd ever seen.

It was also easy to stay awake that night during *Dark Victory* because Frida was on clicker duty, but she was fighting sleepiness and not always getting it right. Frida was one of Melvin's thirteen kids, but somehow she wasn't treated quite as special as his other kids. Maybe this was because her mother wasn't in the Family? We'd read about Rita in Melvin's book *Mirror at the End of the Road* and knew that she broke Melvin's heart. But where was she?

The clicker was a switch attached to the TV by a long wire, created so that when commercials came on, the sound could be muted instantly. It was someone's job—usually a kid's—to make sure that we didn't hear a nanosecond of a commercial but also didn't miss a single frame of the film. A high-pressure gig, especially if you were sleepy. Part of what was keeping me alert that night was that I was nervous for Frida, and so I was sitting on the floor next to her, glued to the TV so that I could nudge her if she wasn't on top of it. The stakes were high here: Commercials were pieces of the World, music and images that could seep into your soul and damage you, sully you, poison you in ways that you might not be able to recover from. I was very afraid of those commercials and always looked away from the TV when they were on—unless I was on clicker duty, of course. Then I would watch every commercial diligently, fingers poised around the long switch, the other hand clasped around the small metal box. I would count the commercials—it was usually three—and pride myself on knowing when the movie would come back on. This usually wasn't very hard, because the commercials were in color and most of the films on the Lord's List were in black-and-white.

Some of my favorite films on the list were *To Have and Have Not, Mr. Smith Goes to Washington,* and *The African Queen.* Truth be told, Bette Davis scared me a little, but I adored Katharine Hepburn, with her clipped way of speaking and her can-do attitude, and I was especially mesmerized by Lauren Bacall. When she leaned in the doorway and said, "Anybody got a match?" I swooned. I thought I might want to be her when I grew up.

Two films that weren't on the Lord's List were exceptions, for very different reasons. One was *The Wizard of Oz,* which was on TV once a year, around Easter. The adults were sentimental about it from their own childhoods, so the kids were allowed to watch it, and for me it was one of the highlights of the year. The Wicked Witch and her flying monkeys gave me nightmares, sure, but not as much as *Invasion of the Body Snatchers* had, and besides, it was all worth it for the dazzling Technicolor of the yellow brick road and the tearful goodbye when Dorothy finally gets to go home. I'd always thought, though, that it was rude the way she said to the Scarecrow, "I think I'll miss you most of all." Though I lived in this world where I rarely interacted with new people, and though I'd rarely been in public except for long road trips from one community to another, my life was full of goodbyes. People were always leaving and coming back, and you were never sure when you would see them next. Missing people was part of the fabric of my life, and the idea of telling someone you'd miss them *the most* seemed cruel. What about all the bonding she'd done with the Tin Man and the Cowardly Lion? I felt if anyone deserved special treatment it was the Tin Man, because after all she had helped him find his heart, and I'd been taught that your heart was much more important than your brain or your courage. We'd often be asked, "What's in your heart?" or be told we had a "dark heart," or that there was not enough heart in our words, our music, our deeds.

The other film that was important but was not on the Lord's List was *The Exorcist.* When *The Exorcist* was on, the kids were told to go to our rooms and stay there, because the devil was in the film, and we could never, under any circumstances, see it. But the adults would always watch it, somber afterward, talking about it into the wee hours. This "devil" we grew up with wasn't Satan with horns, ruling over hell. It was an amorphous threat, something out there that could take you over. It wasn't about whether you were good or bad—the devil was just around, waiting for an opportunity to seize your soul.

CHAPTER 2

I HAD LIVED LESS THAN A YEAR IN LOS ANGELES WHEN I WAS six and the world was going to end. By the time I was nine, I'd been in the community on the Farm in Kansas for more than two years, which was also where I'd lived from the ages of four to six.

This was how I understood the world at nine years old: Melvin was our leader, the Lord. He mostly stayed in the Los Angeles and Boston communities and didn't have much interaction with the kids. At least not us common kids, who were mostly the ones that weren't his. I'd never seen him in person, but framed photographs of him hung on the walls in most houses—a dark silhouette of him playing the banjo here, a close-up of his face staring at the camera there. Before I was born, the Family had a monthly magazine called *The Avatar*, and those were also often on display and usually had a photo of him on the cover. He'd written two books: *Autobiography of a World Savior* and *Mirror at the End of the Road*. We read these books like bibles, struggling to make sense of their philosophies and contradictions. I'd contemplated this passage from *Mirror at the End of the Road* many times:

JANUARY 1963, NEW YORK

We spend our whole lives carefully softstepping from stone to stone taking no risk of getting wet in the crossing and man I just believe in diving right in and seeing how deep the water is, how does it taste, is it cold, man I want to even dig drowning if I go in over my head and am very very tired of cooling it, stepping stones and being oh so careful not to splash any water on my fellow creekcrossers if I should feel like jumping in and going for a swim. I'm saying that there's only one trip to take and only one destination but man the variety of method is infinite. Hop, skip, run, jump, tiptoe, smile, scowl, laugh, cry, hesitate and consider, plan each advance, shut your eyes, run blindly, who cares. Just do it and enjoy it and if you can't enjoy it then don't complain and don't pass judgment and don't put it down because it's *your* trip and *your* choice and if you choose to swing you *can* swing.

This whole paragraph would be subject to harsh criticism if it were read analytically as it contains many seemingly contradictory statements but dig, what I'm saying will still come through because it's oh too simple and doesn't really require analogies and elaboration being only something we all already know but alas do so often forget. Don't you see that analysis and close examination proves nothing and changes nothing. A rainbow *is* if I see it and accept it but if I question it and really examine it closely to see if it *really* is it becomes bigger and bigger and soon disappears and what's left is Zob which is, by definition, me digging a rainbow up so close I can't even see it. Don't you see I have only one message and that it's too big to ever be penned and too small to ever be seen up close. Spend your life digging it or spend your life hiding from it but you're only spending the same thing: Time, and Hey Man, are you having a good time, don't put it off on God or country, I'm asking *you*.

So this just meant enjoy life? The freeness of this was such a sharp contrast to our actual lives, which were full of rules, chores, hierarchies, and very little individual choice. We were accused of "being on our own trip" or "being too self-involved" and lived with the constant specter of "not being in the right place" or "not being in touch with our souls." We lived with contradictions but weren't allowed to ask questions for fear of being asked, "Who the hell do you think you are?" We knew that Melvin lived in his separate chambers, played his music, sometimes came out to lead an acid trip for one of the adults. We knew that we weren't old enough to understand the true meaning of his words, but they were read to us anyway.

Jessie was the Queen, and she was the one who knew what everyone was doing and decided what would happen next. She had dark hair and deep-brown eyes and laughed easily with her raspy voice. She'd been "married" to Melvin once. ("Married" in the Family meant in a serious relationship, and people got married and then broke up a few years later all the time.) Melvin and Jessie had one child together, and since they were the two most powerful people, their daughter, Daria, was essentially our princess. Melvin and Jessie were usually in the same community together, and word of the ideas that came out of their conversations would trickle down to us.

Jessie believed that women should take care of men—that they should serve men so the men could be creative. So that is how it was: Women served men, kids served adults, and everybody served Jessie.

Word traveled fast among the communities about what Jessie said, what she was listening to, who was sick, who was pregnant, who had an acid trip and how it went. "Jessie says" was a constant refrain. It could be followed by "it's time for the kids to take more responsibility for themselves" or "Laura is on her own trip too much these days" or "she's going to stay a little longer on the Vineyard" or "everyone needs to listen—really listen—to 'Yesterday's Tears' again," which was one of Melvin's tapes. A series of black-and-white photos of Jessie hung in the big Farm House kitchen, over the table where we ate dinner every night. In these photos she looked very young and her hair was cut short. A cigarette burned in an ashtray in front of her. In one photo she was laughing, in one she was staring balefully into the camera, and in one she had tears running down her face and a small sad smile. It was commonly known that these were photos of the first time she did acid with Melvin and that he'd taken the photos. It disturbed me that she was crying, that she could cry, that she had ever cried. It didn't fit with the image of the Queen I knew, an all-powerful, almost mystical being who was in constant touch with God (Melvin) and knew what was right for everyone. Jessie said a lot of things, almost daily, but they were certainly never about me.

When I was nine, I heard Jessie's and Melvin's names all the time, but they weren't physically a part of my world. I was happy to be one of the rough-and-tumble Farm Kids, and I spent a lot of time trying not to stand out—to behave well, avoid punishment, and do what I was told. Punishment could mean being sent to sit in a closet for hours, or having a bowl of cereal dumped on your head, or—the worst one— being shunned, which meant no one was allowed to talk to you. We were slapped, spanked, or just given endless angry talks full of impossible questions to answer, like "Where is your soul?"

I'd made up a scenario in my head in which I was the Princess of the Universe, and everyone knew it, but they weren't allowed to tell me until I turned eighteen or until I learned whatever lesson I still had to learn on earth. In my imagination, it was so important that I didn't know who I was that people would get in trouble if they accidentally gave it away. I imagined that right before I walked into a room, people whispered to each other, "She's coming, she's coming—don't look at her or she'll know," and this was why sometimes no one looked at me or talked to me. I took comfort in knowing that my day would come.

CHAPTER 3

M Y MOTHER, BESS, JOINED THE LYMAN FAMILY IN 1967 WHEN
she was nineteen and pregnant with me. My father was her boyfriend
in high school, and I never knew him or anything about him. Once, I
went to the dentist, and while I was sitting in the waiting room I wondered, "What if the dentist is my father? Would I recognize him,
would he recognize me?" If he was, we didn't. My speculation was
more scientific than emotional.

Our idea of family was different. There were a couple of kids in the
Family like me—who only had one parent with us—but it didn't mat-
ter much, because we were all related, really. My mother had my sister
Annalee in 1975, and Annalee's father, Libes, was also the father of
Irene, whose mother was Alison, whose sister was Marilyn, whose kids
Aaron and Corrina were Jimmy's, who had Bellina with Melinda, and
Melinda had Katie and DeeDee with Joey, while Alison had Gabriel
with George, and George had Cybele with Jessie, who had Anthony
with David and then Daria with Melvin, who had thirteen kids with
six different women. My aunt Nell—my mother's sister—was also in
the Lyman Family, and she had Pete with Geoffrey, who had Tom with
Susan, who had Matthew with a man we didn't know. There was a
clear hierarchy among the adults, and though it was ever shifting, two
things were very clear to me: My mother was never anywhere near the
top, and Jessie was, and always would be, the Queen of all of us.

Most of the sixty kids in the Family were separated from their biological parents early. There was no explicit reason given for this—it was just how things were. My mother and I were rarely in the same community. My sister Annalee was seven years younger than me, and we'd never been in the same place long enough to form a bond.

As an adult, I once said to my mother, "Did you know that one of my earliest memories is lining up in the basement of one of the houses on Fort Hill with all of the other girls to get our ears pierced? I remember a man in a lab coat and being scared because the girls were all crying after they got their ears pierced and I was like ninth or tenth in line and didn't even really understand what ear piercing was." My tone was vaguely accusatory. Her response was distracted, and not a little dismissive. "What?" she scoffed. "I wasn't there." That's the thing I remember most about my mother while growing up—she wasn't there. By the time I was three, she'd moved to the San Francisco community, leaving me behind on Fort Hill, where there were lots of other kids. She hadn't been the person taking care of us anyway.

I was born in Boston, shipped off to the Farm at four, and shuttled from the community in San Francisco to Los Angeles and back to the Farm for the next five years.

The truth was that I hardly knew my mother. Once in a while, I would have to talk to her on the phone. Why or when seemed arbitrary—I remember standing awkwardly in a kitchen, overheard by various people as I struggled to make conversation. There were threadbare jokes we had from our limited experience together and long silences. Tiny beads of sweat would form on the back of my neck. I'd talk about a fish that was caught that day or how we went swimming. I would desperately wish for someone to call me away to do some chore so the phone call would be over. Luckily, these excruciating conversations happened only every few months, and she would usually end them by saying, "Well, I don't want to run up the phone bill" or "I better go help the ladies get dinner on the table." I'd heave a sigh of relief as I handed the phone to an adult, instantly putting the experience out of my mind and diving back into my real life.

I didn't love her or hate her; I only felt a slight anxiousness that there was a mother/daughter way of being and I was failing at it. Probably because I'd never seen it. I simply had nothing to say to her and I never missed her.

My mother was Carolee; my mother was Lou; my mother was Jessie.

On the Farm in Kansas, the adults around me were the ones who seemed to wish they were with Melvin and Jessie but weren't important enough or in favor enough at the moment. But people were always coming and going from one community to the next, especially the adults. We didn't question this or feel sad about it. Jessie had a way of choosing people to be where she was on a whim, instantly elevating their status. It was an honor, if a tenuous one.

My favorite ladies were of course Carolee, with her easy, soft laugh, and Lou, who used to be a nun and was very tough and no-nonsense but never mean. She'd tell you to shut up, but usually you realized she was right. She gave rough hugs and then told you to get your ass to bed. She never had a man attached to her.

The kids I was closest to were Katie and DeeDee, who were twins my age and Geminis like me. (Most of the kids didn't have individual birthdays—instead there was a birthday each month for all kids of each astrological sign. So I always had a birthday with Katie and DeeDee.) Like me, they didn't have much status in the Family. I felt perpetually jealous of them—how cool to be Geminis *and* twins, like Super Geminis. I always had a feeling of being the third wheel around them. But they liked to get up to mischief, and that was fun. Corrina was another friend—she was shy and a little goofy, and looked like a frog when she cried. Then there was Samantha, who was a little older than me. Samantha and I had a secret game called The King, which we played late at night, after lights-out. We'd gather dolls and make a boy doll the King, then invent vaguely sexual games for him and the girl dolls. We never talked about it during the day, but often while we were all getting ready for bed, we'd whisper, "Do you want to play The King?" and we'd wait until everyone was asleep and play in hushed tones, tented under a blanket with a flashlight, until we fell asleep with dolls strewn around us.

Her younger sister, Ruby, who was my age, was also my friend.

Their dad was Eben, whose drawings and paintings were in *Mirror at the End of the Road*. Eben was a gaunt man who didn't speak much, but he was untouchable in a way, because he was Melvin's friend before the Family even existed. In *Mirror*, Melvin wrote letters to Eben, joking about always spelling his name wrong and expressing longing for him when they were apart. Samantha and Ruby's mother was Sophie, who was also the mother of Melvin's three oldest kids—Normalynn, Jackie, and Obray—so even though Samantha and Ruby were here on the Farm with us, they had a slightly elevated status. Ruby's name used to be Kalil, but then they changed it to Ruby a year ago, and that's what we called her.

I also loved Frida, who had fallen out of a tree last year, smashing her teeth into her gums. Now she had all fake teeth, which she would take out at night. Adults thought this was funny because her father had some fake teeth too. Frida had long curly blond hair and dimples. Even though she'd fallen from a tree, she would still climb them fearlessly with me. We once climbed a tree and came upon an enormous black snake curled up on a branch, and she said, "Shhhh . . . let's just climb higher than him. He doesn't care about us."

In the lineup of the sixty or so kids that were in the Family, there were about ten who were older than me, twenty who were around my age, and the rest were younger. There were twenty of us on the Farm in the years after the spaceship didn't arrive. We did everything together—worked, played, ate, and slept in the same room. I worshipped the older ones and took care of the younger ones. They were all my brothers and sisters.

CHAPTER 4

*"In all humility I tell you that I am the greatest man in the world
and it doesn't bother me in the least."*

—MELVIN LYMAN, 1967

THE COMMUNITIES HAD SIX PROPERTIES—IN BOSTON, NEW
York, Martha's Vineyard, San Francisco, Los Angeles, and the Farm in
Kansas. Everyone was constantly moving among these places, for reasons that were mostly unknown to the kids. In Boston, the property
consisted of a row of four houses that took up a whole block facing a
park, which had the pointed Fort Hill Tower at its center. We called
ourselves the communities but also the Lyman Family, and sometimes
just "Fort Hill" referred to all of us, sprawled across the country as we
were, though it was also what we called the Boston property. When I
was four, I was piled into a car with Katie and DeeDee and driven to
Kansas by two adults who were not our parents. (As little kids we
didn't know every adult well, but we trusted all of them, at least until
we knew better.)

Fort Hill was where the Lyman Family began, before I was born. It
was the home base and the place people stopped when they were on
their way to the Vineyard or New York communities. The New York
community was a four-level brownstone in Chelsea, and only adults
lived there, most of them working day jobs and coming home to a

completely different life at night. The Vineyard was very much Jessie's domain—she'd grown up there and inherited it from her father. It had three houses on it, and you could walk to the beach in fifteen minutes. There were kids there but usually only the privileged ones. San Francisco was another property where only adults lived, and then there was the Los Angeles property, with a high fence that surrounded two houses, a pool, and a tennis court, with lots more land ready to build on. The Farm in Kansas was the work in progress, a life of roughing it. There were always lots of kids but not any that were too young to work—meaning no babies.

The Farm was enormous to me: We could run and run past fields and pastures and still be on our land, and even when we came to the low barbed-wire fences that marked the property line, we'd just bend a small space open and crawl through to more pastures and fields, where we saw no people—perhaps the occasional gathering of cows huddled under a tree for shade—and we'd keep running. Scratches on our backs from the barbs were common injuries.

When I lived there for the first time, the layout of the Farm was: Farm House, Spring House, Bunk House, barn, chicken house, silo, tree house, woodshed. Then strawberry field, cornfield, three sorghum fields, reefer field, potato field. There was a magical mulberry tree in front of the Bunk House. To get the mulberries out of this grand tree, we would climb high into it, creep out onto its most delicate branches, and shake them, causing the mulberries to rain down on the sheet the other kids were holding below. Our faces, our hands, the sheet—everything would be stained with mulberry juice. Once or twice a day a pickup truck would drive by on the dirt road, kicking up clouds of dust. The nearest town was a half-hour drive and the nearest hospital more than an hour.

I only came to understand how isolated we were the day Gabriel's fingers were cut off. Of the boys, I loved Gabriel the most. We always seemed to be sitting next to each other, laughing about something and being shushed. He had a thick mop of sandy hair that hung over his eyes, and he was fun to talk to because he started a lot of conversations with "What if?" This led to wild flight-of-fancy scenarios where we had wings or were blind. I'd had a crush on him since the day he claimed he wanted to marry me.

He'd said this in front of adults, and when one of them asked, "Well, how would you support her if you married her?" he thought for a moment and then said, "I'd knock out all of my teeth and sell them to the tooth fairy." The adults made fun of him for this, but I thought it was charming, and my future with a toothless and devoted husband seemed bright. In truth, his crush played out more like the time when he claimed that he could kill me with a pencil and I said, laughing, "No, you won't," and raised my hand in faux defense; he accidentally stabbed my palm with his pencil and got in trouble for it. "It was an accident!" I pleaded, to no avail. "Why would you threaten to kill her?" he was asked in all seriousness, and when I said, "He was just joking," I was told to shut up and leave the room.

The day Gabriel had to go to the hospital, the kids were outside chopping wood, a daily task since the houses we lived in were heated by woodstoves. The wood was always cedar, and we loved the beautiful red inside it and the gorgeous way it smelled when you chopped it. We'd invented a game called This Is Your Heart, where we'd find a perfect piece of cedar that could fit in the palm of your hand. We'd put it on the chopping block, and if it was your heart in question, you had to grab it off the block before the kid wielding the ax could chop it in half.

Moments before, I'd already "won," breathlessly snatching the piece of wood and laughing when the blade of the ax landed with a thud into the block and my cedar heart was safely intact in my hand. I put it back in the center of the block and teased Gabriel, "This is *your* heart now." Matthew raised the ax high over his head, and Gabriel lunged for his heart. He grabbed it, raising his hand high in the air in triumph. "Ha ha, I got it!" he said, and then looked around at all of our faces—we weren't laughing with him, only staring in stunned silence. He followed our sight line to his hand, still raised in the air and spraying blood where four of his fingers had been hacked off just above the knuckles. He screamed. We all screamed and ran the short distance up the stairs to the Farm House.

Inside, utter chaos ensued. As adults scrambled to wrap what was left of his maimed hand in a dish towel, they screamed questions at us, like "What the fuck were you kids doing out there?" and "Where are the damn keys to the truck?" Gabriel had turned quite blue in the face and didn't make a sound. "Jesus Christ—where are the fingers?" Somebody shoved a plastic baggie in my face. "Jenny, snap the fuck out of it and go get his fingers!"

I grabbed the baggie and ran out to the chopping block, where the tops of his four fingers lay in a pool of blood. There was no time to cry about it—I threw them into the bag, then ran up to the truck, where Gabriel was being rushed into the passenger seat. Yvonne took the fingers from me and put them into a bucket of ice, and then the truck peeled out and down the dirt road. The other kids were standing wordlessly nearby on the stairs, and I wiped my bloody hands on my overalls and watched the truck disappear on the horizon.

When they came back the next day, Gabriel was in surprisingly good spirits, seemingly excited by the adventure. The doctors had not been able to reattach the fingers, and he had pieces of skin sewn on top of them. "Look!" he said, pulling down his pants and showing us his right butt cheek, where the wounds from four perfect squares were healing. "I have butt skin on my hands now!" He menaced us playfully with his "butt hand," and with that, we decided it was OK to laugh about it.

This was Benton Farm, a gift to Jessie from her father, Thomas Hart Benton. We knew he was a famous painter—his paintings hung on the walls in many of the houses—but to us he was a really nice old man who made Jessie happy when he came to visit now and then, and we loved his wife, Noni, who made enough crochet vests for all of us girls, which was a lot of crochet vests.

In summer, the kids worked mostly in the sorghum fields, which seemed to be in perpetual need of tending. First we weeded them, and once we finished that, it was time to thin the crop so that the strongest stalks had room to get stronger. Then there was mulching time, when we would drag a bale of hay down each row, pulling off enough to create a bed around each plant to prevent more weeds from growing.

When the plants were small, it felt like we were all together, because we could see each other even though we were all in our own rows. When the plants got taller, we could only catch glimpses between the stalks as we worked. But we would always be singing together, our voices carrying across the expanse of the field. "Down in the Valley" was a favorite song in the fields because it had harmonies and lines that repeated in echo, as if we were having a conversation.

Once the plants got big enough, we'd chop off a piece to gnaw on and suck out the sugary liquid inside, being careful not to cut our lips, spitting the leftover pulp into the dirt. Then it would be harvest time— Sorghum Day! Sorghum Day was hard work but also exciting, because every single person on the Farm worked from sunrise until late into the night. After we lined up in height order, the small kids would hack off the lower leaves we could reach with our machetes, and the taller kids would be behind us to hack off the higher leaves. Then the men would cut down the stripped stalks and carry armfuls of them over to a hand-cranked press, where they would be flattened and their juice would spill out into a giant six-foot pan, which was put over an open flame. We brought wheelbarrows full of wood to keep the fire going and then used pitchforks to fill the wheelbarrows with the papery stalks left behind. Sometimes we got to take turns skimming the foam that bubbled to the surface of the sorghum as it slowly boiled. We were told not to eat it, especially at the beginning when the foam was still green, but we snuck tastes anyway, our faces sticky with its bitter deliciousness. It was a long, slow process, and everyone sat around in chairs, the adults talking and drinking into the night, fireflies floating around us.

CHAPTER 5

"Sound is the closest form to the essence, to Truth, to spirit. Sound is the first veil, the first form around spirit. That's why music is the highest art, if you can truly feel the highest music then you are as close to the Truth as you can get without actually becoming the Truth itself. I told you that before, remember I used to say that sound created sight."

—MELVIN LYMAN, 1969

IT WAS A TYPICAL DAY ON THE FARM. WE KIDS WOKE UP AT sunrise to the clanging of a cowbell in the middle of the room. Kay was standing between the rows of bunk beds in the Bunk House, where the kids slept. The Bunk House was going to be the Big House one day— the fancy one made for adults—but for now it was a shell, with plastic taped over the windows and front door, and fiberglass insulation stapled into the raw material of the walls. The bunk beds consisted of one wall-to-wall bed on the bottom, with two loft-like beds over it on each end. You slept wherever you slept, and if you wet the bed, you just moved to another spot. There was no division between boys and girls. I favored one of the top bunks—I liked climbing the ladder up to it and enjoyed the vantage point, high in the corner, where I could see most of the room.

Sometimes the girls woke up with mild headaches—if the night before had been bath night, our waist-length hair was French-braided tight so it would last that way for a week. On the first day after it was braided, we usually felt like our eyes were being stretched to our earlobes, but soon it would relax, and by the end of the week our braids would be frazzled, filled with burrs and often ticks, or still be wet inside from swimming in the creek.

We scrambled out of bed—dillydallying would mean a yanked arm or smack on the butt—and sleepily crowded around the dresser to gather our clothes. There were two dressers, one with girls' clothes and one with boys' clothes, but since we were all putting on overalls anyway, it didn't really matter what you grabbed as long as it kind of fit. I'd pulled my nightgown over my head and folded it, leaving it on the pillow I'd been sleeping on, and climbed down the ladder from one of the top bunks. Samantha was the oldest girl on the Farm right now, and today she was somehow already dressed and annoyed. She was very beautiful to me, with her olive skin and wise brown eyes. "You little kids, hurry up! By God, why are you always so lazy in the morning?" she scolded. "We're not just doing sorghum today—we have about five bushels of corn to shuck too." Shucking corn was not my favorite job, at all. The fussiness of removing all the corn silk made me impatient. I preferred snapping off the tops and bottoms of green beans—another crop we often had in bushels and bushels. Snap, snap—chuck it in the basket. I could snap beans very quickly. I quietly thought I was the best at it but didn't want to appear "full of myself," so I didn't brag.

Samantha started singing "Down by the Old Mill Stream," a song for which we'd invented a call-and-response second verse. We joined in, getting more awake and rowdier as the second verse came around. "Down by the old mill stream," she sang, and we responded, "Not the river but the stream ..." "Where I first met you ..." "Not me but you ..." "With your eyes so blue ..." "Not green but blue ..." "Dressed in gingham too ..." "Not calico but gingham—two not three but two ..." This last verse was fun because it was hard to squeeze the word "calico" into the song, so you had to say it fast, before she said "too"; also, "not three but two" made us laugh.

I fished in the girls' underwear drawer and took a pair, putting two feet in one of the leg holes and almost falling over. I found a T-shirt, but the overalls I chose fell an entire foot past my feet. Samantha's younger sister, Ruby, laughed at this and said, "Ha ha, shrimp—give those to me," and she put them on while I rummaged for another pair. Ruby had burn scars all over the left side of her body—she'd gotten underfoot during one Sorghum Day when we were seven. I'd been standing a few feet away from her when two men were moving a six-foot pan of scalding water from one place to the next, and she made a game of trying to dart underneath it. The scars spread over her shoulder, her waist, and all the way down her leg, and were raised and a lighter color than the rest of her skin. She wore shorts and tank tops and didn't seem to give them a second thought.

"Look at the tag," she said, disdainful. "It says ten to thirteen and you're only nine!" Finally I found a pair with a tag marked "7–9" and put them on. The straps fell off my shoulders. Samantha noticed this and yanked at the buckles to make them shorter, jerking my body in the process. She tossed long-sleeve shirts and jackets at us—it was cold at five-thirty in the morning, even in the Kansas summer—and said, "I'm gonna tell you for the millionth time: Don't leave your clothes in the fields. The Saturday Box will be waiting for you!"

At the mention of the Saturday Box, Katie and DeeDee and I smiled to ourselves. The Saturday Box was a cardboard box that lived in the kitchen, and if anyone found clothes left behind in the fields, they would put the clothes in this box. Over the course of the week, we'd watch it ominously fill up. There was no sneaking into the kitchen to steal your left-behind item from the box—someone was always in the kitchen, and besides, it wasn't like we really had our own clothes. Who could remember what they were wearing three days ago?

On Saturday afternoons, we would be called to gather in the kitchen, where an adult would stand at the front of the room pulling out each item of clothing, holding it in the air, and asking, "Whose is this?" Hanging on the wall was a hand-carved wooden paddle that was made just for these occasions. Painted on one side was a naked woman, viewed from behind, her bare butt cheeks reddened from spanking, her dejected face in profile as tears fell from her eyes and she walked away, leaving footprints made from the tears pooled around her. On the other side was a man wearing a tattered straw hat, also viewed from behind, one hand pulling up his worn jeans, his red butt visible as well, and his head hung low.

The piece of clothing—usually a long-johns shirt or sweatshirt—would hang there in the air until one of us meekly called out, "It's mine," and stepped dutifully to the front of the room to bend over a chair and be paddled—with the gender-appropriate side, of course. Most of the time someone claimed a thing as theirs just to get the whole thing over with. This much we all knew: If no one claimed it, we'd be there for hours, in a deafening silence with our eyes cast to the floor, silently hoping someone would be in the mood to say it was theirs. Not long after this tradition began, Katie and DeeDee and I had an idea: On Saturdays we would put on multiple pairs of underwear—five, six, seven; as many as we could get away with without it showing through our pants—and then the paddling didn't hurt at all. In fact, it made us laugh because we felt we'd gotten around the system, and the humiliation of being paddled in front of everyone was nothing compared to the secret triumph. We'd spend the whole ordeal avoiding each other's eyes so we wouldn't crack up, and we claimed as many abandoned items of clothing as we could without raising suspicion.

This morning, as usual, we tied shirts around our waists and zipped up sweatshirts and we were done. We never wore shoes in summer, proud of our callused feet, often daring each other to walk on a flat rock seared by the sun or on hot pieces of tar paper. At night when we did sewing or needlework projects, we'd test the callus level, pushing a needle into a heel as far as it would go, feeling nothing and making sure everyone saw how tough our feet were.

The twenty or so of us pushed through the opening in the plastic that served as the front door and made our way down the hill to the Farm House, where we knew a giant pot of oatmeal was waiting. The Bunk House was on top of a hill, into which flat stones had been embedded to form a functional if treacherous staircase. Some of us scattered in different directions—we had chores to do before we ate. I walked toward the barn; it was my job to milk Nanny Goat and bring in the milk for the day.

I loved this moment, pleased I had such an important job, because Nanny Goat was notoriously mean and would bite or headbutt most people, but not me. A reddish-brown, portly lady with longer horns than most of the goats, she would send kids screaming as she charged at them with all her might. She'd been known to sink her teeth into the seat of a kid's pants, letting go only when someone pulled her off and the fabric was torn. But in the mornings, when I walked into the barn and into her pen and I was the only human around, she was a different goat, as if the rest was for show and without a big audience she didn't have anything to prove. I walked across the road, past the Farm House, the woodshed, and toward the barn. Three geese waddled across my path. I'd read *Charlotte's Web* and imagined they talked like the geese in the book—busybodies, chatterboxes, not particularly nice. They took no notice of me on their way to wherever they were going.

I stopped at an alfalfa patch and ripped out two fistfuls, stuffed them into my pockets, and headed into the giant barn. The barn's ceiling was infinitely high—even grown men had to teeter atop very tall ladders to hang the reefer plants from the rafters—with stalls for three horses and several cows and a goat pen with ten or so goats in it. Our collie/shepherd mix, Odelia, slept on a pile of hay, lifting her ears slightly when she heard me grab a bucket but soon falling back into a lazy slumber. The sleepy cows and horses eyeballed me. On these quiet mornings, I imagined that only I truly knew these animals and that they liked me the best. Careful not to let the bucket clang again, I stopped to say hello to Stardust, our Shetland pony. I climbed up on a step stool next to her and stroked her nose, staring into her giant gray eyes with their pale lashes. "My Stardust memory . . ." I sang quietly, not to disturb the other animals. She shook her head back and forth, her mane flopping around. I felt like she smiled at me. I kept singing softly to her—"Sometimes I wonder how I spend the lonely night . . . dreaming of a song"—as I made my way over to Nanny Goat.

Nanny stirred a bit, then got to her feet, coming toward me and putting her muzzle into my pockets before I could scramble to get the alfalfa out to feed her. I feared her but tried not to show it—she'd bitten me more than once on our path to friendship—and as she munched with slightly wary eyes trained on me, I pulled over a low milking stool and sat down. From the first time I'd been allowed to milk her, I had marveled at the roughness of her teats—even my callused hands were surprised by the flesh that felt coarse as sandpaper. I faced my stool so I couldn't see the cows. I'd learned the hard way not to get attached to them—I'd see their names on frozen packages of meat in a matter of months, and I didn't like that feeling of eating someone you'd known. Nanny was never going to go to slaughter, so it was safe to get attached to her.

The rest of the day was like most days: We worked in the fields, we came home to do more chores, there was dinner to make and then eat, and after dinner, girls did dishes and boys did whatever they wanted. Tonight we were going to listen to a tape. Melvin had made scores of tapes over the years, many of them live recordings of him performing his own music. He was a banjo and harmonica player. The other tapes were folk music; Woody Guthrie in particular was a hero of his. Still others were collections of forties' and fifties' classics—Bing Crosby, the Andrews Sisters, Ella Fitzgerald, Edith Piaf, Benny Goodman, Glenn Miller, the Platters, and my absolute favorite, Ray Charles. Tonight we were listening to The Jug Band Tape, because Jessie had been listening to it on the Vineyard, and if Jessie was listening to it, word got around to the other communities quickly, and we were all listening to it. When we listened to a tape, we sat in the living room in the Farm House and listened from beginning to end—no talking, no moving, and definitely no sleeping. Sure, babies cried and little kids squirmed, but they were whisked out of the room if they did. Each time Melvin released a new tape, everyone was required to write him a letter about it—how it made us feel, what was our favorite song, something between a review and a thank-you note.

I loved the music. I mean, we *had* to love the music, but I actually did. I learned to listen to the story a song was telling, to let my mind fill with the images it evoked. I was once commended for my description of how Bing Crosby's "Breezin' Along with the Breeze" made me think of sitting under a willow tree. These letters were kept in binders, organized on shelves with the names of the tapes on the spines, such as "Yesterday's Tears," "Blues for the People," "The Early Years," and "The Old Loft and Waltham," the last of which referred to recordings Melvin made before the Family was formed, when he was wandering between a loft in New York and an apartment in Waltham, Massachusetts.

Many of the songs on the tapes were also songs from Lord's List movies. When Marlene Dietrich sang "Lili Marleen," I replayed in my mind her walking down the alley with Spencer Tracy in *Judgment at Nuremberg*. When Fred Astaire sang "Cheek to Cheek," I swooned, remembering how beautifully he dances in *Top Hat* while singing it to Ginger Rogers. But The Jug Band Tape was tricky. It was from the days when Melvin was in Jim Kweskin's Jug Band, and we knew from reading *Mirror at the End of the Road* that Melvin hated being in that band and felt like it was killing his soul.

FEBRUARY 22, 1964, LOS ANGELES, CALIF.

I'm sleeping twelve hours a day and eating all organic raw foods and doing yoga exercises and trying every way I know how to restore my vitality. I'm failing miserably. One set with the Jug Band and I'm a tired old man. The band is descending into Hell and I can't go with them, it wouldn't be right. The dark forces are clutching at my evasive heels as I grope and struggle to keep my footing.

We secretly loved The Jug Band Tape, though—the songs were catchy, and we'd grown up singing many of them with Jimmy. Jimmy was tall and thin with a dark mustache and freckles. He played his guitar and sang with us constantly, teaching us fascinating and hilarious kid songs with elaborate verses that were fun to memorize. Right now he'd gone to play music out in the World, which was mysterious and dangerous to me. He was the only man I wasn't a little bit afraid of.

He'd get out his ukulele and sing "Ukulele Lady" with us, one of our favorites. Just saying those two words together was fun, and the tininess of the ukulele made it feel like it was made for kids. But we dared not tap our feet while listening to this tape—we had to perform solemnity. It didn't really make sense, since it was perfectly OK to sing these songs in our daily lives, but the recordings with Melvin playing harmonica were meant to teach us something I couldn't quite grasp. For all the instruments we played—banjo, guitar, mandolin, fiddle, harmonica, dulcimer, recorder, Jew's harp, ukulele, tambourine—no one ever played the jug.

When The Jug Band Tape ended, we quietly made our way single file up the haphazard steps to the Bunk House, carefully finding each flat stone in the dark. And then we heard the familiar creak of the Farm House screen door, way down at the bottom of the hill, and when the bang of it closing echoed in the night, we naturally turned around to see who it was. "Hey, you guys!" Gabriel's voice called up to us, his voice giddy with the news. "The Caravan is coming!"

CHAPTER 6

THE CARAVAN WAS COMING IN A WEEK, WHICH MEANT THAT
our daily routines were put on hold. Jessie migrated with the seasons—
Los Angeles in winter, Martha's Vineyard in summer, with a stop at
the Farm for a month on her way across the country. Usually about
twenty people traveled with her. This time, on their way to Los Angeles, it would be her three children, Anthony, Daria, and Cybele;
Anthony's father, David, and Cybele's father, George; Jessie's current
husband, Richie; and Melvin's oldest kids, Normalynn, Jackie, and
Obray. Also Jimmy; Sophie, who was the mother of Normalynn,
Jackie, and Obray (her other three kids—Jesse, Samantha, and
Ruby—were already here on the Farm); and Faith and Delia, who
were Jessie's right-hand women. Melvin was already in Los Angeles.
He used to travel with the Caravan, but he hadn't for the last few
years.

The Caravan consisted of four vehicles. The "point car" was a silver
stretch limousine called Saturn, with the license plate UR ALL 1. It was
followed by an orange van that could fit a few people and was full of
camping supplies and instruments. Jessie and the adults rode in Mercury, a giant tricked-out luxury camper. Finally, there was Jupiter,
which was a converted school bus for transporting the kids. Jupiter
had a mural depicting stars and planets painted on the side of it, along
with the words "Venus or Bust." This time they were coming from the
Vineyard, and they would either drive in shifts or decide to camp.

We'd certainly get news from the road, but we had to be prepared for them to get here as soon as four days from now.

All else came to a halt while we prepared for the arrival of Jessie and her entourage. The crops could wait. Jessie's room had to be painted, or someone needed to drive the hour and a half to Topeka to get the caviar she loved. We cleaned like mad and made up extra beds. Some of the ladies would share rooms while the Caravan was here, and some of the Farm Kids would be sleeping on floors in adults' rooms to make space for the other kids who were coming. We worked hard on gifts for Jessie—a hand-carved cigarette box, an embroidered blouse. This time, we decided, we would put on a performance of poetry for her, and we set about choosing which poems we'd memorize. There was an air of nervous excitement. Everything had to be perfect.

The last time the Caravan came through, when I was seven, Normalynn and Jackie brought their new Ouija board with them, and it was the first time I got to talk to Faedra. There were many other spirits the adults talked to, but the kids weren't allowed to be present for those. All the conversations with spirits were transcribed as they happened, then put into giant binders labeled with the date and the name of the spirit, each page in its own protective sleeve. Every community had shelves and shelves of these notebooks, and we weren't allowed to read them, but sometimes they would be pulled out and pieces would be read to us to emphasize some lesson. There were dozens of spirits, and sometimes new ones would appear, but only Faedra spoke to kids.

Cleaning up after dinner one night, Jackie and Normalynn were gushing about the new Ouija board they'd made with Obray. We begged them to let us see it, but they said it was packed away in Jupiter and would be a pain to dig out—they would take it out when they got to L.A. Because Normalynn and Jackie were Melvin's children and also the oldest of all the kids, they were big sisters but also authority figures. We dared not push them, but we *really* wanted to see the Ouija board. Without even discussing it, Samantha and I began to mope as we dried the dishes, silent, perhaps even dropping a dramatic sigh for effect here and there. "I've never talked to Faedra," I said wistfully, and Samantha said, "You always learn so much . . ." and trailed off. At this,

Normalynn seemed to fall into reverie—a hopeful sign. I was in the middle of dragging a chair across the floor so I could stand on it to put away dishes, but I stopped, not wanting the scraping sound to interrupt her trance. She was considering it.

"It could be a Faedra night," she said to no one in particular. We held our breath and then Jackie said, "Yeah. I think I can feel her already. I think she wants to talk to these kids."

A half hour later we'd fetched a group of kids and gathered around one end of the dining room table in the Kids' House. It was mostly girls and a few younger kids. We marveled at this new Ouija board. Carved out of dark wood and sanded to perfection, its kidney shape was inlaid with mother of pearl, the alphabet and numbers hand-painted, and the whole thing finished with a shiny lacquer. The pointer was covered with purple velvet, its tip adorned with a sparkly gem. We oohed and aaaahed over the board until Jackie gently put her hand on the pointer. "OK, shhhhh, you guys. She's not going to talk to us if you're all over the place. Be quiet and let her in." We hushed up and waited. Normalynn sat with pen poised over paper, ready to transcribe whatever Faedra said to us.

The pointer started to move slowly. We held our breath, the only sound in the room now the soft swoosh of the pointer's felt-tipped feet. We craned our necks to see which letters it would frame in the little circle of glass. The pointer picked up speed, and soon it was hard to keep up. "Aaron," said Jackie, her voice a little surprised, "how . . . old . . . are . . . you?" We all looked at Aaron, a sweet, freckled boy who didn't usually get much attention and cried easily. He was surprised to be singled out, his eyes widening. The pointer was making more swooshing sounds. "She wants to know how old you are, Aaron." Aaron's eyes lit up—he knew the answer to this one!

"I'm five," he said proudly. We all waited as the pointer swooshed around the board more. I wondered how Jackie could even read that fast.

"Five . . . is a . . . magical . . . age. You are lucky." Aaron beamed a kind of "who me?" smile, the gap where he'd recently lost a tooth showing. The rest of us stole glances at each other, silently asking,

"Why Aaron?" The pointer kept moving. "Enjoy . . . every minute of it," Jackie read. "You will . . . never . . . be this . . . age again."

I sulked inwardly. Why had no one told me that I was at the most magical age when I was five? I'd squandered being five! Now I was just a boring seven-year-old. I smarted at the injustice of this. Faedra chose a couple of other kids to talk to. She told Corrina, "Your mommy misses you every day," and to DeeDee, "You have a special gift that will start to show itself soon, so don't get lost on your own trip or you'll miss it." We all nodded solemnly at these precious bits of wisdom, envious of those who'd been singled out.

The pointer stopped moving. We remained silent, hoping for more. Jackie kept her hand on the pointer, but it wasn't moving anymore. "I guess she's done for tonight," she said. "You should be very thankful that Faedra came down to talk to us. She doesn't always come. I guess we were all in the right place for it and she felt our openness." But the pointer started to slide slowly again, and Jackie said, "Oh . . ." We all watched as more words were spelled out.

"Oooh, Jenny—she's talking to you now." As the pointer started to swish, I looked around the room and up at the ceiling. Faedra was *here*, in this room. She could see us; she could see me. I squared my shoulders in anticipation, suddenly wishing I'd had time to put on nicer clothes. "Jenny . . . you . . . are . . . a . . ." All eyes were on me. Was she going to tell me I was special or destined for greatness? Was she going to tell me how many children I would have or that I was really good at singing? Jackie continued: "lazy . . . little . . . girl." Jackie looked at me with raised eyebrows. What could she do? Faedra had spoken.

Lazy! I was mortified. I thought about how much I hated carrying heavy baskets of laundry up all the flights of stairs, how the pillowcase I'd been embroidering was taking weeks, how sometimes when I was coming back from the chicken house with eggs, I dawdled, daydreaming, even though I knew people were waiting for the eggs so they could make breakfast. I was a horrible, lazy person. Everyone was looking at me now, and I could see they felt sorry for me. I was the only one Faedra said something negative about. I darted out of the room, ashamed.

I didn't actually know where I was going, but eventually I found myself walking up the stairs, legs leaden. I sat on the landing between floors with a heavy heart. My laziness must be *really* bad if Faedra had to point it out. But what was I doing, just sitting here? I had to stop being lazy immediately. On the landing was a small table with a lamp on it and an ashtray that held a few cigarette butts. I'd start here! I grabbed the ashtray and ran down to the kitchen to empty it, then washed it, dried it, and ran up the stairs to put it back, placing it carefully in the center of the crocheted doily on the table. I spent the next hour running around the house, working up a sweat as I emptied ashtrays and put them back just so, aligning one perfectly with a nearby table lighter or dusting off the top of a silver cigarette box. I knew Faedra could see me and hoped she understood that I would never be lazy again.

This was the kind of exciting thing that might happen when the Caravan came. We were being graced with the presence of important people. Even though back then Faedra had called me lazy and I had to work extra hard to make sure that everyone knew I was trying not to be, a spirit had spoken my name, and I would live forever in the notebooks that cataloged our conversations with the spirits. We knew that whatever happened while the Caravan was here, we'd be talking about it for months afterward, rehashing moments and quoting things that were said. We'd savor the brief sheen of the visitation, and though we would feel loss when they finally went on their way, we'd also feel great relief. The adults we lived with would become less tense, and life would go back to normal until the Caravan came back around in the spring.

CHAPTER 7

ONE OF THE MANY THINGS THAT THE ARRIVAL OF THE CARA-
van meant was chicken slaughter. There would be many more mouths
to feed, and of course everything had to be fresh—the best we had to
offer—so we'd have to kill at least twenty chickens.

I was afraid of chickens even when they were alive. It was often my
job to retrieve eggs from the chicken house in the morning. I'd grab a
bucket and walk down the road to the low-ceilinged structure about
ten minutes from the Farm House. I had to hurry, because the ladies
were waiting for me, but I didn't want to hurry at all, because I dreaded
going in there.

As I approached, I could see the rooster and some of the chickens
milling around their fenced-in yard; their jerky way of moving and
pecking at the ground always disturbed me. They had this way of lifting their feet slowly and deliberately as they walked, as if being a
chicken was beneath them and having to touch their yellow claws to
the dirt was something they'd never really accepted as their lot in life.

I'd steel myself and open the screen door to the chicken house, and
the chickens would start to make their anxious and vaguely threatening noises the second they heard the creak of the door hinges. Inside,
there were two tiers of nests, built like shelves along both walls, and
there was a chicken in every one of them—forty or fifty chickens—
none of them happy about the intrusion. The lower tier was at just
about my waist level, and the higher tier was at eye level. Most of the

chickens would be making a low warning tone, like "Don't you even think about taking these eggs I'm sitting on," and then one would suddenly let out a "Bock!" so loud I'd gasp and jump back, only to rile another chicken on the other side. Their heads moved more jerkily the more agitated they got, and all eyes were on me. Well, not *all* eyes— just one of each of their eyes. That's the weird thing about chickens: They don't stare you down by looking straight at you—they turn their head to give you one pitch-black shiny eye, like lizards.

But eggs had to be retrieved, and though these menacing creatures were at eye-pecking level, I bravely reached underneath their bodies, wrapping my hand around the eggs I found and gingerly taking them. Sometimes they yelled at me for it, sometimes they flapped their useless wings and left their nest in a huff, and once or twice I'd had a vicious peck on the back of my hand. The eggs would be disturbingly warm and covered in a combination of slimy chicken feces and the hay that stuck to it.

I didn't eat eggs for all these reasons, which didn't matter much— eggs were mostly for adults and special occasions anyway. But my fearful repulsion toward eggs was solidified when, a few months before, I'd seen one of our eggs cracked into a frying pan and watched as a bloody chicken fetus plopped onto the hot surface, the white around it instantly sizzling.

But all of this was child's play compared to what happened on Chicken Day. On this Chicken Day, in anticipation of the arrival of the Caravan, the mood was light and giddy. The chickens to be slaughtered had been brought down in a cage from the chicken house to the clearing just outside the woodshed, where the chopping block was. They beat their wings against the edges of the cage and each other as one by one they were taken out, held down on the block, and beheaded—usually mercifully in one blow, but not always. On this day they didn't chop off their feet right away, thinking it was funny to show us that it's true: Chickens really do run around with their heads cut off. I did not find it funny at all to watch a headless creature with blood spurting out of its neck hole run silently in circles until it fell over, but I seemed to be alone in this sentiment.

Every single person on the Farm was here for Chicken Day, so when I panicked and wanted to get away, my quiet exit to the nearby woodshed went unnoticed. I opened the creaky door to the tin shed just enough to slip in. The dark, damp space with the dirt floor was a temporary relief, until I realized the voices and the panicked chicken sounds were only amplified and warped by the corrugated-tin walls. There was a little closet in a corner where the rakes were kept, and I went inside to the very farthest corner of it and covered my ears.

I knew I could only do this for a few minutes. Soon I would be sought out for the next step: an assembly line where we would pull the guts out of the chickens and then pluck their feathers. I'd demonstrated an ability to be very patient with one of the last stages: picking the finest, tiny under feathers from their bumpy yellow-pink skin. This was the last step before they were hacked into pieces and wrapped in white paper. At least I didn't have to do any hacking.

I listened until I couldn't hear any more chickens screeching and came out a few minutes later. Near the chopping block, the adults had "planted" chicken heads and feet in the ground. They were arranged in neat rows in the dark, newly tilled soil, the vacant eyes staring out of the heads, the toes of the chicken feet curled in resignation. "Look," they laughed, "we're growing chickens!"

I tried not to look as I passed them on my way to the garage, where the assembly line had started. I took my place at the end of the line, arriving just in time for the first headless carcass to be plunked down in front of me, with only its tiniest feathers left to be plucked.

CHAPTER 8

A FEW DAYS LATER THE CARAVAN ARRIVED IN THE MIDDLE of the night, and after dinner the next evening, it was time to perform our poems for Jessie. I had chosen Edna St. Vincent Millay's "The Little Hill." I was very nervous, particularly because my poem had the word "Gethsemane" in it, which was hard to pronounce. But this was also going to be my triumph—I'd chosen it precisely because it had this word in it. I aimed to impress. I certainly didn't understand the poem, in which Edna St. Vincent Millay muses that she might be the mother of the hill that Christ died on. I didn't understand if Christ had been a real person or not. I'd never read the Bible or even seen one.

Everyone was gathered in the living room of the Farm House for our show as we stood in a single-file line in the hallway outside. The overalls we wore daily were now replaced with dresses we'd helped to make. My dress fell to just above my knees, and even though the fabric was a little rough against my skin, I loved the orange-and-blue paisley pattern and the big bell sleeves. This was the rare occasion when we wore our hair down, and most of us had hair long enough to touch the top of our underwear.

Corrina finished her poem and sat down on the floor, and it was my turn. My heart was beating a bit faster than normal, but mostly I was high on the idea of performing and that, for these forty-five seconds (I'd timed it, of course), all eyes would be on me. When I was younger,

I'd learned the words to Shirley Temple's "Animal Crackers in My Soup" (it was on one of Melvin's tapes), and someone found it cute, and soon I was frequently being asked to perform it for adults. I remembered knees, men's knees, at my eye level and sometimes being pulled into one of their laps as I sang. I would timidly walk into the room and sing the song, feel a golden moment of approval, and then be quickly ushered out and forgotten. I laughed at the thought of it now—I was so young then! But tonight I knew what I was doing.

I made my way to the center of the living room. Jessie sat in a wing-backed chair in a place of primacy, her dark hair falling loosely around her face, which was a rich golden brown from a summer on the Vineyard. She'd kicked off her leather sandals and Frida was sitting on the floor, rubbing her feet. Her band of travelers sat on each side of her and behind her—everyone with red wine in hand, their lips and teeth purple from a fourth or fifth glass. On her right was Delia, her chair pulled so close to Jessie's that the arms touched. On her left was George, to me the most powerful of the men besides Melvin himself. He was Gabriel and Padrick's father and also the father of Cybele, who was six years old and one of Jessie's three kids. The kids were sitting on the floor, and Lizzie hovered around, refilling men's wineglasses when they wordlessly demanded it by raising an empty glass. The air was thick with cigarette smoke.

Jessie's eight-year-old daughter, Daria, sat on a footstool next to her mother, clutching her favorite bear, Barnaby. Barnaby was almost half her size, and his stuffing was so worn that he folded practically in half over her arm. She was six months younger than me, but we'd never lived in the same place for very long and I didn't know her at all. But everyone knew about Barnaby and how he was always with her. Her honey-colored curls poked in every direction, wild and tangled.

I cleared my throat and began, "Oh, here the air is sweet and still/ and soft's the grass to lie on." My voice had a bit of a tremor to it, and I willed it away for the next two lines. "And far away's the little hill/ They took for Christ to die on." Jessie raised her eyebrows, an amused expression creeping over her face. "And there's a hill across the brook,/ and down the brook's another," I continued. Daria fidgeted now, her eyes darting around the room for something—anything—interesting to look at. But I couldn't let that derail me.

I made it through the word "Gethsemane," and as I uttered the last words of the poem—"grieves still the hill that I call mine/I think I am its mother"—I heaved an involuntary sigh of relief.

Jessie let out a surprised laugh. "Well, aren't you the little forty-four-year-old?" she said, not without affection, and laughed again, shaking her head. She herself was forty at the time, so I guessed forty-four was very old to her. Her proclamation made sense, though, because of what I'd been told about being on this planet so many times and not learning my lesson. So on the one hand, I was stupid because I hadn't learned this mysterious thing for lifetimes and lifetimes, but on the other hand, I was wise because I'd been here so many times? That sounded like a compliment to me, or I chose to hear it that way. And so I became "the little forty-four-year-old," because if Jessie said something about you, it was a badge of honor, and it stuck.

The Caravan had been here for a week, and while the Farm Kids still had our chores to do, the adults were paying less attention to us, and we had an influx of new kids to play with.

Geordie was older than me, the son of David and Faith and the brother of Clotilde (they had the same two parents, and then Faith had kids with other men and David had kids with other women). He was tall and kind and didn't speak down to me. While he was there, he taught me how to do this whistle trick with your hands—if you cupped them together and made them airtight except for an opening where the thumbs met, you could make a sound like an owl or, when you got good at it, a mourning dove. I practiced this endlessly but still couldn't do it as well as he could.

On a few nights, Geordie and Anthony, Jessie's only son (with David), came up to the Bunk House to play music with us kids. Anthony played the guitar, and when he did, I was always struck by how much he looked like the famous painting of his mother as a young woman playing guitar, which I knew hung in the house on the Vineyard, though I'd only seen it in photographs. Loren and Lyman sometimes came up too; they were Melvin's twenty-one-year-old twin cousins, who were dwarves. Loren played the fiddle and Lyman played the mandolin, and they were full of jokes, cracking themselves up with their barky laughter. Those of us who didn't play an instrument would grab a tambourine or Jew's harp to play along with them. We'd sing at the top of our lungs, all clapping and stomping on the floor so hard the half-finished building would rattle. We loved Woody Guthrie's "This Land Is Your Land," singing verse after verse and sometimes just starting over from the beginning and singing the whole song several times, improvising between the lyrics with a "hallelujah!" or a repetition of the words.

> *This land is your land, this land is my land*
> *Hallelujah!*
> *From California to the New York island*
> *From the redwood forest to the Gulf Stream waters*
> *Gulf Stream waters!*
> *This land was made for you and me.*

We'd learned a lot about Woody Guthrie and how this song was his response to the Great Depression. He also wrote a song called "Tom Joad," which was about the movie *The Grapes of Wrath*, which was of course on the Lord's List. Woody was sacred to Melvin, and as such we also revered him.

One night we were stomping and carrying on, kicking up clouds of sawdust, when Gabriel came in and sat down next to me, his hands cupped in a way that I could tell he was holding something alive. "Look," he whispered, and opened his hands just enough for a tiny pink nose to poke out. "I found a mouse—I think he's sick. Do you want him?" He opened his hands a little wider now, and as the mouse jumped out, I instinctively put out my hands to catch him. His little round body fit perfectly in the palm of my hand. I could see that under his soft gray fur he was crawling with fleas—every inch of the flesh under his fur was in motion with them.

"We have to save him!" I said. "What do we do?"

Gabriel shrugged. "I don't know—he's probably going to die anyway. I just thought you'd like to see him."

"He can't die!" I cried. "I'm going down to the Farm House and I'm going to make him a little house and figure out how to get the fleas off him." Gabriel was clearly surprised by my vehement reaction.

"I'm sorry. Maybe he'll—he might not—die?" he said, but I barely caught the end of his sentence, because I'd jumped up and headed to the front door, shouldering aside the plastic that hung there, the mouse cradled in my hands.

Outside, I headed down the treacherous stone steps in the dark, fireflies twinkling around me. "We're gonna save you," I whispered into my fingers. "What is your name?"

On the thirty-fifth stone down the slope (I'd counted them, so I knew), I decided his name was Ratso Maroo, from a poem that Melvin had written in *Mirror at the End of the Road*. I'd memorized the whole thing, because it was fun to say and sounded kind of like a song. In the sixth stanza, it went:

> *Ratso Maroo, a humble soul*
> *Wearing patches and snatches of rigamarole*
> *With a toe and a tail and a tale to tell*
> *In disguise ears and eyes and a fur and a bell*
> *Hippo hair hollyhock nimbery bimbery poo.*

"I'm sorry, I know you're not a rat," I said to him, "but you have a tail, and I know you must have a tale to tell." I was standing at the door to the Farm House, and even though we weren't allowed to just waltz in there, especially when the Caravan was here, I felt emboldened by Ratso and his crisis. "Hippo hair hollyhock nimbery bimbery poo," I said to the night air, prying the screen door open with my foot because my hands were otherwise occupied, feeling strengthened by the words.

"Oh God, what now?" was the first thing that Lizzie said to me in the kitchen when I opened my hands and showed her the weak little mouse. Lizzie was the only lady not taller than most of the kids, and she had long dark hair and was always in the kitchen. "What on earth are you doing in here?" she said, her voice lowered, so as not to be heard by everyone in the other room. I could hear them laughing and talking and felt relieved that it sounded like everyone was in a good mood. Lizzie was barefoot, in a long skirt, kneading bread, her arms covered in flour. I whispered back urgently, even quieter than her, "It has fleas—we need to help it! Can you help me find something to make a nest for him in?" She leaned down to get a closer look, then shrieked, "That's disgusting! Get that thing out of here!"

"But . . ." I stammered, closing my hands around Ratso while my eyes welled up with tears. "I can't . . ." Richie came into the kitchen, smiling and curious, a little drunk. Richie was a handsome guy with wispy strawberry-blond hair down to his shoulders and rippling muscles. He used to be not so important but now he was with Jessie, and they would disappear in the afternoon into her bedroom, emerging with dreamy smiles. It seemed like Richie always wore a tank top, and the blond hair on his arms only made the muscles more defined, as if he were some kind of fairy-tale prince.

"What's goin' down in here?" he asked Lizzie, and then looked at me and Ratso. Lizzie shook her head, as if to indicate that it was nothing important. I opened my hands to show Richie. He chuckled and snatched Ratso by the tail, holding him up to his eye level. "What are you doing with this little fucker?" he asked, mostly to the mouse.

My heart was in my throat, watching Ratso dangle like that, his tiny feet flailing in midair. Richie must have seen my anxious face and put him back down into my hands. "Sorry, bad trip for the guy," he said. He patted me on the head and walked out.

"Oh Jesus," said Lizzie, "there's probably a shoebox or something in the hall closet." She went back to kneading her bread.

I found a haphazard collection of shoeboxes on a high shelf in the closet, and I jumped to reach for one, finally catching hold of it and bringing several other shoeboxes down with it while holding Ratso in the other hand, trying not to squeeze him with the effort. "Shhhhhhh!"

I said, and then stifled a giggle as I looked down at him. Ratso was, of course, quiet as a mouse.

I placed him gently in the box and whispered to him that we would go to the barn and get some hay to line it and make him a home. He was very still, and for a moment I thought he was dead. I stroked him gently with one finger and he still felt warm. "Don't be afraid of the dark," I said, putting the lid of the box over him gently. "It's only for a minute." I tiptoed into the kitchen, hoping to slip out of the house without anyone noticing, but now several adults were wandering around in there. I'd almost made it to the door when Bruce noticed me with the shoebox tucked under my arm.

"Whatcha got there, kiddo?" he asked, tapping an unlit cigarette on the back of the silver cigarette box he'd picked up from the kitchen table. Bruce lived on the Farm, rode tractors and fixed things, didn't say much, and hardly ever hung out with the kids. As with most of the men, I don't think I'd ever had a conversation with him. He wasn't ugly, but he wasn't handsome either. He lit his cigarette and was already reaching for my shoebox, and I was powerless to stop whatever was going to happen next. I wordlessly held it out toward him.

His cigarette dangled off his bottom lip as he lifted the lid, peering inside. "Mice can't see for shit, you know," he said. "We're all just giant scary blobs to them." I wanted to get out of there so badly. I was sure that I wasn't just a big scary blob to Ratso. He had to know I was trying to help him. "Why you carting him around like that?" he asked as he took a long drag of his cigarette, the shoebox lid in his other hand. I managed to eke out that he had fleas and Bruce nodded thoughtfully—endlessly, it seemed—and then said, "What you gotta do is dip him in olive oil. That's what you gotta do. The fleas will choke on it. Drown in it."

By now a few other adults had gathered around in drunken concern. "Mice carry a lot of disease, you know," said someone, and someone else said, "You oughta put that thing out of its misery." Devora was already pouring olive oil into a Folgers coffee can, and she put it down on the table. I had hope—at least people cared. I picked up Ratso and lowered him gently into the oil, careful not to get it in his eyes. He trembled slightly. When I brought him back out, his fur slick with oil, the fleas were all the more visible, crawling around on his body, and not at all dead. "Guess I was wrong about that," Bruce chuckled, and everyone wandered away, leaving me alone in the kitchen. I raced to the sink and rinsed Ratso off, to no avail. He looked extra pitiful with his matted fur. I sat down on the floor with him, tears streaming down my face, trying not to make any sound.

And then little Daria appeared, standing over me in red footie pajamas that zipped up the front. "Why are you so sad?" she said, and then saw Ratso in my hands, oily and still. "Oh no!" she cried, and then took him from me, studying him closely. "You just have to give him love. A lot of love. And then he won't die." She addressed the mouse: "Hey, little mousey, hey, everyone loves you. Everyone loves you so much."

"His name is Ratso Maroo," I sniffed, wiping away my tears. She chuckled.

"Ratso Maroo! A humble soul . . ." She sat down next to me on the floor, and we studied the mouse together. "We love you, Ratso," she said, and then, "Let's sing him a song." She thought for a minute, then started singing "You Are My Sunshine" to him, her voice very soft and low. After a moment I joined in: "When skies are gray . . ."

"Let's go up to the bedroom," she said. "We'll close the door and no one else will be allowed in." In spite of my sadness, I was excited that Jessie's daughter was paying so much attention to me and also that she could close a door and not let anyone in and not get in trouble for it. I picked up the shoebox and followed her upstairs.

"We should decorate his little house," she said, "and maybe we could teach him to do tricks!" I was getting hopeful, imagining his future. "Yeah, he'll be like Stuart Little!" I said. "Oh, Mr. Maroo," she cooed at him, "you are going to have a very fabulous life!" "Fabulous" was a word Jessie said a lot.

We went into the bedroom she was sharing with her sister, Cybele, and closed the door. Daria's suitcase was exploded on and off a nearby armchair, and her bed was strewn with several teddy bears. On the floor between the twin beds was a mess of cut-up construction paper and glue, clearly abandoned midway through. She pointed to it. "I was trying to make a picture for my mommy when something made me come downstairs. I think this moment was meant to be."

"Where's Cybele?" I asked.

"Oh, she's sleeping in Mommy's bed like a baby," Daria replied. "This is just our room right now."

She took the box from me and set it on the nightstand, putting Ratso gently inside. "He needs covers!" she said, her eyes searching the room. "Oooh—I know!" She grabbed the pair of scissors from the floor and picked up a corner of the quilt on her bed. The scissors were giant shears and she struggled with them, tongue sticking out, as she cut off a tiny rectangle. I was scandalized. She saw my shocked face and laughed. "No one's gonna notice. Just watch. Anyway, I'll be gone before anyone sees it."

She put the little piece of quilt over Ratso so that just his head was peeking out. "Say good night to Ratso," she said to me. I swooned—she understood! She cared about Ratso like I did. I leaned down and whispered good night to him. "Tell him you love him," she said. "Love is going to save him."

"I love you, Ratso," I said, but I felt like I was saying it to her, and I meant it because I loved her so much in that moment.

"You should sleep in bed with me tonight," she said then. "You're too sad to sleep in that messy old Bunk House with all the kids." I must have looked a bit anxious, because she announced, "I'll go tell the ladies," and marched out of the room. She came back and gave me a pair of her pajamas and we got into her bed, with Barnaby, of course. "You should read to me," she said, and pulled a book from a pile on the nightstand. "I've heard this one a thousand million times, but it's really good and I like to hear it before bed sometimes." She handed me *Where the Wild Things Are*. I also loved this book, but I pretended not to, because it was a kids' book and I didn't want to be perceived as a kid. I'd recently read every word of *The Once and Future King*, though I hadn't understood one bit of it.

"The night Max wore his wolf suit and made mischief of one kind and another," I began, "his mother called him 'WILD THING!' and

Max said 'I'LL EAT YOU UP!'" Now Daria made a very impressive monster growl, and I growled back, but mine wasn't as good.

"I can do it much louder," she said, "much louder! But I don't want to scare Ratso." By the time I got to the part where Max was having the rumpus with the Wild Things, Daria was sound asleep. I wondered if she would still like me in the morning.

CHAPTER 9

I WOKE UP AT DAYBREAK, EAGER TO GET BACK TO RATSO. DARIA was sleeping next to me, facing away, her mass of curls fanned out over the pillow. She'd kicked off her covers, and her footie pajamas were unzipped down to her belly button. I saw that Barnaby had fallen to the floor and I tiptoed around to pick him up, placing him gently next to her and putting the covers back over both of them. She pulled him close and squeezed him tight but didn't wake up.

I went back around to my side of the bed and peered into the shoe-box. Ratso didn't have the little blanket on him anymore and was wedged into the opposite corner of the box. "Your covers—" I said as I picked him up. His body was cold and stiff. I gasped and dropped him. The fleas were still crawling all over him. Ratso was dead. I put my face in my hands and sobbed.

Daria woke up and said, "What's wrong, what happened?" and then she looked in the box and saw his lifeless body. She burst into tears. "Oh no! I loved him to death!" she wailed. We sat there crying for some time.

"We have to give him a proper funeral," she said solemnly after a while. Neither of us had ever been to a funeral, but we'd seen them in movies. "Get dressed, and let's go find a good place for his grave." We put our clothes on quickly and tiptoed down the stairs, through the kitchen, and out the front door. We decided on a spot behind the barn where no one ever went. "Only we will know where he is, and we can visit him every day," she said as we dug a hole in the dirt with our hands. We carefully placed the little blanket she'd made him at the bottom of the hole, and I laid him gently on it.

"I can't put dirt on him. It's too sad," I said, starting to cry again.

"But we have to," she said. "Here, don't look—I'll do it." I wandered a few feet away, weeping at the injustice of it all, daring to be mad at the adults for not caring. I found a milkweed pod, half-opened, its silken fluffy seeds bursting out. I broke it open completely and let some of the seeds drift off into the air. "OK, it's done," Daria called to me finally. She'd put two small sticks in an X shape on top of the grave. I opened up my hand and scattered the milkweed seeds over the little mound, and they mostly flew past us and into our hair, twinkling in the morning sunlight. We stood back, contemplating our work.

"Let's make up a song for him, a secret song that only we know," she said. "Today is September 4, 02, right? Let's call the song 'September 4.'" She started singing it, as if it was a song she already knew. It had a sad four-note melody, and its only lyrics were "September 4 . . . September 4." I joined in, a bit timid at first because the song had only just been invented. "September 4," I sang, and then decided to sing it like a question, in harmony. "September 4?"

"And now let's make a promise, something we do every day to remember him by." She thought for a moment, then said, with surprising conviction, "Let's always skip the third stair on every staircase we ever walk on." This somehow made perfect sense to me.

"OK," I said. She took my hand and stared intensely into my eyes.

"But we have to do it forever. For the rest of our lives."

Still holding hands, we wandered back toward the Farm House. "What do you want to do today?" she asked.

"Oh—well, I have to do my chores," I said. "First Nanny Goat, and then Carolee said we have to do all the Caravan laundry, and then we have almost three bushels of elderberries that the boys picked from the woods yesterday and we have to take them off the stems before they go bad, and then today we're supposed to go all around the Farm and find all the thistle plants and chop their heads off."

Daria wrinkled her nose. "Oh," she said. "That sounds boring."

I was about to say, "It's not, really," but decided not to contradict her. "But we go to the creek around noon every day—do you want to come do that with all the kids?"

"Yeah, maybe . . ." she said, dropping my hand. My heart sank. "But can you just help me brush my hair first?"

I looked over at the barn, where I knew Nanny was waiting for me. "Yes," I said. "I can do that, then chores after. I got a lot of milk from Nanny yesterday, and anyway Jesse milked the cows the day before—"

Daria was walking ahead of me already, though, and I hurried to catch up. We'd come to the steps of the Farm House, and she stopped me at the bottom with an outstretched arm. "You almost forgot," she said, and I said, "Never!" We hooked arms and walked up the stairs, careful to skip the third one. I skipped the third stair well into my teen years.

Inside, Lou was stirring a giant pot of oatmeal, and Katie and DeeDee were setting bowls around the table. Lizzie was frying bacon in two big pans over the woodstove. We never had bacon when it was just us regular people. Lou told me to put the spoons on the table, and Daria disappeared up the stairs. I stopped in front of the silverware drawer to count how many kids were on the Farm right now, saying everyone's name under my breath as I extended my fingers one by one. "Normalynn Jackie Obray Anthony Geordie Jesse Frida Samantha Corrina Katie DeeDee Caitlin Ruby Anna Irene Erica Matthew Gabriel Padrick Cybele Aaron Marlon Bellina." Twenty-three. Oh, and me. Twenty-four. And maybe Daria. Twenty-five.

I counted the spoons from the drawer and set one next to each bowl. "Did I count wrong?" I asked Katie. "Why did you put twenty-six bowls?"

"Lou, dummy!" she said, nudging me with her elbow. Overhearing us, Lou chuckled from the stove.

"Ya can't forget Ol' Lou," she said quietly, and I went over to her and wrapped my arms around her legs, leaning my head against her hip. She smiled but said, "I got hot things in my hands, girl; you better keep your distance. And get the milk and the molasses on the table." She shooed me away.

I was carefully cradling a very full milk jug with two hands and making my way to the table when Daria came downstairs holding a Mason Pearson hairbrush. "Come on," she said, and grabbed the jug from me with her free hand. The jug slipped so she was only barely holding on to the neck, and as I lunged for it, milk splashed all over the floor. I glanced up nervously at Lou, who just shook her head. Daria managed to get the jug to the table, but it landed with a loud bang. DeeDee was instantly crouched on the floor, wiping up the milk with a dish towel. Daria grabbed my hand. "I need her," she said to no one in particular, and pulled me into the living room.

In the living room she said, "You go there," pointing to a footstool, "and I'll go here." In one seamless motion she was sitting cross-legged on the floor, holding up the brush for me to take. I sat down behind her on the footstool and took the brush, contemplating my approach. At the back of her head was a giant matted chunk of hair.

"I think a burr got in there," she said. "And maybe some honey."

"How'd you get honey in your hair?" I asked.

"Don't ya know I'm a bear?" she said, and let out her raucous laugh. "Bears don't care about honey in their hair!" She paused for a moment, then broke into a low chant—"honey in their hair, bears don't care"— wiggling and dancing where she sat. "Bears don't care, bears don't care."

I was pretty good at untangling things—all of the girls crocheted and embroidered, and sometimes the yarn basket would be one big mess and someone would have to fix it before we got back to our projects. I'd untangled morning-glory vines that were strangling young sorghum stalks and some of the ladies' necklaces when they ended up in knots and they were too tired or impatient to fix them. But I really didn't want to hurt Daria.

"Don't be afraid of hurting me," she said, as if she'd read my mind. "I'm very tough, like John Wayne." Thankfully she'd stopped dancing, and I got to work, first with my fingers, easing sections apart, and then brushing them, starting from the bottom. "You know, I have a Bear House in L.A.," she said. "My own house, just for me and my bears. It has lots of pillows and so many bears I can't even count. I could only take a few bears with me on the Caravan, so I asked them all who wanted to come, and could you believe it, some of them just wanted to stay in the Bear House and wait for me to get back." She went on chattering like this as I worked, until eventually we fell quiet, the only sound in the room the whoosh of the brush as I worked my way through her knots.

Finally her hair was tamed. The process had produced a massive fluffy mane, and though the part with the honey was still a little matted and would need to be washed, my work was done.

"There," I said. We'd been at it for almost an hour. Daria put her hands up and felt the scope of her hair now and laughed, jumping up.

"It's sheer madness!" she said, loosely quoting the Lord's List movie *The Bridge on the River Kwai*. She charged over to the mirror on the opposite wall and planted herself in front of it, like she was daring it to give her bad news. Peals of laughter, a few more shakes of the head, and she roared at herself, claws out on each side of her face. "I look like a Leo!" she said. This was funny because she was a Sagittarius and not at all like a Leo. Everyone knew that!

"Will you let me braid it," I asked, "just until someone washes it?" She was raking her fingers through her hair, from scalp to ends, trying to make her mane even bigger and more dramatic.

"No one will ever be allowed to wash it again!" she cried, shaking her head gleefully back and forth with her hands on her hips.

"Then you should really let me braid it," I said, and she said, "Yes!" and in a heartbeat she had placed herself in front of me, cross-legged again. She wiggled her butt back and forth for a few seconds.

"I must be perfectly comfortable," she explained, "and now I am," and then she was still.

"Would you like two?"

"Too girly-poo."

"Would you like French?"

"My hair doesn't stay in those."

"One regular braid coming up, then," I said, as I combed my hands through her hair in preparation.

"Regular, but special," she said, and I said, "Oh, special, of course," and arranged my knees around her shoulders.

As I gathered her hair from the top of her head and then scooped it up from behind her ears, she leaned into me like an animal, lost in the joy of being petted. Sitting above her, I watched her eyelids get heavy, blinking slowly and then more slowly, until finally they were closed. But I could tell she wasn't asleep—her palms were rested on her knees, quietly alert. Out of nowhere a new feeling washed over me—a feeling of perfectness. Here was Daria and she wasn't mean or scary, and she trusted me with her sumptuous hair in my hands, and maybe we were friends, and my heart felt full.

And then, melancholy. "This perfect moment will go away soon," I thought. "It will go away any second, and I can't ever forget it." My hands were braiding her hair slowly, but my eyes were darting around the room for something to latch on to, something that would make me remember this moment for always. I saw the green glass lampshade, the bargello pillow, the ashtray full of cigarette butts with the silver table lighter beside it. I wondered if it needed lighter fluid. I quickly became frustrated, because everything was too familiar in this room and couldn't possibly serve to make this day stand out from any other day.

I turned my head toward the window and my eyes landed on the barn, far in the distance. "I know you too, Barn," I thought, briefly mad at myself for being mad at the barn I so loved. "So you won't be any help at all in saving this moment for me."

Then a squirrel caught my eye, scampering up the branch of the glorious oak tree that grew just outside the window. The squirrel paused on a branch, lifting its nose to the wind. "I have to remember this squirrel forever," I said to myself. I took a photograph of it with my mind, getting swept up in the idea that we live so much of our lives and don't remember the moments, and how I wanted to be different, but was it possible to remember every single moment, even if you really tried?

I was tying a rubber band around the end of Daria's braid when Jessie came into the room, several people following behind her, as there often were. She was holding a mug of coffee, smoking a cigarette, and saying, "I had this incredible dream about a voluptuous lady carved out of wood. I think Anthony could make it for somewhere in the new house, maybe a—" Daria jumped up now to give Jessie a hug, yanking the end of her braid out of my hands. Jessie wrapped her arms around Daria and then marveled, "Your hair! Who brushed your hair?" She looked up at me, sitting there with a hairbrush on the footstool in front of me. Was I in trouble?

Daria pointed to me, and Jessie said, "Fantastic! How on earth did you get this wild child to sit still? We've all been trying for a week!"

I smiled and shrugged, wishing I had an elaborate tale of my magic powers over Daria, but I hadn't had to try at all.

"Something very sad happened, Mommy," Daria said, and as she started to tell the story of Ratso, I got up to leave, behind on chores and nervous about it. I walked through the kitchen, which was empty now, every dish washed and put away. I had to go figure out what everyone was doing, where I should be, and try to slip in unnoticed.

I saw Carolee hanging things on the clothesline and headed toward her. Then Daria called out, "Hey!" from the doorway of the Farm House. "Come find me for creek time and see if I feel like coming!"

"OK, I will!" I said, and she said, "So long, Eningstine!" I did not know why she called me this, but I had learned since last night that she loved to make things up on the spot, and I was thrilled that I had a nickname.

For the next few days, I rushed through my chores to be with Daria. Soon I was sleeping in bed with her every night, reading to her until she fell asleep. One day Barnaby got a hole in him somehow, and Daria cried and cried. "He's bleeding!" she wailed. "Barnaby is dying!" I convinced her that it was a good thing—he needed more stuffing anyway, and we would find some. We went around the Farm gathering things to stuff him with: We brushed the dog and saved the fur that came off her; we collected tufts of down from where the geese made their nests in the barn; and we even braved the chicken house to gather some of the scraps they made their nests with but decided it was all too dirty. We busted open milkweed pods, and when we'd finally gathered enough material, I solemnly laid Barnaby on the kitchen table, ready for surgery. Daria watched anxiously as I stuffed him back to normal shape and threaded a needle to sew him up. "It's OK, Barnaby, it's not going to hurt," she said, then to me, "It's not going to hurt, is it?" I knew it wouldn't hurt him, but I thought I shouldn't act like Barnaby couldn't feel things.

"Barnaby is a bear!" I said. "He can take anything." She seemed pleased by this answer.

Soon I was being summoned to make sure she brushed her teeth or to have a special tea party with her and Barnaby and the other bears. (She loved that Barnaby could sit upright in a chair now that he was properly stuffed.) We stole strawberries from the patch to eat secretly in the tree house. We visited Ratso's grave every day.

Two weeks later, the Caravan was going on its way to Los Angeles, and it was somehow known that I was going with it. There wasn't a formal announcement or much ceremony around it—Jessie must have said it on a whim to someone who told someone who packed my bags. Before I knew it, I was stepping on to Jupiter with a little suitcase and on to a new chapter of my life. I was moving to the Los Angeles community with the royalty. I was elated. Being chosen to be in Jessie's orbit was nothing short of magic.

CHAPTER 10

ALL OF THE VEHICLES IN THE CARAVAN HAD CB RADIOS installed so that we could communicate with each other. Everyone would play a guessing game called Botticelli, in which one person would say initials and we'd have to guess who they were thinking of. Someone would say, "I'm thinking of someone with the initials BC," and you'd have to answer by making them guess who *you* were guessing. So someone from another vehicle would say, "Are you a lady known for baking?" and then the person would think and come back with, "No, I am not Betty Crocker." Then from another car someone would ask, "Are you a character played by Paul Newman in a Lord's List movie?" and someone would say, "No, I am not Butch Cassidy." We'd go on like this until finally, in this case, someone said, "Do you sing 'Just One More Chance'?" and the person would say, "Yes, I am Bing Crosby!" I wasn't very good at this game—it was hard!—but I loved to listen to everyone playing it.

On my second night of the Caravan, Jimmy was driving Jupiter, and he let me sit up front in the passenger seat and stay up as late as I wanted, listening to the crackling voices of truckers talking to each other in the middle of the night. All the other kids were fast asleep. I was asking him questions about the language truckers used to talk on the CB. I learned that "Breaker 1–9" was how they began when they were about to give some information—to whoever was out on the road listening—and that "10–4" meant you understood. The truckers would mostly be talking about the presence of cops to warn each other when to slow down. A "Kojak with a Kodak" was an officer with a radar gun; "Evel Knievel" was a motorcycle cop; and state troopers were "Bears," because they wore hats like Smokey the Bear. When they said, "Someone spilled honey on the road," it meant there would be a lot of state troopers on the road ahead. I thought this was all very clever.

Jimmy seemed tickled by my steady stream of questions and happy to answer them—after all, I was keeping him awake as he drove through the night. He was talking back and forth with George, who was driving the point car, Saturn (the truckers called the first car in a convoy a "rubber duck"—hilarious!). He held the CB mic in his hand as they planned a quick pit stop because George needed a "10–100."

"What's a 10–100?" I asked.

"He's gotta take a leak," said Jimmy, "and come to think of it, so do I." He handed me the mic. "Here, say '10–4' back to George." I grasped the mic, which was almost too big for my hand, and said "10–4" into it. Jimmy laughed and said, "No, press the button on the side, then talk," and I pressed it and said, "10–4." It was thrilling.

George's voice came back. "Who's that little lady talking now?"

"Jenny," I said, and George came back with, "Well, I'll be." I looked at Jimmy—what do I do? He said, "Say over and out!" and I did, feeling like the coolest kid in the world. I handed him back the mic and he put it in the dashboard mount.

He glanced over at me and saw my big smile and said, "Look at that shit-eatin' grin. We should come up with a handle for you if you want to keep talking on the CB." I *really* wanted to keep talking on the CB.

"What do you think it should be?" he asked. "Something that says something about you, but a letter and a number." My mind raced, intrigued by the challenge of it. What did I know about myself?

"Well," I said finally, "I like dogs ..." and he said "K9!" and then said, "No, that doesn't make any sense," and then, "I got it: J9, because you're Jenny and you're nine years old!"

"J9," I said, feeling it out. "I'm J9."

A few minutes later, George's voice came over the CB, but it was hard to make out what he was saying. "Ask him, 'Come back?'" said Jimmy, gesturing toward the mic. I pulled it out of its mount with some effort and said, "Breaker 1–9, this is J9. Come back?" I could hear George chuckling through the crackles when he said, "Brake check, Jupiter; think there's an accident ahead." I relaxed—we understood him now—but Jimmy said, "How are you gonna let him know we heard?" I shrugged, nervous. "You just learned this!" he said, and I pressed the button and said, "10–4, Saturn," and looked at Jimmy for approval. He mouthed the words "over and out" as if anyone could hear us, and I said, "Over and out," and then handed him the mic, afraid if I had any more airtime I would mess it up somehow.

I suddenly felt very sleepy and content, and I yawned. Jimmy said my yawning would be the death of him, so I climbed to the back of the bus and into bed with Daria and Barnaby.

The next morning we were headed to Shiprock in New Mexico. Shiprock was a beautiful massive rock formation in the desert, Jessie said, and it was a magical place where spaceships had landed before. The plan was to camp as close to it as we could, hoping to see a spaceship or two in the night sky.

But first we visited Four Corners, where New Mexico, Colorado, Utah, and Arizona meet, and if you wanted to, you could be in four states at once. There was a giant granite circle embedded in the pavement, and we took turns straining our limbs so our hands and feet could touch each of the four corners at the same time. When it was my turn and my feet and hands were in all four states, I craned my head around to see what was inscribed on the outer edge of the circle. HERE MEET IN FREEDOM UNDER GOD FOUR STATES, it said, and I felt genuinely disappointed that it didn't say something more profound. You could literally be in four places at the same time here—this was mind-bending. Why wouldn't they write something about the incredibleness of that?

As we approached Shiprock, Jessie wanted everyone to be listening to the same thing: Melvin's famous performance at the 1965 Newport Folk Festival—a twenty-minute harmonica version of the song "Rock of Ages." When we could just make out Shiprock on the desert horizon, Jessie's voice came over the CB and said, "OK, start now." Jimmy pressed PLAY. As Shiprock loomed larger and larger through the windshield, the mournful strains of Melvin's harmonica filled the bus. I thought of this passage from *Mirror at the End of the Road:*

FEBRUARY 1964

1. Playing my Hohner Harmonica is like making love

2. Playing my Hohner Harmonica is like making love
    a. To my cat?
    b. To my self?
    c. To my mother?

3. My Hohner Harmonica is only an extension
    a. Of my self
    b. Of

4. I don't play my harp
    a. It plays me
    b. It sucks me
    c. I blow it
    d. I suck it

5. I don't suck my harmonica anymore
    a. It blows me
    b. I suck
    c. I suck myself
    d. I don't blow anymore
    e. I sucks mashself!!

6. I feel like I'm eating it
    a. When I play
    b. When I'm blowing it
    c. When I'm sucking it
    d. When it's sucking me.

Listening to him play, I thought, did sound almost private. Like he was crying about all the sadness in the world when he played. I knew he had felt lost at the time, because right before this concert, he'd written in *Mirror:*

> How can one tell if one is asleep or awake when there is no way to tell? I am like a ship without a rudder, I am drifting and I am no longer strong enough to take hold of the wheel. Once I climbed up to the wheelhouse but I fell asleep on the stairs. I think it's probably good for me to be confused. I know that chaos leads to order, I feel that I must be on the verge of some vast new order, but as yet I am unable to get a foothold.

But he had found himself, we knew, and the clarity that came after this sad moment and this beautiful performance was part of the story of why we were here, together, and why we lived this way. This thought made me feel hopeful and thankful, and I opened one of the side windows on the bus and stuck my head out to get a better look at Shiprock, my hair whipping around in the hot desert wind. They had intentionally timed it so we would arrive around sunset, and now I could see its red-and-orange peaks glowing in the golden light. It was glorious. Some of the other kids stuck their heads out of the windows too, and Geordie said, "We have to climb to the top!" and we all agreed, our excitement mounting. Finally, when we were at the base of Shiprock, Saturn pulled over in front of us, the sunset reflected in its long silver body, and the other vehicles pulled over in line behind it.

Jimmy swung Jupiter's doors open, and the kids burst out of the bus, running at full speed toward Shiprock, determined to climb it. After a few minutes of running, we were still only at the bottom of the mountain Shiprock sat on. We stopped, doubling over and out of breath, and marveled at how the closer you got to it, the more you could see how far away it was and how massive. We looked back and saw the adults, tiny in the distance, leaning against the vehicles, puffs of smoke around them as they admired the giant rock. We sat down on the ground, talking about spaceships and pointing to places where we thought they might land. We compared it to the rock formation in the film *Close Encounters of the Third Kind*, which was the only movie we'd ever seen in a movie theater. Shiprock was better—more magical, we decided.

When the sun finally set and Venus appeared, the first star in the sky, we all closed our eyes and made silent wishes on it. "I hope I get to stay with Jessie forever," I silently wished. "I wish I wish I wish."

We drove to a campsite nearby and set up camp, working quickly to pitch the tents and build a fire because, now that the sun was down, it was surprisingly cold. We lit kerosene lamps, heated up beans, and tore chunks of bread off homemade loaves, just like we'd seen cowboys and outlaws do in films like *The Treasure of the Sierra Madre*. The men drank whiskey and the women drank wine, sitting around the fire in camping chairs and making plans for what time we would leave in the morning and talking about how good the sound system was in the new van for listening to tapes. Geordie played his harmonica, Anthony drew in his sketchbook, and Jackie held her embroidery in her lap after she'd realized the work was too intricate to see in firelight.

I was sitting on a blanket near Jessie when she absentmindedly started stroking my hair. Eventually she looked at me and said, "J9, huh? You liked talking on the CB." I nodded and she studied me with her unwavering stare, the kind where I wasn't sure if it was better to keep eye contact or to look away, in case it seemed disrespectful. I decided to keep eye contact—I didn't want her to see me as weak—but I hoped it looked like adoration and not defiance. We stayed looking at each other like this for a moment, and then she said, "Why do we call this girl Jenny, when her real name is a queen's name? Look at her— I think she's ready to live up to her name. Let's call her Guinevere from now on. It's what Bess named her, after all." I knew my given name— the name my mother gave me—was Guinevere, but I'd always been called Jenny, which was the nickname King Arthur had for Guinevere in the Arthurian legends.

"It's why I call her Eningstine!" Daria chimed in, excited. "She just seems like she needs a big fancy name."

Jessie laughed at Daria's insight. "And she has had one all along. Guinevere it is," said Jessie, and no one ever called me Jenny again.

That night I was sleeping with Daria again in Jupiter, where if you lay in bed just so, you could see the stars in the pitch-black sky out the window. I was on my back, soaking in how wonderful my life was at the moment, Daria falling asleep next to me. I wondered what I had done to deserve all this. Here I was, having these fascinating adventures, learning new things, and Jessie had given me back my name, a queen's name, and Jessie herself was a queen. I asked Daria, "Why do you think I got to come on the Caravan?" and she yawned and said, "Oh, I just asked if I could have you," and then rolled over and fell asleep.

CHAPTER 11

IN LOS ANGELES WE WERE ALL GIVEN DIARIES AND TOLD WE
should write in them every day. I loved the idea of a diary—it was
almost as if my words mattered. I decided to name mine Lavinia,
after a girl in *A Little Princess*, a book I adored. Lavinia was only a
minor character, and a mean one at that, but the name sounded fancy
to me, and the diary made me feel like a fancy girl. I took great pains
to cross out the gold embossed "1979" on the cover and etch in "04"
with a ballpoint pen the best I could. This is how I began on January 1, 04:

—EARTHQUAKE—
—LOS ANGELES 04—

My Dear Lavinia,

*At 3:14 PM an earthquake hit us. We were sitting in the school-
house and oh boy did it wobble! It was a 4.6 magnitude. Also today
a spaceship was seen 4 miles behind an airplane for two minutes.
Wow! What a way to begin the year. The earthquake was wonderful. I miss Frida too much, and Samantha. I love diaries. Everyone
in the whole school is using them. Jessie said January 5 will be a
great day because it was exactly four years from then that we were
supposed to leave this rotten planet.*

It was 04 and I'd been with Jessie for almost a year and a half now, traveling with the Caravan three times back and forth from Los Angeles to the Vineyard; I would be eleven in May. Lately I'd been consumed with the desire to be treated like one of the older kids. I was desperate to prove that I deserved more access to what was really happening with the adults, to have more authority over the younger kids, and, of course, to have a later bedtime.

But my world still revolved around Daria, who had just turned ten a month ago. These days she'd started to seem more and more young to me, with her tantrums and fits of silliness, and I struggled to strike a balance between keeping her happy and not being perceived as childish myself. We were best friends, but of course the power imbalance between us informed everything about the friendship. It indeed felt as if I belonged to her, and my fate seemed to be largely wrapped up in her whims.

Still, even though I had a bed in the Kids' House, I often slept in Daria's room in the Big House, which we also called Jessie's House or Melvin's House. I knew when I was there that I was at the nerve center of it all, witnessing the moods and overhearing the conversations that would determine other people's fates across our communities. I had come far in life since my humble days sleeping in the Bunk House and working in the sorghum fields.

It also made a big difference that Jessie sometimes did things that indicated to everyone I was special.

She'd recently gotten excited about bargello—a form of needlework made with yarn and a mesh canvas with colorful geometric patterns, usually in shades of the same color so that the shapes appeared to have dimension. The finished pieces were used for pillows or the seats of furniture. I took to this skill easily, and Jessie would invite me to come work side by side with her on our respective bargello projects, comparing our progress and collaborating on color choices.

She'd also given me a banjo for my tenth birthday. I'd struggled playing adults' banjos before—my arm barely reached the top of the neck, and the massive drum eclipsed my midsection. But the banjo she gave me was made for kids—kids who really played, not a toy—and the weight of it in my lap felt perfect. The tuning pegs were made of mother of pearl, and there were also pieces of mother of pearl embedded between the frets. My banjo came in a case that had been newly lined with protective foam and then covered in royal-blue satin. Inside the case was a little compartment made of cedar, which was for picks and extra strings, and when I opened the case to play, that gorgeous smell wafted up at me. I would always close the case quickly, hoping the cedar smell would stay forever, because it reminded me of my friends who were still on the Farm.

Getting an instrument was already an honor, but getting a banjo—Melvin's instrument—was truly special. I'd learned "Skip to My Lou" first, then "Down in the Valley," and I was working on "Cripple Creek," which was challenging because you had to slide your fingers down the strings for parts of the song. There was a song called "The Warm-Up Tune" that Melvin had written and performed on one of the tapes. This song was considered sacred, and people were only allowed to play it if he taught it to them, but I dreamed of one day being given the privilege. The banjo was a spiritual instrument, and when I practiced, I practiced with reverence.

CHAPTER 12

"If a woman is really a woman, and not just an old girl, then everything she does is for her man and her only satisfaction is in
making her man a greater man. She is his quiet conscience, she is
his home, she is his inspiration and she is his living proof that
his life, his labors, are worthwhile. A woman who seeks to sat-
isfy herself is the loneliest being in God's creation. A woman
who seeks to surpass her man is only leaving herself behind. A
man can only look ahead, he must have somewhere to look from.
A woman can only look at her man."

—MELVIN LYMAN IN *AVATAR*,
DECEMBER 2, 1972

THE ONLY OTHER PERSON CLOSE TO MY AGE WHO LIVED IN
Jessie's House was Clotilde, who at thirteen seemed wise. Clotilde had
giant eyes and wispy blond hair that almost touched her shoulders.
She was tall and had the elegant bone structure of her mother, Faith.
Clotilde lived in Jessie's House because two years ago she'd been chosen by Mel to be his "wife," and she slept in a room you could only get
to by going through his bedroom.

We never saw Mel, only heard what was going on with him through
Jessie. A few years ago he'd declared that he no longer wanted to live
on a daytime schedule and that he would only be awake at night. This
meant Jessie and one of his right-hand men, usually Terry, David, or
George, would go into his room and close the door, sometimes not
coming out until dawn. David was Clotilde's father and had been
Mel's close friend before the Family was even formed.

We weren't allowed to cross the threshold of Mel's room into Clotilde's, and the door to the whole suite was always closed. But one day she snuck me in, so I knew what her room looked like. "He's meditating in the pyramid for the next few hours," she whispered, peering over the balcony to the downstairs to make sure no one noticed and then opening the hallowed and mysterious door for me. "You can't ever tell that you came in here," she warned me as I walked reverently across the threshold and into his bedroom, barely daring to look at the details. There was a giant bed, raised high, and a worn gray velvet armchair; his banjo with the famous (to us) groundhog-skin head was hanging on the wall. She led me to her own room, which was furnished with her bed and a six-foot-wide wire cage for her pet squirrel Joad, who was named after Tom Joad.

Usually when Clotilde came out in the morning and closed the door behind her, Joad was perched on her shoulder, tail twitching. Like Daria, Clotilde was exempt from most of the chores and punishments the rest of us lived with daily. I desperately wanted to be her friend.

JANUARY 19, 04

I think that Clotilde and I are going to become very great friends. If it wasn't for her I would really be in the dumps, you know what I mean? Well I would have no one, like I had Frida to, well, sort of take care of me. I mean like I always need somebody that is older than me to be with, because if I am with someone smaller, I take care of them in a way. Take for instance Daria. If she were older than me Clotilde wouldn't be so important to me, but I take care of her.

The thing that was most interesting about seeing Clotilde's room and going through Melvin's room to do it was this: I knew Melvin was dead.

A year ago, I'd been instructed to go and meet Daria in the Bear House. I rushed out to the lawn and crawled into the doorway, which was barely big enough to fit through. I found her crying, clutching

Barnaby close and wiping her nose with his raggedy paw. Daria never cried—why would she? She did whatever she wanted and got whatever she wanted. Her crying scared me. I hugged her and she cried a little more, then blurted out, "My mommy just told me Melvin is dead." I was stunned and confused. Had the spaceship secretly come to take only him? Now she got very serious. "But you can't tell anyone. Only Mommy and a couple of the men know. And now me. And now you."

"Clotilde knows, though, right?" I asked, hesitant.

"I don't know!" Daria wailed, falling into my arms, crying again. But of course Clotilde knew—she had to; she lived in a room off Melvin's room.

That was the unspoken part of the dynamic between me, Daria, and Clotilde. We all knew he was dead, but Clotilde didn't know that Daria and I knew, and Daria and I knew that Clotilde was living off the room of a ghost but wasn't allowed to say.

So committed was I to pretending not to know that he was dead, I wrote this in my diary on the anniversary of his death:

MARCH 19, 04

Today is a very special day but I haven't been told why. I did not ask though because I can very easily guess and I don't want to write about it. All we did all day in school was read Melvin's poems and memorize them. It is very hard to say them correctly. To express them as Melvin writes them. I am tired but I cannot sleep and I am restless. My mind is in a flurry and I am unpeaceful. I cannot explain it. I have tried time and time again to express myself in words like Melvin and Jessie. I can't really explain myself to a blank book with dates on the top.

Now he had been dead for over a year, and it still seemed like almost all of the adults didn't know. I'd only ever had one interaction with him—I was nine, on Fort Hill while passing between houses. Of course I knew what he looked like—his gaunt face and unwavering stare looked out at me from framed photos in nearly every room—but I'd never encountered him in person. I felt fearful when I saw him coming and kept my head down as we were about to pass each other. He let out a low laugh as he meandered across the courtyard and approached, saying, "God, you look like your mother." This was a monumental occasion, and one that I'd recounted many times to others. Mel Lyman had an opinion about *me*—it was almost like we shared a joke. This was social currency.

MARCH 26, 04

Dearest Lavinia,

Heavys Heavys and more heavies. I don't know what any of them are even about! Skip that sentence. I do know. But I don't quite understand. Clotilde just told me. I think they have something to do with faith in—whatever, just faith—and that people need to go behind the surface, the horridness of everything and everyone and see if it's truth that is behind it, I guess. Now I feel <u>very</u> guilty. I just realized something. Clotilde said I am lies, cheats, and self, yes SELF, and just now I said to myself "I can't be that bad," but if I am, then I am such a lie, and I've cheated so much that I can't tell the difference between me and my "outer shell". Oh! I am a ghastly person! If what I discovered is actually true, then I am worse than I ever thought I was. She asks me if I care, and before I can properly answer she jumps to the conclusion that I don't. Now, I do—but—ah yes, that is the key. I must learn to show it. I care, but no one sees that because it is sealed in my little locket of feelings that I have locked and melted the key. But somehow, no matter what it takes, I will get that key, open my little locket and show it to the world!

"Heavies" were when the adults would spend hours and hours behind closed doors and people would come out crying, or at the very least looking very fraught and being short with us.

Clotilde had a habit of taking whatever she knew from the adults and having her own mini heavies with me. I wrote what she said partially knowing she would read it but also because I was genuinely confused and wanted to be better, but I didn't really know how. Everything was so abstract, and I thought that things didn't make sense to me because I was somehow lacking. Clotilde's frequent and haughty admonishment rattled around in my head: "How *could* you understand? You're only ten. You haven't had any experiences."

MARCH 27, 04

My Dear Lavinia,

Why can't I do what all of the other children do? That's what I want. I try and try to put out so much but I don't seem to be communicating. I have to literally hide so I won't get sent to bed early, and people always count me as "a little one". What have I done? Maybe I am just not ready. Maybe it's just that I'm "only ten", (and I have heard that phrase a lot), and not experienced enough to be around the grown ups and know what's going on. That is another thing—I just wish people would let me know what is happening. For God sakes. They let Daria—well she's an exception for anything.

About a year after Mel chose Clotilde, some of the other powerful men took on young "wives" of their own. Frida had already been given to George when she was twelve and then banished to a different community when something went wrong. David had Anna, who was also twelve. She served him silently, seemingly always in trouble. These men also had adult wives, and the arrangements seemed tense and mysterious to me. The girls were talked about as being in "training" to be women, and it was considered an honor to be chosen by one of the four or five upper-echelon men.

Part of me wanted this for myself—after all, it would mean I was closer to being perceived as an adult—but I was also scared because I didn't really know what happened to my friends behind closed doors.

I knew that Frida had been miserable, and once George chose Saman-tha, she went from being my friend to being sullen and closed off to me. The girls didn't seem happy, but they were treated with more re-spect. I speculated that being an adult was a serious matter and that maybe I wasn't ready, but for a while I thought if I had to have some man take me on, I would want it to be George.

Like most of the powerful men in the Family, George was intimi-dating to me, but even though I heard scary things about him beating up other adults and flying into rages toward his wives, to me he'd al-ways been nice, even playful. Also, I liked him because he was Gabriel's father, and I loved Gabriel.

One day I was standing in the hallway of Jessie's House, contem-plating a framed black-and-white portrait George had taken of Jackie, when George was suddenly behind me, asking, "You like this photo?" I wondered how long he'd been standing there. "Yes, I love it," I said, flustered by the attention.

"Why?" he asked, in a tone that felt like a challenge. What I was really thinking as I gazed at the photo was "When will I be beautiful and grown up like Jackie?" but I wanted to say something that proved I was a deep thinker, so I said, "Because you can really see her soul through her eyes."

He paused for a long while and then said, "I'm about to go down to the darkroom and develop some new photos. Do you want to come hang out with me and see how it's done?" I'd passed the test! He thought I was worthy company. I followed him down to the basement, wishing that someone was around to witness this moment of being singled out by George. My mind raced, thinking of smart things to say, desperately wanting to be an interesting companion in the sanctity of the darkroom.

I'd never been in the darkroom before—kids weren't allowed, at least not kids like me—and at first I was overwhelmed by the smell of the chemicals. The light was an eerie red, and as my eyes adjusted to the darkness, I peered up at the photos already hanging on a wire above the big developing trays that lined the counters. There was a photo of Marilyn standing with her arms outstretched in front of the tower on Fort Hill; here was a photo of Richie, Big John, and Padrick working on our new schoolhouse when it was still just a foundation and some beams. George was explaining the process to me, step by step, and when he put a wet piece of paper into the tray with the chemicals that made the image appear, I strained on tiptoe to see it. He noticed this and said, "Here, let's get you a better view," and pulled over a small step stool. He put his hands around my waist and lifted me up onto the stool in one swift motion, and I was aware of his size and strength and how little effort it took for him to physically move me from one place to another.

But I was soon swept up in the process, watching images magically emerge under the liquid as he gently prodded the piece of paper with a pair of tongs, then lifted it from the tray, let the water run off, and hung it up to dry. I was standing there on the step stool when he put another photo into the tray and said, "You can handle this part, right?" and gave me the tongs. He put on a timer and said, "Just make sure it stays under the fluid, but try to only touch the sides of it, not where the image is. We take it out when the timer goes off." He busied himself with something else as I focused on the task at hand, hoping I would do it right and not somehow destroy the photo and the moment. The room was completely silent except for the tick tick tick of the timer—we were in a far corner of the basement, with double doors between us and the rest of the world. A tendril of fear worked its way into my stomach, but I dismissed it as being about developing the photo properly. The ticking of the timer suddenly felt very loud.

I heard him chuckle in the darkness across the small room, and he came up behind me. "You don't have to be so tense," he said. "I can practically hear your heart beating from over here." He put his hand over mine, guiding it through the process. "Even if you fuck it up, we can always start over." Now his whole arm was touching mine, and I could feel the heat of his body around me, just inches away. I could smell coffee and cigarettes on his breath, a smell I associated with men being too close to me.

I started to panic. Was this it? George already had Samantha, but was this the moment he was going to choose me too? I suddenly knew, with every fiber of my being, that it wasn't what I wanted. But what did I know—maybe this was part of it, the fear. Was I supposed to just let it happen, even if I was afraid? And what exactly was going to happen? Part of me wanted to want it, to be "ready" for whatever this next phase of my development was, but that was my brain. My body, my animal instinct, was screaming no. I had to get out of there.

The timer went off, a piercing *ding!* in the quiet that made me jump and filled me with a sense of urgency, because—what now? I'd tried so hard to act like a grown-up, and this is where it had gotten me. My only recourse was to do something, anything, to remind him I was a kid.

So I giggled, the most childlike giggle I could muster, and said, "I think the chemicals are making my brain feel silly," and it worked. I felt the mood shift, and he took his hand off mine and said, "Oh yeah—maybe you better get outside and get some fresh air." I jumped off the stool, and for a minute I actually did feel dizzy but probably just from relief. I put my hand to my forehead and steadied myself, making sure to laugh again as I said, "Whoa . . ."

"Go on upstairs," he said, sounding annoyed, and turned back to his work. "Only open the door the tiniest sliver, and do it quickly," he said, and I slipped out and up the basement stairs, so happy to see daylight in the doorway at the top.

CHAPTER 13

Instinctively I knew that our diaries weren't *really* for our private thoughts and feelings, because they could be read by anyone. I didn't consciously think, "This is a perfect opportunity to show how good I am," but that is what I used it for. In addition to writing down who came and went, and what films we saw, and what tapes we listened to, I used it to agree with whatever the party line was, to express regret or self-judgment if I was in trouble or admiration for appropriate things. It's not as if I was lying—the idea of privacy was foreign to me, and what I felt *was* what everyone else felt, in a way. But I was halfway writing it as a newsletter, the underlying project being to show what a model citizen I was.

JANUARY 9, 04

My Darling Lavinia,

I wish that I was not restricted to write in my diary because there is so much I could write about certain people that I can't write, just because I feel that way. There are things I won't write because of certain people I am afraid would read it. Really jerky, huh?

I was in a perpetual friendship triangle with Daria and Clotilde. Yes, Daria's father was a secretly dead man who kept Clotilde sequestered away, and Clotilde's mother, Faith, was one of Jessie's best friends, and yes, Clotilde's father, David, also had Anthony with Jessie. Oh, and I was a nobody—with a mother far away in New York who had no power and a father who'd never been there at all—but none of our tensions had anything to do with those things. We were just nine-, ten-, and thirteen-year-olds, living out the intricate power dynamics of three girls, each with our separate kind of power—my power, of course, being the most tenuous, and theirs etched in stone.

They would each sneak my diary and write notes in it, sometimes on pages that were months ahead, sometimes so that I would find them the next day. "Your diary isn't dumb, Guin," Clotilde wrote after I'd berated myself on the previous page for having nothing to say. "I find some pages quite interesting. xxC." I swooned over this tiny acknowledgment. Daria would be more inclined to write things like "Hello, Sweet Ermengarde," the name of the Little Princess's best friend, a way of saying I was her best friend. Clotilde would write, "Be full of love today," on the top of the page, and Daria would draw an arrow pointing to it and write, "What a dumb thing to say." Clotilde would tell me Daria made me act like a baby; Daria would tell me I was "stuck up" around Clotilde, and it all mattered very much to me.

Daria would hover over me when I wrote in my diary—she rarely wrote in her own. It was as if my diary was also hers, and she'd often get excited, saying, "Oooh, write this down! Write this down!" I didn't mind—I thought she was funny and it would make my diary more interesting. She'd pace around, dictating words, cracking herself up.

JANUARY 15, 04

Daria Benton Lyman would like me to write a quote from her. Here it is. "I want you to know and remember me by this quote. I am very beautiful, a little on the pudgy side, exciting blue eyes, a flaming red mouth, a warty nose, a great sense of humor, good character, IQ of zero, golden hair sparkling in the sunlight. I want you to remember me because I am a great success in America."

But I was passionate about my diary nonetheless, writing faithfully in it every day, pleased whenever I had the chance to write something that had to do with Jessie.

JANUARY 5, 04

Dear Lavinia,

I woke up to the pitter-patter of rain beating on the windows. The morning was rather horrible, mostly because Daria was being just awful. As the day went by it got better and better until finally I heard that Jessie invited Daria, Gabriel and I over at 8 pm sharp for a small party and chat to chat. She told us that she planned to stay here til March 24 and then go to the Farm. Then we would stay there for about a month and go to the Vineyard. We all got drunk and had a wonderful time. Daria did the "Devil Disco" dance and we all sang to it. It was wonderful.

I had to go to bed so darn early just because of Daria. I can't STAND that. She makes me look so young and immature. I hate it.

I must write in my diary this so I never forget. FP said for my 15th birthday I can go to Rome, Italy for a birthday present. Lavinia, you must remind me or I will forget and so will he. I love Jessie and I wish we could hang out with her more often. I miss Melvin.

We hadn't really gotten drunk—we were just allowed a couple of sips of wine and were high off the idea of it more than anything. The only other adults at this party were Richie, Jessie's husband; Delia, who was currently Jessie's best friend and never left her side; and a man named FP.

FP never would have been invited to Jessie's House if it wasn't for the fact that he was having a not-so-secret affair with Delia. This was all a bit confusing to me, since "officially" he was married to my mother, and he lived with her in the New York community. FP was a "low-level guy." ("Low-level" was a term Daria had coined. I'd first heard it two years before, when she said to me, "Aren't you glad you don't have to be with the low-level people anymore?") Like Bruce or Mike or Jay, FP was one of the fifteen or so adult men who I perceived as something like worker bees. None of them had kids, and maybe for this reason I didn't feel very connected to them. FP had red hair and gnarled hands from working in the construction company on whatever community he was sent to. He'd been a late addition to the Family, and no one talked about him much. He was never invited to travel on the Caravan. I figured he said that thing about taking me to Rome because he felt guilty about being unfaithful to my mom. I didn't care about any of it. I mostly felt annoyed that he was there, because at this point it felt like I was close to being one of the important people, and his presence made it seem that just anyone could be invited.

He and Delia were an odd pair. While he was something of a charmer—chatty and full of jokes—Delia had always been tightly wound. Thin, with the erect posture of a dancer, she was often the most femininely dressed woman in the room, though nothing else about her was particularly girly. Her short hair was always impeccably in place, and the rare laughter she allowed herself was usually ironic. She made me nervous—it was obvious that for some reason she didn't like me. Maybe it was the same kind of hidden resentment I felt toward FP. Maybe she was thinking, "What the hell is so special about this girl that she gets to be around us?" Whenever I was in Jessie's House, Delia bossed me around and corrected me, going out of her way to treat me like the help.

CHAPTER 14

Dear Lavinia,

My life is strange and I am confused. I wonder if anyone ever understands life. I want so many things. I want friendship, and I don't want Frida to be so messed up, and I want Daria to quit acting the way she is, and I wish Obray would stop bothering me and leave me alone. I wish so many things my thoughts are turning into a whim. Lou embarrasses me in so many ways. It seems that she likes to, but I know she doesn't. My mind is full of crazy thoughts and I am restless. I miss all my friends. I wish we could see more of Jessie. I wish people would explain things to me. I wish I knew what was going on in other people's lives, because I hate my own. The thing about Daria is that she is loving and kind one moment and the next moment she goes and tells everyone what I said. I don't make sense to myself, strangely enough. I wish I was with Frida, Corrina and Samantha. I wish I was always around George but I guess I am not old enough on the inside to experience that and it makes me sad not to be a part of it. I want to be like all of the other girls but something is missing inside me. I guess it is the part (as Lou says) that doesn't want the responsible part of growing up. I wish—oh I had better stop being a whimsical fool and grow up. I'm too much of an "I wisher". La-

vinia, did you know that George said Samantha loves him much
more than Frida? Now that is just plain amazing since Saman-
tha only got to be with him since about October. Just shows her af-
fection. I'm lonely these days.

Obray was Melvin's third child and eldest son. His mother was
Sophie, who was also the mother of Normalynn, Jackie, Samantha,
Jesse, and Ruby. (And another son, who was older than all of them but
had disappeared from the Family when I was much younger.) Obray
was seventeen, with sandy-blond hair and dimples, and he was moody
and dramatic. He was named after the famous folk musician Obray
Ramsey, who had been Melvin's friend.

Obray was another person who wrote in my diary often, which also
meant that I knew he read everything I wrote.

On January 31, 04, he wrote (in my diary):

Dearest, you are the only one. You make my life worthwhile and
are the only one who cheers it up. I love you dearly and hope you
feel the same towards me. I don't know what I would do without
you. You are the only one who I can talk to freely, and spill my
heart without worrying. I feel very lucky to have you even though
you do drive me up the wall most of the time. If you were older I
would marry you today, but for now all I ask is that you love me
and make me happy, cause you know I will always love you. And
for the nosy bastards who read this in Guin's diary, may you keep
your mouth shut and don't get any ideas unless you know the
whole story, okay?

Although I didn't feel romantic toward Obray, I did like the romance of his affection. I got a certain thrill out of his writing to me
this way, especially because it was something of a public declaration,
despite being written in a diary that we were all pretending was private.

After I opened my diary and read what he'd written that night, I
wrote:

Obray wrote all of this. You know I am very sorry for not introduc-
ing him to you. He is a boy of 17 and (as he says) "head over heels"
in love with me. It is a long story but bit by bit I will tell you.
Today he is not feeling well and as you can probably tell, very ro-
mantic. Every night he comes up into my room and talks with me
for an hour about God Knows What and then kisses me on the cheek
when he leaves. People always start to think their little dumb
thoughts when they see us talking. As this diary goes on you will
find out more about him.

The other boys made fun of him for it, and the girls teased me re-
lentlessly. I liked the idea of it all—especially because he was Melvin's
son, and the next Lyman boy after him was Lincoln (named after
Abraham Lincoln, of course) and he was only five. But in actual daily
life, I was torn between feeling flattered by Obray's obsessive attention
and annoyed by it. My days were long and often exhausting. I had
chores and homework and the endless wrangling of Daria and the
navigation of the mercurial world of the adults, and sometimes when
he came up to talk to me at night, I just wanted to go to sleep.

One night we were listening to a tape, sitting in the living room, as
we always did, quiet and still as we absorbed the music. We knew that
the adults would dub it a "good session" or a "bad session," and we'd
have to listen to the tape again the next day if the session was bad. I
didn't mind if we heard a tape two days in a row—we'd heard them all
a hundred times, and they were the soundtrack to our lives. I knew all
the peaks and valleys the order of the songs created, and I cherished
the lyrics, all of which of course I knew by heart. Melvin hadn't released a new tape in over a year (which was unusual, but no one seemed
to ask why), so we were hearing the old ones over and over, almost
daily. I loved it. For an hour or so there were no chores, no nothing, just
absorbing the music. I liked trying to remember how a song had made
me feel the first time I heard it versus how it felt now.

We also knew that across the communities, whatever time zone
they were in, people were listening to the tape at the same time. I loved
to think of Katie and DeeDee and Corrina and Frida on the Farm

and pictured them sitting in the living room on the floor at the Kids' House, all listening to the same song I was, wondering if the music was making them as happy as it was making me.

Tonight we were listening to the tape "Yesterday's Tears," and the opening twangs of Hank Williams's song "Lovesick Blues" came on.

I closed my eyes, listening to Hank's warbling voice:

> *I got a feelin' called the blu-oooo-ooooo-ooooes,*
> *Oh Lord, since my baby said goodbye.*

I could feel eyes on me, and I opened mine to see Obray staring balefully at me, as if the song had been written for us. Our eyes locked for the line "Such a beautiful dream," and I looked away quickly, not wanting him to think this was some kind of special moment between us.

His affection was volatile, though, and sometimes he would scold me like I was a child and he was an adult.

FEBRUARY 21, 04

Dear Lavy,

Last night, even though it took him a lot of courage, Obray sure laid a big heavy on me! You wouldn't believe what he called me, it really hurt my feelings. He called me a cold, stone hearted bitch! Now I can't be all that bad. He said I don't care about anyone and I shouldn't be around Clotilde. But I have to be around Clotilde. Who else do I be with? Well actually if not Clo I can be alone. He said he doesn't even know why he likes me. And I don't know either. He didn't have to include Daria in it though.

He'd gone on that night to lecture me about how Daria made me seem younger and I needed to learn how to make her behave better. I tolerated these long-winded speeches from him—I could tell they made him feel as if he had authority over me and that he was just trying on the position of grown-up. But he didn't scare me. Unlike the adult men, he was emotional and often very sweet. I just had to be careful to be kind but not romantic, and maybe I would marry him someday? I didn't want to destroy the chance of that, but I knew whatever he wanted, I didn't want it now. I also worried that if I pushed him away too much it would somehow lead to me being sent back to the Farm. He was a Lyman after all.

When I was at the height of my crisis about him—trying to neither piss him off nor encourage him—Jessie must have heard about it; everything got back to her. She pulled me aside one night after dinner in the Big House. I was helping with dishes when she came into the kitchen and took my hand, led me into the living room, and shut its glass-paned double doors so no one could overhear us. She had a glass of wine in her hand and her mood was light and conspiratorial, so I didn't think I was in trouble. If I was in trouble, I wouldn't have been in her house anyway. As she talked to me, I saw people casually walking by to try to see what was going on. But she was sitting with her legs crossed under her in an armchair, leaning in to me and taking my hand as if we were just friends having a good talk. I basked in her attention.

MARCH 18, 04

What a relief! I had a long talk with Jessie about boyfriends and Obray. She answered all of the questions I ever wanted to know, and much more. She said "Come here, Guinevere, I want to have a girly talk with you." Then we got into the living room and she said "About your love life, can you tell me about it?" I said yes, and I told her about how Obray would come up at night and talk. She asked me about what and I said, "Whatever was happening." Then I told her about the time he got furious at me and called me a cold hearted bitch because I started to get tired of him, and she said that he had no right over me whatsoever. She said that he was clinging to me because I was much more of an interesting person and more interested in life and he needs someone alive to be around all the time.

She said I will have so many like him, but they shouldn't be stuck to me. She said it would be a bore to be stuck to him while I will have so many men to choose from. And that if I am stuck to him, I will miss the beauty and godliness of falling in love, really in love. She said that he is lazy, stupid and inconsiderate and that his mind is only stuck on me, so all he does is mope around and be a lazy bum. She said that she could guarantee to me that by the time I am 17, I won't be interested in him anymore, and if he were my husband he would bore me to tears. I have to tell him that he is to be my friend, and only that. Please don't think that this passes me like nothing. It is painful, but the truth is always painful. He just has to learn. Jessie told me so much, much more but I cannot write it all because I am exhausted.

After this, Obray sulked around me endlessly, sometimes writing me lovelorn notes and surreptitiously handing them to me when no one was looking, and sometimes completely ignoring me for days. But he didn't come up to my room anymore, and I was grateful for Jessie's intervention and looking forward to the beauty and godliness of really falling in love in the way she spoke of.

CHAPTER 15

IN THE PAST YEAR, A SCHOOLHOUSE HAD BEEN BUILT ON THE Los Angeles property. Because the Family had started a construction company eight years before, the boys my age were all raised learning how to build things, and they were good at it. I was excited that this meant we might actually have school every day, with grades and everything.

Before 1974, we'd had sporadic experiences in public schools: a brief stint in kindergarten in Kansas, a disastrous couple of weeks in elementary school in Los Angeles, and my own solo foray into the first grade in San Francisco, when I was briefly sent to stay in the community there just before my sister Annalee was born.

In all cases, we were ill-equipped to socialize with other kids. We'd cluster together on the playground at recess and get stares from students and teachers alike. But now that I was older, I understood—or somewhat understood—the real reason they had pulled us out of World School for good. In the summer of 1974, I'd heard, a reporter from *Rolling Stone* magazine came to write a piece about the Family. Apparently he had hung out for days, seeming like a cool guy who really got what the Family was about. But then his article came out and it compared us to the Manson Family and generally got us all wrong, painting Melvin as an acid-crazed lunatic and his followers as mindless but dangerous weirdos.

I was confused by this story—I knew the Rolling Stones were an evil rock 'n' roll band; was this a magazine about them, and if so, what did that have to do with us? We learned to have disdain for being called hippies or compared to Manson and his followers, but I didn't really understand what those things were. The adults didn't like to talk about it, and so we all just accepted that with this article, World People had shown who they truly were—manipulative, conniving, and untrustworthy. The men started building high security gates around our properties in Boston and Los Angeles, and it was ordained that there would be no new people—no coming and going and casual visits. You were either in or out, and all of us kids were most definitely in.

The new three-story schoolhouse was just a five-minute walk from the Kids' House, behind the tennis court, and inside it smelled like sawdust and looked so very pristine. Some of the windows still had stickers on them from—well, I didn't know where windows came from, but the stickers told me they weren't homemade. In my world of hand-me-down clothes and cluttered old houses, the schoolhouse stood out. It had desks, chalkboards, clean walls, and new carpet.

But our schooling still consisted of the erratic, often incoherent teachings of the adults who happened to be around us. Owen had been a speechwriter for Henry Kissinger. He was supposed to be teaching us history, and the way he did that was to analyze the astrological charts of the U.S. presidents. We learned that both Abraham Lincoln and Franklin Delano Roosevelt were Aquarians and that FDR had a lot more signs in Mercury, which explained the New Deal. I was pleased to learn that John F. Kennedy was a Gemini like me but was immediately admonished: Kennedy and I also shared Venus in Gemini, which meant we were flirtatious, superficial, and untrustworthy. George would read to us from Melvin's writings—Melvin had written detailed liner notes for every tape he issued, much of it about his own history of traveling with his music before the Lyman Family was formed. Big John was meant to teach us science, but he had no books and would sit at the teacher's desk, rolling cigarettes and talking about whatever came to his mind. He didn't give us tests. Once, Jessie came to teach us geography for a few days; Delia taught us composition for a while; and some days school "just wasn't happening."

My Darling Lavinia,

*George read The Loft stories to us. He asked us some questions like
why was Melvin a World Saviour, and those kind of hard ones. Of
course, I never said a word, but just thought thoroughly about each
thing he said, although I did not understand it all. I was thinking
today, about the banjo. What I can play on it, (and have worked on
for two years), anyone could learn in a week! I used to think I was
really hot stuff to be able to play it but it is NOTHING. Anyone
can pick up a banjo and pluck out a couple tunes, but few can make
it really sound beautiful. I've got a lot to learn, more than I will
ever know. In Mirror at the End of the Road, Melvin talks about
taking steps on your way to God. I used to think that every step you
take it would get easier but My God! I know now it gets harder, I
know!*

Some days we actually ate breakfast, walked to the schoolhouse,
and wrote in our diaries before our first lesson. But the structure never
lasted or stayed the same. School just didn't seem to matter that much.
Life was school. Being on Planet Earth was school.

I was already scared of Delia before she trained her sights on me,
but once she made my expulsion her mission, my fear bordered on
obsession. It began in the schoolhouse in her writing class.

A few weeks before, I'd decided to capitalize on the classified
knowledge I had that Melvin was dead. I wrote a short piece about an
encounter with him, but not a real one. I made one up. The story involved me working alone in a row of sorghum on the Farm a few years
earlier. In the story, Melvin wanders down my row and puts down a
folding chair, deciding to sit and meditate as I work. I'd seen a photo
of him doing this, so it felt possible. I didn't dare put invented words
in his mouth, choosing to have it be a scene of silent connection between us. "What can anyone do?" I thought. "He's dead. I can't get
caught for this." But the lie gnawed at me. I would study Delia anx-

iously. She clearly knew he was dead—but did she know that I knew? I wondered if she knew my Melvin story was a lie but couldn't risk challenging me. Or maybe her absolute confidence that the lowly likes of me would never be privileged to know such information meant that she didn't think twice about it. After all, she was Jessie's best friend, and I was just some stray Jessie had taken in.

Delia's writing assignment on this particular day was to choose a painting from one of the many giant books we had of the work of Thomas Hart Benton and to write a paragraph describing it. On this day, I chose to write about Benton's painting *July Hay*. I'd always loved its lush images and the way the perspective made me feel like I was playing hooky, peering ever so briefly out from the woods to watch the farmers harvest hay. I finished my paragraph before everyone else (I'd thought about this painting before) and was gazing out the window, chin in hand. Delia didn't like this. I'm not sure exactly what part of what I was doing got under her skin, but she startled me close to screaming when she snatched the piece of loose-leaf paper off my desk.

The sudden movement made the whole class look up. Or maybe it was my gasp, which seemed to annoy her even further. Her eyes scanned the page, and then she read my first sentence aloud. "The farmers were working laboriously." She lifted her eyes from the page to look at me with disdain, and with what I immediately understood was suspicion. "Who the hell do you think you are, using a word like 'laboriously'?" she demanded, her voice indignant but controlled. She was standing very close to my desk now, her hands close enough to smack my face, and she had certainly smacked me many times before.

I could smell the sandalwood perfume she always wore, a smell that I'd come to associate with danger. I stared at her hands, trying to will her attention away from me. She didn't like my hesitation and raised her voice insistently. "*Where* did you get this word? Do you even know what it means?"

"Working really hard?" I answered ever so cautiously, hoping I sounded unsure. It would have been more strategic to pretend I didn't know, but I thought of that two seconds too late.

She scoffed and slapped the piece of paper back on my desk, speaking to the whole class now. "Using big words doesn't mean it's good writing. Don't use words if you don't know what they mean."

But I forgave her for continuing to act like I didn't know what "laboriously" meant. I forgave her because I knew something about her and that she was probably sad. I knew this because of Daria. Jessie told Daria everything, and then Daria told me. Because of this, I sometimes knew things most adults didn't know.

What I knew about Delia was this: She had very recently been forced to have an abortion she didn't want to have. It was a complicated situation—she got pregnant with FP, the man who was officially in a relationship with my mother. Delia was told to have an abortion, and FP was told to stay with my mother. It didn't occur to me in this moment that Delia was lashing out at me because she was likely full of rage at my mother—I just thought she was sad that she didn't get to have that baby. Plus she already had a baby—Luka—who had recently been in the hospital for weeks and almost died.

But I was always told I looked a lot like my mother, and Delia did have to look at me daily since I'd been living wherever Jessie was. If Jessie was the Queen, Delia was her right-hand woman. In a room full of drunk adults (the kind of room we were in often), she seemed the most sober and the least likely to join in on a joke. While other adults got progressively more raucous and more likely to break into fights or jump into the pool fully clothed, Delia was quiet, tense—an observer—and as such she wielded significant power. Just as Delia was Jessie's handmaid, I was Daria's. We were both privileged to be in proximity to Jessie. We had versions of the same job. I assumed it was Jessie who'd said she had to have the abortion (she was the only one who had that power, after all), but Delia couldn't afford to be angry at Jessie (there was no such thing as being angry at Jessie), and so began Delia's campaign to get me out of her sight permanently.

CHAPTER 16

WHEN JESSIE DECIDED IT WAS TIME TO MAKE THE JOURNEY across the country again in April, school was instantly over, and we were on our way. There was the usual chaos in the days leading up to getting twenty people ready to leave on a weeklong camping trip and an underlying melancholy from those who would be left behind.

APRIL 1, 04

My Lavinia,

Goodbye Los Angeles, Hello Martha's Vineyard. We're on the move! The morning was crazy and all the ladies were so grumpy and have been at my throat since last night. I wish Jessie would pack me, Lou won't help and I did it all wrong. My feet hurt like hell today. But anyway, when we finally got it all together today, it was great! I feel so much more at home on the Caravan than locked up in LA. We are in the desert and close to the border of California. We drove 210 miles today. Oh God I can't wait to get to the Vineyard. I hated saying goodbye. Poor Aaron, he was crying.

We stopped at the Farm, as usual. I hadn't been there since we passed through last September, and it felt like a lot had changed—

both the physical place and the kids I'd lived with. It seemed like the girls my age and I had come to a new awareness of our stations in life, and I watched Jackie, Clotilde, and Daria all turn into hyper-regal versions of themselves, alternately being dismissive of or bossing around the kids who lived there, especially the girls.

APRIL 5, 04

The "Bunk House" is so beautiful! It looks like some kind of rich house. God—the kids here are under such strict rules. First of all they can't go anywhere without permission. Number two, they can't come to this house (Jessie's house) without being invited. Oh well, I guess it's good for them. I didn't like today. I don't know <u>what</u> we're going to do here. Might as well Bargello all day. Jessie seems so much more happy here than on the Caravan. I'm glad to be settled too. Everything is just gorgeous here—in comparison with LA. Katie and DeeDee are getting into their dumb things about low class people. It is really stupid. God! This afternoon we heard a session of Reflections. God! I couldn't believe it! The way all of the children listen to tapes here is surprising. And the way they let those babies act! My God, they talk and read and clap and everything. All I did all day was wander around.

Katie and DeeDee had indeed joked with me when we were alone in the kitchen about how they were just the low-class people and I was part of Jessie's world now. For some reason, though I knew and understood that in the deeply ingrained hierarchy of our Family I was above them now and I didn't used to be, I was uncomfortable with it when it came out of their mouths. Because of this I brushed aside their talk of being low-class people, which only underlined their point. "You used to be like us," their betrayed eyes seemed to say, "and now you're different."

I still had to help with dinner and dishes afterward, but I was mostly in Jessie's House, where the regular Farm Kids weren't often allowed, and I meandered from room to room, marveling at the new beautifully carved staircase, sliding my hand up the banister, picturing where our plywood bunk beds used to be, and thinking about the nature of time. I was turning eleven next month and I was taking that very seriously, contemplating life as I imagined eleven-year-olds did.

APRIL 10, 04

Life is an eternal passage of change. Every time you take a step you think "Oh God, this has to be the last one, I can't go any further," but there is always something more that you haven't discovered.

> *Tomorrow will be Yesterday*
> *Once Yesterday was tomorrow*
> *And tomorrow and Yesterday*
> *Are sometimes today*
> *And today goes on in the same way*
> *Until it is Yesterday again.*

Of course, Daria and I visited Ratso's grave. It was a year and a half later, but we still sang the September 4 song to each other sometimes, though I'd seen her forget about our pact and carelessly step on the third stair when she was tired. Behind the barn where we'd buried him there were now several pieces of farm equipment—a giant yellow backhoe and a shiny green tractor parked almost on top of the hallowed grave site, surrounded by the prints of heavy work boots.

We leaned against the tractor, contemplating the short life of Ratso, and sang "September 4" to him in low, melancholy tones. "No one understands," Daria said quietly, but she was soon distracted, sitting in the seat of the tractor. "Look at this!" she said, pointing to the gearshift. "It has a turtle for slow and a rabbit for fast." I looked at the little icons as she put her hands on the mini steering wheel, making loud tractor sounds, declaring, "I'll tell them we want to ride it later." Here on the Farm she didn't need me as much. There was a fresh crop of people catering to her every whim, and she didn't need to throw tantrums to get attention. My position was starting to feel tenuous.

Clotilde was behaving with extra imperiousness, alternately giving me the cold shoulder and giving me lectures. Obray was also on the Caravan, and Clotilde had daily ideas about how I should treat him. I was trying to defuse the whole thing—Jessie had made it clear that I shouldn't be concerned with Obray's attention, so I was nice to him but didn't seek him out. This was easier said than done, since we were in a room full of people together every night, and of course I would know him for the rest of my life, so I couldn't alienate him completely. But Clotilde would stoke the flames, reading his diary and reporting back how miserable I was making him.

She insisted I write him a note to tell him that I still cared about him, and I was hesitant. "Can you be friends with someone who is in love with you?" I asked her, and she scoffed, "You have to," and then nonchalantly added, "Anyway, he also wrote that he thinks I'm very beautiful and he thinks he's falling in love with me but he knows he can't." She of course had no romantic intrigue in her life and never would—it was an unspoken rule that she would be Melvin's forever. No boy ever dared flirt with her, and no adult man could "take her on." I wondered if this would change once everyone knew that Melvin wasn't alive, or would that be a secret forever? Would Clotilde be married to a dead man for the rest of her life?

Once I heard that Obray thought he might be in love with Clotilde, I refused to write him a note. I didn't want anything to do with him romantically, but I still felt slighted. Now I realized the truth—he was just eager to pine after someone and was clearly choosing impossible people like me and Clotilde so that he could mope around without fear of getting what he was pretending to want. So I refused to write him a note and Clotilde was mad at me. We didn't speak to each other for a full day, and she wrote this on the top of one of my diary pages:

Really don't know what's gotten into you since we've been here. You're such a shithead and so self involved. Really not the same person at all. Now don't think I read your stupid diary because I really don't care to.

She knew that being self-involved was the highest of crimes, and adults accused me of being self-involved often. "It's all that Aries in your chart," I'd been told. My moon was in Aries, which I always thought was cool because Melvin was an Aries. It was supposed to be the sign of my "soul," after all. But my Saturn was also in Aries, and Saturn was the planet of discipline, which meant my Saturn made me impulsive and impatient—undisciplined. Once when we were watching *Sesame Street*, a short segment called "The Most Important Person" showed young kids playing and doing things like blowing out birthday candles, happy and carefree. The lyrics were: "The most important person in the whole wide world is you, and you hardly even know you." I was scandalized by this song, thinking, "Wow, they really teach World Kids all wrong. No wonder the World is such a bad place, with all these little kids walking around thinking they are the most important person." Clotilde knew being called self-involved would cut me to the core, and it was also her way of mimicking adults in an effort to assert authority over me.

When I read what she wrote in my diary, I ran to find her, eager to make up with her and ask her how I could be less of a "shithead." I found her crying upstairs in a bedroom in Jessie's House. She'd rescued a litter of baby mice the day before, and now they were gone. She stood over a bloodstained towel in the corner of the room where she was keeping them. "That stupid cat Pretzel ate my babies," she said, sobbing. She was devastated by this, and her uncontrollable crying made me wonder if it wasn't just about the baby mice.

I hugged her and she leaned her head on my shoulder. I considered telling her about Ratso and how I understood her pain but then thought better of it. She clearly wasn't mad at me anymore, and the mention of Daria might send her into some kind of angry fit, and right now she was treating me like an equal. "Do you want to take a walk to the creek?" I asked, and she nodded wordlessly. I led her outside and we held hands and didn't say much as we made our way down the hill to the road, across two fields and to the creek. Eventually she said, "Please don't think I hate you or anything, I don't. I'm sorry if I've been on edge lately. I love you." I squeezed her hand, relieved, as we sat down on the bank of the creek.

*Clotilde and I took a wonderful walk. It wasn't very far but it was
so nice just to stand out there in nowhere and listen to the stillness.
You really can't call it stillness, so much is really happening here, it
is such magic and yet it is there every day for anyone to hear. The
creek flowing, the wind rustling through the trees, the crickets singing. So many little things. It really freshened us up.*

As we were walking back to Jessie's House, Clotilde no longer crying and our friendship repaired, she asked, "Are you excited that you
and Gabriel are going to visit your mommies in New York in a few
weeks?" I said I was, which was true, but then she said, "Well, I heard
through the grapevine that you and Gabes might stay there for the
whole summer." My heart sank. It had already been decided that Geordie and Jesse would stay on the Farm for the summer, but we all knew
that "for the summer" could turn into a much longer time.

CHAPTER 17

ONCE THE CARAVAN WAS ON ITS WAY TO BOSTON, WE MADE the trip in three days with no camping, only pit stops. Jessie was eager to get to the Vineyard and out on her boat to do her favorite thing in the world—fish for striped bass. She'd seemed troubled on the Farm, always staring out windows and not talking as much as she usually did. One day she was doing this in the kitchen and several of us girls were hanging around, busying ourselves just to be near her or maybe over-hear something she said that we could tell everyone we'd heard first-hand. That day she suddenly said, "Out! All of you!" shooing us away with her hand. "Go do something constructive with your lives!" We scattered quickly, ashamed.

But now she had a spring in her step. She grew up spending summers on the Vineyard, on this very piece of property, which wasn't true of any of the other places we lived, and it clearly felt like home to her. This time she was really limiting who came with her. "I don't want a lot of people just hanging around," she said, and so at first it would be only thirteen of us, though we knew people would be invited to visit and, if they were lucky, go out on the boat to fish with Jessie. Still, it felt *very* important to be selected as one of the few who were coming with her and staying all summer.

I was supposed to go directly to New York to visit my mother, but now Jessie said we should wait awhile because there was "too much going on there and it's not a place for children." I wanted to know more, but I knew better than to ask. I just hoped it wasn't my mommy who was in trouble, because there was always the danger that the trouble would trickle down to me.

But my mother seemed to be more in favor these days than she had ever been. After Delia had the abortion and FP was commanded to go back to New York and be with my mother, Jessie said to me, "Your mother is full of hell, and I love her!" This was the only time I ever heard Jessie talk about her, and I felt proud of whatever it was my mother had done. I assumed it was fight to get her guy back? I'd seen this before with Jessie: She'd command that someone do something, and sometimes when they fought back, she respected it. And sometimes when they didn't fight back, she would berate them for being spineless. Maybe Mommy had said fuck you to FP—if he wanted to have a baby with Delia, then she didn't want to be with him?

In the few days we had in Boston, I got a clearer sense of what was going on in New York, my most reliable source of information being the older girls who loved to tell me things to prove how in-the-know they were. Jackie was the one to give me the scuttlebutt.

MAY 8, 04

Jackie said she thinks everyone in New York is in trouble because Lyman got drunk a couple days ago and went walking out in the streets and got picked up by a cop and the cops put him on a drug and put him in the Looney Bin until we came and picked him up. They are in trouble because it is carelessness and dangerous carelessness.

Lyman and his twin, Loren, were exceptions in the Family—in their twenties, and Melvin's cousins, they were treated as somewhere between adults and kids, probably informed by the fact that they were dwarves and had significant medical problems over the years. This meant they got away with a lot—they didn't do chores or work on the construction sites, but they were talented musicians and funny guys. I shuddered to think of Lyman in a loony bin, as the adults called it. All

I knew of mental hospitals was in the Lord's List movies *The Snake Pit* and *One Flew Over the Cuckoo's Nest,* and they seemed like horrible places to me. But I was relieved that my mother wasn't in trouble, at least not specifically her.

We went off to the Vineyard, and I was delighted.

MAY 9, 04

Packing for the Vineyard was kind of hard but when it was done I was very thankful. Thirteen people came to the Vineyard plus two cats, two dogs, one hamster and one bird. It was really squished inside the van. Coming was just like home. Clotilde, Samantha, Padrick, Daria Cybele Lou and I came down to our house and then had dinner, just the seven of us. Jessie and us girls decided that we should cook all of the dinners and she will help us and we will learn to cook. Oh, it is so great to be here.

There were three houses on the Vineyard—the Kids' House, Jessie's House, and a building called the Moskie House, where most of the boys and men slept. There was a shed where the fish were cleaned, and a lot of woods to wander in. Behind the Kids' House was an elaborate tangled grapevine, and we loved to stuff ourselves with the fuzzy grapes that grew there. Menemsha was the nearest town, with a few restaurants and shops that were only open in the summer months and the dock where Jessie kept her boat. This was my second summer on the Vineyard, and it was definitely my favorite place.

Days on the Vineyard were mostly pretty easy and lovely. We girls always had to cook, clean, and take care of the younger children, but there was usually a beach trip, or sometimes we were allowed to walk into Menemsha to wander around on our own, with just enough money for an ice cream sandwich. People in town seemed to know who we were and didn't treat us like freaks, the way people had when we tried to go to public school. Jessie knew a lot of people on the island, which meant we sometimes had guests from the outside world come for dinner. There was a PBS show called *The Pallisers,* and we sat down to watch it each week; the attitude toward television was more relaxed here, though the only television on the property was in Jessie's House, so it was up to her when it was turned on.

Daria and I would ride our bikes down sandy paths into the woods, just the two of us, spending hours inventing worlds where fairies lived, before coming home dirty and exhausted. We had a fresh crop of things that were just our own, inside jokes and characters we'd conjured, and I felt relieved that she was back to treating me like her best friend.

Everyone usually ate dinner together in the Kids' House, but we'd often end up in Jessie's House to watch TV after dinner, where the famous painting of her as a young woman playing guitar hung over the fireplace.

Jessie went fishing almost every day with a few others, and we all waited for her return once the sun started going down. If she caught a bass—if anyone caught a bass—she would step out of the car beaming, her eyes sparkling as she regaled us with the story of the catch.

That summer I decided I would take a scale from each fish that was caught and glue it into my diary, diligently writing down the statistics: who caught it, what kind of fish it was, and how much it weighed. I'd keep an eye out for the car and rush down to the shed where they cleaned the fish. I marveled at the catch laid out on the table, then carefully plucked out a big scale from the fattest part of the fish. There were bluefish, sometimes scup or flounder, but when someone caught a bass there was a celebration. The men got used to me loitering around the cleaning table, and soon they were helping me out, saying things like "That one was Anthony's" or "This one really put up a fight." I'd admire the fish and watch them weigh it, and then someone would call out, "Seventeen point three pounds!" and I would hurry back to the house, reciting the number to myself so I didn't forget, the precious scale between my fingers.

The trip to see my mother had been indefinitely postponed, until out of the blue Jessie told me I was leaving for New York the next day. She also said Gabriel's mother, Alison, was coming to the Vineyard, so Gabes didn't need to visit her. It would be just me going to New York.

I was quite panicked about this development. I hadn't been in trouble on the Vineyard so far, but was there something I didn't know? The New York community had no kids in it, and the adults there were people like my mother who had full-time jobs, except for the couple of women who maintained the house. What would I do with myself if I had to live there? I tried to find reassurance in reminding myself that kids never lived in places where there weren't other kids. You were never the only kid. But there was a first time for everything, and I couldn't think of a sadder life than one that was only populated by adults.

After I'd packed a small suitcase, my banjo, and my bargello project, I got into bed and fretted in my diary.

MAY 11, 04

Maybe they are trying to leave me alone in New York for a reason. What have I done wrong? Oh! I am so full of guilt, guilt, guilt!

There wasn't anything specific I was guilty about—the possibility that I'd done something wrong was always there.

CHAPTER 18

THE NEW YORK COMMUNITY WAS A THREE-STORY BROWNSTONE on 15th Street in Manhattan. The inside of it felt somber to me—the curtains were heavy velvet and usually drawn, and the floors were a dark wood. I was looking forward to seeing my mother, but that was also woven in with the anxiety of not really knowing what to say to her. I hadn't seen her in almost two years.

My mother was working on Wall Street during the day, leaving before I woke up and coming back around dinnertime. The only people who were home were Lyman, medicated and sullen, and Carol, who was one of the ladies I really liked. She had stringy black hair and a gap between her front teeth, and her eyes squinted to nothing when she laughed. Her little kids, Leelia and Dean, were in the Boston community, and I'd spent a lot more time with them than with her, so I found it amusing that she looked like a giant little kid. She was really into bargello too, and we spent some of the days working on our pieces together.

But mostly I played the banjo and waited for everyone to get home, helping Carol with dinner preparation and talking about life on the Vineyard. I was careful not to seem too at home and took the opportunity to sigh and stare out the window when I felt like someone would notice.

My mother would come home exhausted and then get right into the business of domestic chores, waiting diligently on the men, especially FP. FP seemed like the most happy-go-lucky guy, considering only a few months before he'd been faced with Delia's abortion and being forced to go back to New York. I'd heard that he was sad about it, but he certainly didn't seem sad now. He joked a lot with me and playfully teased my mother, who did seem to lighten up a bit around him, though mostly she seemed distracted.

MAY 16, 04

Mommy doesn't seem too happy here. I hardly ever see her. She seems so sad—like something is wrong.

I called Jessie every night, anxious to remind the New York people where I really belonged and to make sure Jessie didn't forget me. The first two nights the phone just rang and rang on the other end, which I told myself was no big deal. Everyone was probably listening to a tape. On the third night I finally got to talk to her, and she told me about catching a herring and how she was getting up at 3:00 A.M. to go fishing the next day. "How's my little forty-four-year-old doing in the big city?" she asked, and I told her how we were planning to visit my grandmother and how much progress I'd made on my bargello piece, and she said she missed me. I felt a small bit of relief after we hung up—she didn't sound like she was planning to make me stay.

The next day Carol said she would take me to the bargello store and then she had a surprise. The bargello store had rows and rows of yarn, organized impeccably by color, which I found very beautiful. I hadn't been in stores much in my life and so it was exciting and a bit over-whelming.

One of the only times I had been in a store was in Los Angeles when I was nine. I was with Yvonne in a place that sold greeting cards, candles, and fancy things for the bath. I was well aware that adults "lifted" things often from the outside world, and when I saw a package of colorful bath beads that were just like the ones we used at home, I decided I would impress Yvonne by stealing them. There weren't many people in the store, and while Yvonne was buying something at the counter, I glanced around and then slipped the little circular container under my jacket. Once we were safely walking down the street, I pulled out the bath beads, triumphant. "Look what I got for us!" I said.

Yvonne looked confused and then horrified. "What? Where did you get those?"

"I lifted them," I said, now a little nervous.

"No!" she said, grabbing my hand and pulling me back toward the store. "We're going in and you have to give them back."

I felt humiliated when we walked back into the store and she made me go up to the counter and hand over my stolen goods. "I'm sorry," she said. "My daughter took these when she wasn't supposed to." I hung my head in shame as the lady in the store shook her head in disdain, but what I was really feeling was confusion. Adults stole all the time and laughed about it! I was expecting praise and instead I was in trouble. I made a mental note that not everything adults did was OK for kids to do and wondered when I would be old enough to steal.

Because of this, my association with stores was fraught, and as I wandered around the bargello store, wanting things, I reminded myself that it was not OK to steal them, as if I might do it by accident. When the lady in the store saw me pull out my bargello piece to make sure the new yarn colors would match, she said, "Well, look at you!" and gave me a huge smile. These World People were so confusing— I knew they didn't have souls, but some of them seemed really nice.

Finally Carol told me the surprise: She was taking me to visit Mommy at her office. I was wide-eyed as we approached the giant glass building downtown, the street bustling with men in suits. I'd never been near anything like it—an elevator to the thirty-fifth floor, a room full of metal and glass and strangers. I felt shy when we found Mommy at her desk, and she hugged me in a way that seemed different. It was dramatic and felt fake. Her co-workers stopped by, talking too loud when they leaned down and said, "And who's this?" and "Where'd you get those pretty blue eyes?" The blue-eyes question always threw me—adults asked it urgently, as if they genuinely expected an answer, and I didn't have one, so I would just shrug.

As the women stood around me chatting, I wandered off to look out the floor-to-ceiling glass windows at the street below. Incredible. I'd seen it in movies, but here it was in real life—people looking far away and so tiny as they rushed around having city lives.

But the thing I marveled at most was an object on my mother's desk: a framed photo of me at seven years old, holding a troll doll and grinning from ear to ear. "She lies to all of these people she works with," I realized, amazed. "They think she goes home to me at night." I hadn't really understood until now that she led a double life. I knew that some of the adults went to jobs where they didn't talk about us, but the jobs and lives they led outside were abstractions—I'd never seen the other side—and it had never occurred to me that they were all lying. It had been drilled into our heads that lying was bad, but it was OK to lie to World People? I wondered if she'd invented a fake father for me and why she didn't have a picture of Annalee, who was four at the time and living in Boston. Was upholding the fiction of going home to two kids one lie too many? What would her co-workers think if they knew she had two young kids who lived in different cities than she did? I felt anxious—she hadn't shared the extent of the lie with me, and what if someone was about to ask me a question and I messed up somehow? I said I had a stomachache, which wasn't a lie, and Carol and I were soon on our way.

That night, back on 15th Street, the adults decided to listen to The Jug Band Tape for the second night in a row. They settled in the living room to listen, and I was struck by how everyone in this place was so serious and there wasn't much laughter, except for Carol, who seemed to be permanently amused by life, and FP, who continued to go out of his way to be nice to me.

As the adults settled in the living room, FP hung back, then leaned in to me, conspiratorial. "I already got what I needed out of The Jug Band Tape last night—let's go watch a movie." Alison was still in the kitchen, refilling her wineglass, and overheard him, and the three of us quietly slipped down to the lower floor to watch *The Outlaw Josey Wales,* which was a transgressive thing to do because it wasn't on the Lord's List. FP was chummy, laughing at some of the lines and quoting them; he'd clearly seen this movie before. I felt guilty when I teared up when Clint Eastwood's young companion died—if this movie wasn't on the Lord's List, then it shouldn't make me feel anything, right? It would be one thing if Jessie said it was OK to watch it, but FP? I wasn't comfortable being in league with him like this; I had a sense of his lowly status being contagious and vowed to listen to whatever tape the adults listened to the following night.

When FP heard that I'd visited Mommy's office that day, he scoffed and said, "That must have been really boring! We should do something fun tomorrow—let's go to the circus! Have you ever been to the circus?" Of course I'd never been to the circus; what kind of a question was that? And I didn't particularly want to go. This was all becoming too much for me, and I was itching to go home to the Vineyard.

At the circus the next day with Mommy, FP, and a couple of other adults, I was overwhelmed by the Madison Square Garden crowds and alarmed by the noise. I didn't like the way the animals were treated—they couldn't possibly tolerate all this loud music and yelling. I watched the high-wire and trapeze acts in awe, keenly aware that one of the performers could fall at any time. FP and Mommy got into some kind of fight, but I didn't know what it was about, because I couldn't hear what they were saying.

MAY 18, 04

When everyone finally got into it, we went to the circus. They had some good acts, a couple, but everything was so modern.

The best thing about this day was hearing "The Old Loft and Waltham". It is so much. It has so much inside of it—God—how can I describe it? Sometimes I feel like I don't deserve it. Tonight, deserve it or not, I needed it so badly. I missed everyone so much, I found myself talking to them. Really, while I was playing the banjo, I would play a song, then out loud dedicate it to one of the people I miss dearly. Pretty crazy eh? But the Old Loft was such a comfort. SO full of love Ray Charles's voice is. I was weeping through the whole tape. I love it so much.

On the weekend, we drove to visit my grandmother in New Jersey. My mother told me I'd met her once before, when I was three and she visited Fort Hill, but I didn't remember that visit. My grandmother's house was on a quiet tree-lined street in a small town, and she lived there with my uncle Dennis, who was in his twenties. My mother and my aunt Nell, who was also in the Lyman Family, had grown up in this house. I knew that my grandmother blamed my mother for Nell joining the Family—my mother had joined first, and Nell followed a year later, as soon as she graduated from high school. My grandmother would forever be mad at my mother for luring her favorite daughter into this alternative life she didn't approve of.

But as we sat in her living room, eating homemade lemon squares and drinking iced tea, none of this tension was evident. In fact, they didn't talk about the Family at all or even acknowledge that it existed. My grandmother sat down in a high-backed armchair with a hectic floral pattern, clearly "her" chair, and told us tales of intrigue from the Singer sewing store she'd worked in for thirty years and shared tidbits about Uncle Dennis, who was at work. When she spoke of him, she gestured toward the empty armchair parallel to hers, chuckling that he'd recently bought an electric guitar and she'd banished him to the basement to play it.

In her early sixties, my grandmother wore her long gray hair twisted into an old-fashioned chignon ("Like Eleanor Roosevelt," I thought), and her piercing blue eyes had a little twinkle of mischief that belied her formality. Today she was wearing a crisp lavender jacket and skirt set she'd made herself and a string of pearls. She spoke with an almost British accent, and the stack of finished *New York Times* crossword puzzles by the side of her chair was almost as tall as me. "Your grandmother finishes the *New York Times* crossword puzzle every morning," my mother said, and my grandmother waved the statement away in a gesture of false modesty. I didn't know what *The New York Times* was, but I could tell I was supposed to be impressed.

I'd only met a few old people in my life—Jessie's parents and a guy named Red, who used to bring carp to the Farm when he had caught too many for his family to eat. But I'd never had the full attention of an old person or sat with them for hours in their home. I tried not to stare at her wrinkled hands or the way the skin was loose around her neck. I felt a little afraid of what an old person looked like up close, and this added a layer to my awkwardness. Unsure of what to talk about, I asked her about the paintings that hung in every room of her house—large and colorful framed images of landscapes and sailboats. "Paint by numbers," she said. "Your grandfather couldn't get enough of them." The hint of bitterness in her voice was the first time I'd seen a crack in her very proper demeanor.

On the car ride home, my mother told me how when she was four months pregnant with me at nineteen, she'd come home from college for Christmas break and tried to hide her pregnancy from her family. On her second day home, my grandmother had said, out of the blue, "Don't tell your father, and don't bring that child into this house—it will kill him." It was my first inkling that maybe my mother had become a part of the Lyman Family out of desperation and not adulation of Melvin and his teachings. I realized maybe she'd simply had nowhere to go. My grandfather died when I was three, having never known I existed. This gave me a melancholy feeling and I looked out the window, wondering if it really would have killed him to know I existed. My mother glanced over, saw my expression, and said, "You didn't miss out on much. He was an asshole, and I didn't go to his funeral."

Finally it was my last night in New York. I would ride to Boston with a couple of adults the next day and be back on the Vineyard soon after. I was supposed to hang out with Mommy that night—she said she'd teach me how to make lemon squares like the ones we had at my grandmother's. But something shifted in the mood during dinner, and suddenly everyone was just sitting around browbeating Lizzie, and it went on for hours. This was the problem with being the only kid—people completely forgot about you. In my normal life when a heavy started, they told us to go upstairs, and we were happy to oblige. Heavies were scary but also kind of boring and repetitive.

MAY 19, 04

Lizzie had a small heavy laid on her tonight. I happened to be sitting right in the middle of it. And I had all I could do to keep from bursting out with laughter because of the expressions on Carol's face and then every once in a while she would laugh, too, which made it really hard.

I was off to Boston the next morning, and Lizzie had been added to the trip, because apparently George had heard about the heavy and wanted to talk to her in person. Lizzie barely said a word for the whole ride.

But when we got there, Lizzie was off the hook, because a guy named Wayne was in big trouble. Wayne was kind of a quiet guy who seemed older than the other adults, but that may just have been because he was the only one with thinning hair. He was always extra nice to me because he'd been in a relationship with my mother, but we both seemed to understand that this was obligatory and didn't mean much. Because the adults were having a heavy with Wayne, us kids were sent upstairs, and Frida told me that she heard Wayne was thinking about leaving the communities for good. Wayne had been friends with Melvin from the very beginning—the preface to *Mirror at the End of the Road* was a letter to Melvin from Wayne, in which he wrote:

> For me to approach this book and read it is already an awesome responsibility. I stand in awe of its greatness and purity. I can't believe it. It's full of miracles and its greatest miracle is in its reality. It really is the new bible, born to be read again and again, inexhaustible in its capacity to teach.

Wayne leaving was a very big deal. For as long as I could remember, no one had left.

*This morning Devora came up and told us what happened with
Wayne. It went on til 5:15 in the morning and George was making
Wayne tell the pure truth, making him let out the part of him that
hates Jessie and Melvin, and pretty soon it wasn't just Wayne that
was the focus, it was <u>everyone</u>. And it was plain truth. When
George moved into the kitchen, everyone did except Wayne and
George asked him why he was alone, and if he could love Melvin
and Jessie, and Wayne said, "No." He left. He is gone. Poor, Poor
George. Devora said he wept, and it was so hard for him. At ex-
actly the time Wayne left, Jessie caught her first bass! Oh, and then
Richie caught another. 18 lbs, and then a 21 lb!*

*Later, George, Bruce, Kay and I left Boston and came to the
Vineyard. Oh what a wonderful thing! I came home just in time
to eat the first bass, and Jessie said if I hadn't I would have a gap
in my soul.*

CHAPTER 19

DELIA HAD FLOWN AHEAD OF THE REST OF US TO THE Vineyard, sent to make sure everything was in order, and once we'd arrived she went back to being glued to Jessie's side, often leaning in to whisper in her ear. When I was in Delia's presence, I could always feel her eyes on me, like she was willing me to make a mistake. But also, as Melvin had said, I looked like my mother. This couldn't have been easy for Delia, so maybe she was just willing me out of existence because she couldn't stand the constant reminder of what she'd been through.

One night Jessie was in a good mood because her bass had been caught and prepared and eaten. She was stormier when she hadn't caught a fish, and we all felt that storm. Nothing terrible—she just wasn't radiating the way she did when she caught a bass. Bass were magic, we were told. We were all lucky to be eating this fish. I didn't like seafood of any kind, and though in my life I'd caught and shucked thousands of mussels, I'd sneakily managed never to eat one. I'd peeled skins off catfish and then later moved their cooked flesh carefully around my plate, chunks of it often ending up wadded in napkins in my pockets. But I always choked down the bass, thinking it sacrilegious not to, and thinking less of myself because I didn't enjoy it. What was wrong with me? I kept my repulsion a secret. My repulsion for this failing of mine was, after all, stronger than the one for the fish.

When everyone settled in after dinner, Jessie usually wanted her feet rubbed, and it was an honor to be the girl (always a girl) chosen to do it. On this night it was me, and I was relishing the task, and feeling the envious eyes of some of the other girls. I was usually invisible (or attempting to be invisible), and it was a moment to be in the spotlight, or adjacent to the spotlight. I sat on the floor, her foot in my hands, attempting to be invisible and perfect all at once as she held court in her usual fashion.

Seemingly out of nowhere, she reached down and took my face in her hand, her wineglass in the other. She had this proprietorship over our bodies, our daily lives, and our futures. Anything could change at any moment. "What are we going to do with this beautiful little Guinevere?" she asked everyone and no one in particular. She stared into my eyes for a moment, studying me. The room went quiet. This might have been the most attention I'd ever gotten, and it was intoxicating. "Let's make her Miss America," she said. She laughed her raspy laugh at this idea and dropped my face as she made a sweeping gesture with her arm. "Miss America. That's what she'll be." She was serious. She elaborated—she liked the idea of one of us infiltrating this American institution. She started to sing the Miss America theme song, raucously and grandly: "There she is, MISS America . . ." And everyone drunkenly joined in: "There she is, your ideal . . . the dreams of a million girls who are more than pretty . . ." They stumbled through the next few words, no one really knowing them, someone yelling out, "Something with Atlantic City!" and then disintegrated into laughter, and my golden moment had passed. I glanced over at Delia, who looked away, feigning nonchalance.

While other people, adults and kids alike, embraced the idea of me being Miss America, Delia began to use it against me. "You're not Miss America yet," she hissed at me days later. "So stop acting like you're better than everyone else and go empty the ashtrays in the living room." I didn't feel like I was better than anyone else, not by a long shot, but I had taken to dreaming about being Miss America. For the talent portion, I'd play my banjo. I swore that, win or lose, I wouldn't make a spectacle of myself and cry. I'd seen the show once before, and I thought the way some of the contestants cried was undignified, but

I also thought the ceremony was the most glamorous thing in the world.

And then things really started to turn, without any particular incident, as far as I could tell.

JULY 8, 04

I'm so confused. Daria told me that Jessie doesn't like me these days and that I was too full of myself and I guess that's why Delia is acting angry at me too. Tonight Delia said Daria and I could talk to Faedra after we cleaned the kitchen, but in the middle of it Daria went up to Jessie's house, and when I asked Lou if I should go up she said no. I felt so terrible. She is sleeping up there. I don't know what to do, or what is happening and I feel terrible because I guess I don't deserve to talk to Faedra, but I wonder if Daria is talking to Faedra. I am so confused tonight. I think I am going to cry.

I keep having nightmares, so disgustingly sickening that I can't even write about them, but they keep me awake at night.

Delia's watchful eye had me increasingly on edge, and in the days that followed I began to make mistakes. I washed baby Henry's hair with adult shampoo, and it got in his eyes. His screams echoed off the bathroom walls and through the house, and with each one my stomach sank. I desperately tried to calm him, but to no avail. After that, Delia decided that I wasn't allowed to handle the babies anymore. "If you're not responsible enough to be careful," she said, "I don't want you around the little ones. It's dangerous. You don't love these kids—you're just one big Gemini con." This was a big deal; there were probably five kids under the age of one year old, and now if one of them needed a diaper change or to be taken out of their high chair, I wasn't allowed to do it. The other girls began to resent me, though of course they didn't dare complain. I worked doubly hard on other tasks to try to make up for it. I thought I felt Jessie's attention toward me waning. I wondered if this was all because of something Delia had whispered in her ear about me.

Daria did talk to Faedra the other night. Faedra told her that I was too into myself and didn't care about the other children. I don't know why, I must really be unconscious that I don't even notice that. At first it made me all grumpy, but I thought about it and then I knew that Faedra would be very disappointed in me so I changed.

Delia doesn't seem to be angry at me anymore, but I had better watch my attitude. I am just a selfish person. Why did I have to have that bad quality? SELF. Yuck. I hate it. A selfish deadhead, disgusting. Absolutely revolting. I have got to change my ways.

It seemed like everyone was getting more in trouble these days, kids and adults alike. Corrina wasn't allowed to go to the beach because she hit Sylvie, and soon afterward, Sylvie was sent to Boston because she lied too much. Lou was constantly yelling at us because we didn't clean well enough, and a kid named Ricky got sent back to Boston for "being a deadhead." We were all getting a lot of speeches. FP came to visit, got in trouble for something, and was sent back to New York two days later. George took Clotilde aside and talked to her for hours, and when she came down she was sullen for days but wouldn't tell me what they talked about.

One night Delia didn't like the way the kids listened to a tape, and she told us we were all "asleep" (not literally—we wouldn't dare), and that we had to "give to the music. It's not just going to make you feel something." She said she had a paper for us to write that would make us think deeply. The next day she gave the assignment: It was "What Kind of Person Are You?" We had a few days to write it and I agonized over it, knowing that if I just wrote about being a terrible, selfish person, I was in danger of getting in trouble for that too. When we all handed them in, Delia sat in front of us and read each one to herself, commenting here and there but not on mine. When she was done, she said, "You should all send these to your mothers," but when Gabriel asked if we could send ours in the same envelope because our mothers both lived in the New York community, Delia pretended not to hear.

A few weeks later, in the hustle-bustle of the predinner kitchen, I was making salad dressing. Delia walked into the kitchen in a pretty purple wrap dress, and I tried to sink into the background. My heart beat a little faster as I poured the vinegar into the carafe, then the oil. I started to shake some dried basil into it, and she was at my side, her tone just short of disgust. "Don't be lazy—measure the spices," she scolded, then walked across the room. I'd made this dressing a million times and never measured the spices. I didn't know where I would even find the official amounts to put in.

One of the other women took pity on me and handed me the measuring spoons, speaking in a kind tone. "Just do a half teaspoon of each and we'll taste it." There was a tiny victory here—it was an acknowledgment that Delia's request was unreasonable—but even that could be scary if it didn't sit well with her. I dared to glance over at her; she was leaning into the refrigerator and thankfully hadn't heard. I measured the spices as quickly as I could, dying to get out of that kitchen, desperate not to make another mistake she could latch on to. I closed the lid of the carafe and shook it to combine the ingredients. But I didn't close the lid tightly enough, and as Delia closed the refrigerator and turned around, I sprayed oil and vinegar all over the front of her dress. For a stunned moment we watched the oil spread into larger and larger spots on her dress, and then she looked up and barked, "Just get out. Get out of this kitchen and out of this house. I can't stand to look at you." I put down the carafe and hurried out the screen door into the summer night.

Outside, I wondered what to do with myself and what would happen next. I walked around the house to the big bay window of the dining room and sat underneath it, where I couldn't be seen. I willed myself to cry, hoping that Delia would come out and see my remorse.

But too much time went by, and I didn't feel like crying anyway. I felt numb. I could hear everyone as they settled in for dinner, then the muted clank of forks against plates and bursts of laughter here and there. As the sun went down, a light went on inside the house, forming a big glowing rectangle on the lawn in front of me. I looked up at the stars and listened to the katydids as they sang to each other. An hour went by, maybe two. I could hear that dinner was over, and I imagined myself getting up and walking inside. But my legs were made of lead, and I couldn't bring myself to do it. What if I was kicked back out again, and she was twice as mad at me for coming back in? She'd said she couldn't stand to look at me. How long would that last? Forever? I knew it was because she didn't want to be reminded of my mother, the woman who was with FP instead of her. "I can't stand to look at you" was probably the most honest thing she'd ever said to me. It also meant the aversion she had to me wasn't going to go away, and I was doomed. I wondered if they would make me sleep out here. I wondered if they'd forgotten about me entirely, as if I'd never existed.

Finally, mercifully, Daria came outside. "What are you *doing*?" she asked, her voice a pleading whisper. She sounded so genuinely sorry for me, so desperate for me to make things right, that I let out a small sob and pulled her into a fierce hug. She hugged me back but pulled away pretty quickly. "Just go inside and tell her you're sorry. She's in the kids' room with Mommy."

"OK," I choked out, wiping away my tears.

"But wait a few minutes," she said, still whispering, "and don't tell them I came to talk to you." She darted away and around the side of the house.

And with Daria's words, I knew. If she wouldn't, or couldn't, stick up for me, I didn't stand a chance of staying here in Jessie's world. I pulled myself together and willed my feet to go inside. I walked into the bedroom where Jessie and Delia were sitting next to each other on a bed, clapping as one of the kids danced around in his pajamas. I *really* didn't want Jessie to see this abject performance, but I had no choice. I managed to choke out the words "I'm sorry, Delia. I'm so sorry."

They looked at me as if I were a piece of gum stuck to a shoe. I was really crying now—out of frustration and relief but hoping I was selling it as remorse. I was crying at the injustice of it and because I was so afraid I was going to be kicked out, away from Jessie and Daria, back to the lesser life I'd had just two years before.

"OK, OK," Delia said, and I could hear in her voice that she was embarrassed for me. "Jesus—I didn't expect you to stay out there for *hours*. You shouldn't get into a whole heavy trip about it. Now go make yourself useful and help the girls finish up the dishes." She shooed me away with a dismissive hand.

That night I wrote shakily in my diary.

JULY 27, 04

I have two Gemini sides and they <u>con</u> each other and that is a big problem. Sometimes I can't control my thinking and I smack myself to stop. But I still think. I go crazy trying to stop thinking. Sometimes I wonder if it's possible for me to stop thinking. What a Gemini. I'm going to get it soon. I can feel it.

The next day I tried to be invisible, which wasn't hard because no one would look me in the eye. George had been teaching us about Melvin's history, and today we were gathered around the dining room table, where he'd spread out a huge map of the United States, drawing lines and dates while he lectured us about Melvin's journey before he started the Family. "In the spring of 1967, Melvin traveled from Portland to Oklahoma. Who can point to Oklahoma on the map?" My hand shot up. George looked past me and around the table. "Samantha? Can you show us Oklahoma?" I meekly lowered my hand. Samantha got up and correctly pointed to the state.

Later in the day, I was relieved when Lou handed me Henry to take care of. Perhaps all was forgotten! I put him in my lap, and he smiled at me as he curled his chubby hands around my thumbs. At least this baby wasn't mad at me anymore. I silently thanked him for looking into my eyes, for helping me prove I was still worthy, and for not being blinded by my shampoo mistake. A half hour later, Lou hurried into the room and snatched him out of my hands. "You're not al-lowed to do anything, because you just don't care enough," she said, and then I was alone in the room, shrinking into the couch, wondering how to prove that I cared. How could I prove that when I wasn't al-lowed to do anything? Was there laundry to fold? (There was always laundry to fold.) I could go and clean the bedrooms—but would that get me in deeper trouble? Stuck, stuck, stuck.

I didn't have long to agonize over my situation, because Delia came into the room. "What are you *doing*?" she demanded, angry and full of disdain. I stammered a bit before I said, "Lou said I am not allowed to do anything, so I'm not—"

She interrupted me, furious. "You are a little coward weakling," she said. "Go and see Jessie. She wants to talk to you." She said this last part in a way that made me positive it wasn't good news. I stood up, quickly smoothing the couch cushion I'd been sitting on, erasing the slight dent I'd left from sitting there. I rushed up to Jessie's House with a pounding heart.

Five minutes later I was standing in front of Jessie in her living room, slightly out of breath. She had been working on her bargello piece, and she sighed and put it down. "You are bored here. I can see that." It was not a question and it was not my place to speak, though of course I was never bored. I was often happy, often tense, always thrilled I was allowed to be around Jessie, always dreaming of my fu-ture as Miss America, often in the woods with Daria creating magical secret kingdoms. Never bored.

"You just aren't enthusiastic enough toward life, and so it's time for you to have a new one. I'm sending you to Boston. Or maybe the Farm." She spoke for a long time, elaborating on why this was the right choice, seeming not to notice the sobs I was only half-managing to control. Eventually she seemed to get bored with telling me how bored I was, and she trailed off, her eyes narrowing as she looked out the window. "The thing is"—she paused briefly to find the words—"I used to love you, but I don't love you anymore."

Five days later I was woken up at five-thirty, handed my suitcase, and driven to the ferry. Only Lou was awake to see me off. She said very little until I was getting into the car, when she took my head roughly in both hands and said, "You have to face the fact that you blew it. But you know, even though you are a horrible shithead creep, I love you." After a car ride, a ferry, a ride to the airport, a flight with a woman named Lisa who was one of us but I didn't know very well, and another three-hour car ride, we arrived at the Farm at 3:00 A.M.

CHAPTER 20

I WAS EXPECTING A LIFE OF SHUNNED DRUDGERY WHEN I arrived at the Farm, but what I found instead was that the other kids, especially the girls my age, greeted me with warmth and excitement. Anna, Ruby, Katie, and DeeDee followed me around from room to room, asking questions about life on the Vineyard, hanging on the stories I would tell, seeming to bask in the Jessie-glow that I didn't know I'd brought with me. While I'd been living and traveling with Jessie and her entourage for the past two years, these girls had all stayed right here, working on the Farm and looking forward to the next time the Caravan would pass through. I felt I didn't deserve this kind of attention and in fact felt anxious that it would somehow get me in trouble.

My first night there I stayed up late with Anna, confessing everything that had happened to me, assuming things would change once everyone knew I'd been banished and began treating me accordingly. But Anna only said she was so happy I was there and told me how she was always getting in trouble these days and that she'd been beat up a lot.

Geordie and Jesse were the oldest boys on the Farm and had evolved to be kind of the leaders of this pack of kids. Jesse soon asked if I wanted to milk the goats with him in the mornings, knowing that had been my job when I was there last. I was thrilled to be allowed to work. The days I spent not being allowed to do anything on the Vineyard had made a deep impression on me, and I dove into every task with fervor and gratitude, shuddering at the memory. I played Jessie's words over and over in my head: "You just aren't enthusiastic enough toward life." I was determined to fix that about myself.

Geordie suggested all the kids camp out a few nights later, because it was a full moon in Aquarius. We all ran around the side of the mountain, hiding behind trees and calling out to each other with that special owl sound he'd taught us to make with our hands, then sneaking away to another spot so as not to be found. Once we exhausted ourselves and tucked into our sleeping bags, Geordie played the harmonica for us until we drifted off to sleep.

Days were spent working in the garden or collecting elderberries in the woods and then gingerly rolling them off their delicate stems. Nights were big dinners, with most of the adults up the hill at the Big House, now barely recognizable from the bare bones of the Bunk House I'd slept in when I was younger. We played music together and sang our hearts out at night. I felt both elated and guilty; suddenly life was fun again and no one was mad at me. In fact, I felt special. Geordie even said I could go fishing with him and Jesse.

AUGUST 7, 04

I am just trying to be alive and enthusiastic and not follow any
stupid ideas. I just want to be alive. Tonight I miss Jessie so much
but I led myself to the Farm and so here is where I have to make a
new life.

The girls kept following me around, and I started to notice that when we'd walk into a room, giggling and joking, adults would walk out. I tried to quiet them, but it didn't work. I took a few of them aside individually, telling Ruby, "You're just very loud and obnoxious all the time, and it makes me not feel good inside." I was anxious to appear grown up and not call attention to myself, and this was not helping. Ruby only laughed and got louder. The adults here didn't seem to notice us much, as long as we did the chores. The adult people on the

Farm were, like me, not privileged enough to be where Jessie was or to travel with her, and maybe because of that they also didn't seem as poised to discipline us or even to pay much attention to what we did.

Except Eve. With the wispy blond curls that framed her face and her impish smile, you wouldn't think she could be scary, but she could be. I wondered why Eve was there—she had always been part of Jessie's inner circle, until recently. But these were not questions us kids asked. Eve had two kids with Mel Lyman, which may have been a part of her power. The women who had kids with Mel Lyman—all six of them—seemed to have a kind of protected status.

One night after dinner, I was huddled in a meeting with Geordie and a few of the girls. We'd decided to put on a play, and we were very excited about it. The concept of the play was that there was a button that ended the world, and while some regular guy sat in front of it trying to decide whether or not to press it, he was visited by various historical figures who gave their opinions on the subject. Woodrow Wilson, for some reason, figured prominently, and I was to play Eleanor Roosevelt, who was going to disagree with Woodrow's line of thinking. "Woodrow, what is all this foolishness about buttons?" was the line we'd written for Eleanor's entrance, and I was beside myself looking forward to having this moment onstage. We were laughing, talking over each other, and I was writing things, then crossing them off, and then dramatically crumpling up the page and tossing it aside, as I had seen people do in films. This was the excitement of creation, and Geordie and I were at the center of it.

In the midst of this fervor, Eve poked her head into the living room to tell us it was bedtime in half an hour and then motioned for me to come talk to her. I'd been struggling with writing a letter to my mother to tell her everything that had happened, and Eve wanted to read it. I'd been struggling with the letter for two reasons: First, because I didn't know how to tell my mother what was really happening to me—that I'd been dismissed and disgraced, didn't really know why, and was now curiously having the time of my life. Second, because I was haunted by something I'd once said and was afraid it had gotten back to her. Earlier in the year I'd been in trouble for something, and George had asked me, "Do you want to live your mommy's life?" What he meant was without Jessie, and kids, and isolated in the New York community where she was, and I said no I didn't. When he asked why, I said, "Because it is too lonely." For some reason this answer had enraged him, and I worried that it had gotten back to her and I had hurt her feelings by calling her life lonely. But I had finally written the letter, and I showed it to Eve. She read it carefully and then looked up at me. "This is great," she said, in a kind voice. I'd written all about how I failed Jessie and was doing my best to be better while on the Farm, and for this I had Eve's approval. I'd gotten very good at figuring out what adults wanted to hear, or at least sometimes I was good at it, apparently. "But I must tell you," she continued, the moment of approval so fleeting, "that you are so wonderful around the grown-ups but you act like a queen around the other girls."

But they were treating me like a queen! And I'd tried, I really had, to make them stop. I was very busted, though, because I also knew I liked it and was quietly reveling in how swiftly my status had changed. "I know what happened on the Vineyard," she said, "but now you have something special to give to the girls from Jessie—you've brought a piece of her here and you have to honor it." She put her hand on top of my head. I wasn't sure if it was a gesture of kindness or domination or both, but I was trying not to cry so I put my head down. "Don't pull away from me!" she said, sounding genuinely hurt. "It seems like you don't even want to be friends."

As I sat writing in my diary that night, I could hear David down the hall playing "Danny Boy" on his banjo, and it made my eyes well up with tears.

AUGUST 19, 04

Everything just makes me so confused and I'm tired. I just feel so lonely and I miss so many people.

CHAPTER 21

BLISSFUL DAYS, STILL. THERE WAS INTERMITTENT "CLASS," where we learned about Melvin's history and copied it down in our own words. David, one of the men who had been with Mel the longest, told us some of his stories. It was a great privilege, hearing the stories of how the Lord became the Lord from someone who was actually there when it happened, before any of us were born, and we took it very seriously. This was the history of how we were formed, in a way, and why we lived the way we lived.

Some days we harvested potatoes from the fields, a favorite task of mine, digging in the dirt and discovering them like buried treasure, then tossing them into the wheelbarrow until it was overflowing and someone had to wheel it back to the house. There was endless corn to shuck and all those fields of sorghum to tend to.

We usually started very early in the morning, and around noon some adult would say, "All right, kids, it's too damn hot to work," which was our signal that we were free to run to the creek. We'd race across the field, down the road, across another field, and into the woods just a little bit, peeling off our clothes as we ran. I don't know why the other kids ran, but I ran because if you got there first, the water was perfectly still and clear, and you could see tiny schools of minnows swimming in it and every single rock on the bottom. A perfect stillness, with the roar of the rest of the kids only seconds behind, and then they would descend, practically flying into the creek, and within minutes it would be nothing but a chaotic muddy pool. We dove off rocks, landing on top of each other, our cries of pain or injury drowned out by the din and soon forgotten. Someone would find a leech on their leg, and someone else would scream, "Leeches!" and the fastest runner would tear back to the house to get salt to pour on it. In the shallow brook that fed into the creek there was watercress, its leaves perfectly swaying on the surface with the tiny tide, and we would yank it up, eating half of it on the walk home, the peppery taste mixing with the gravelly texture of the fine silt still clinging to the stems.

But also, almost daily, there was trouble. Once, the phone rang and there were no adults around, and none of us knew if we were allowed to answer it. This was the *real* phone, not the buzzer. The real phone hardly ever rang, and when it did it was either someone from the World or an adult from another community wanting to talk to an adult in this one. Nothing to do with us. It rang and rang and rang. We looked at each other and started saying, "You answer it. No, *you* answer it," whipping ourselves into a frenzy and laughing until DeeDee bravely picked it up, then panicked and hung it up again. Eve rushed into the room and said, "Who was it? What happened?" No one said anything for a moment. Did we pin it on DeeDee, even though it could have been any one of us? We knew from experience that if no one owned up to a perceived misdeed, everyone would be punished. We also knew we might all be punished for letting it happen, regardless of the actual culprit.

Mercifully, DeeDee eked out, "I hung it up. I didn't mean to."

Eve was furious. "What if that was Jessie?" she asked, horrified. She yanked DeeDee by the arm. "If you want to act like a child, you will be treated like a child. You will follow me around from now on and not do anything unless I say you can." DeeDee accepted her fate wordlessly, the implication also being that she wasn't allowed to speak. But this was normal for us, and though our hearts went out to her, life went on. We'd all been there in one form or another. Someone was always in trouble. I silently made a note: If the phone ever rang, I would run out of the house and down the road, pretending I didn't hear it, because I was pretty sure you could be just as punished for answering it too.

Geordie didn't believe I'd be up early enough or be tough enough to go fishing with him and Jesse and playfully teased me that it was only for boys anyway. Of course, he knew those were fighting words and that they guaranteed I'd be all in. The first morning we went, I shot up at the crack of dawn and we headed to the river, laden with gear. On the Vineyard, fishing on the boat with Jessie was a privilege, mostly reserved for adults and older boys. I'd never gotten that privilege and was very eager to prove myself worthy, even if it was in a river, from the shore, and no one saw but these two. Geordie showed me how to set minnow traps in the shallow part of the water, then handed me a coffee can and sent me to catch grasshoppers for bait. I came back a few minutes later with twenty grasshoppers, their bodies making panicky clanging sounds against the inside of the can. Next he showed me how to put the bait on the hook. You took the grasshopper in your hand and plunged the hook into the top of its thorax, maneuvering it so that it poked out at the bottom. I was actually quite afraid to do this, repulsed by the green goo that oozed out of the living thing and how its delicate legs flailed pointlessly on the way to slow death. But I hid all that, and once I did it myself and saw how amazed the boys were at my completely manufactured nonchalance, I became a brutal grasshopper murderer over and over, showing off. Then Geordie taught me how to cast—starting with the pole behind you and flinging it forward into the water. I wasn't very good at it, and I was grateful that he didn't make fun of me for that.

Eventually Geordie's rod bent and he reeled in a giant catfish, struggling at first, until it was thrashing on the shore. I'd never seen a live catfish before, with its strange skin-whiskers retracting and extending out again, and I instantly loved it. "Oh, please don't kill it," I begged. "Can't we just put it back?"

"Look at all those hook scars," said Geordie, pleased with himself. "I think this guy has been put back enough times. But maybe—" He was already pulling a knife from the holster on his belt, and he stabbed the fish swiftly on top of the head. It was immediately still. I'd seen hundreds of chickens slaughtered; I'd even pulled guts out of their headless bodies. I'd seen flat, dried toads in the middle of the road with tire marks across them and tossed them like Frisbees for fun. I'd thrown live mussels in boiling water, and just this morning I'd heartlessly gouged many grasshoppers. But this catfish made me sad. "Poor boy," I said quietly.

We headed back, talking at length along the way about what Abraham Lincoln would say to the Guy with the Button to End the World in our play. We'd studied Lincoln's life and astrological chart extensively in our schooling and speculated that, whatever he'd have to say, it would be long and philosophical. His rising sign of Capricorn would make him feel the burden of being responsible for so many deaths, even if it was a world of horrible people. "Wait," I said, "is the world of our play full of horrible people?" Geordie thought about it for a moment. "Well, yeah. I was thinking it was just the World."

As we rounded the bend in the road and the Kids' House came into view, we could see someone chopping wood, and it looked like that was Yvonne hanging wet clothes on the impossibly long clothesline strung up between two trees, the center of it almost touching the ground from the weight of all the clothes. Kids seemed to spring out of every door in the house and come toward us, waving. They crowded around us as we got closer, wanting to see the catch. My melancholy about the fish was gone now, and I was eager to regale everyone with the tales of our adventures. Yvonne called over to me: "Guinevere! Come help me finish hanging up these clothes." I was ever so reluctant to tear myself away from this mini moment of glory, but I did, handing Jesse my fishing rod and getting over to where she was.

I reached into the basket and started hanging a pair of wet overalls from the massive pile she was working on. Such a pain to hang, overalls. You wanted to just throw them over the line, folding them in half, no pins needed. But no, each strap had to be carefully detangled and pinned. We worked in silence, me eyeing all the fun I couldn't hear as I watched the kids follow Geordie into the shed to see him clean the fish.

After they'd all gone inside and it was just us, Yvonne said, out of the blue, "You aren't helping enough around here." I wanted to say, "But I'm learning to fish, which means soon I will catch some, and then I will be helping because I will be bringing in food." But I didn't say that. Even though I meant it sincerely, I knew it would sound smart-ass. I didn't say anything—just felt my heart sink. I was back here again, a disappointment. Was I wrong to go fishing? Were things only considered helping if they weren't fun?

"OK" was all I said, wrestling with a pair of inside-out overalls, vexed at the unyielding feel of wet denim.

"Where are you?" she said. "I can't feel you." How on earth does one answer such a question? But I wasn't really scared of her. Sure, she could hit me or yell at me, but she didn't have any real power, and nobody cared what she thought. And anyway, there wasn't another place I could be sent for punishment. I was already here.

CHAPTER 22

A FEW DAYS LATER I WOKE UP, MILKED GOATS, BRAIDED SOME younger girls' hair, and hurried through the rest of my chores so Geordie and I could get back to working on the play.

That night I was in the Kids' House at dinner, a chaotic ruckus of twenty of us eating and laughing, with only a few women around to keep the unruly pack in line. We heard the buzzer and someone answering it. Yvonne approached the table and told me forebodingly, "They want you up at the Big House."

Everyone got quiet. There was no way this was good news. I assumed I was in trouble, though I was pretty sure I hadn't done anything wrong. Of course, we were all used to being in trouble for nothing concrete: I was punished once for looking at someone "with that Scorpio soul in your eyes."

I went out into the summer night and started the long walk uphill, listening to the crickets, pulling anxiously on my braids. I felt like I wanted to be alone in the quiet, on these smooth pieces of slate embedded in the grass, forever. But I didn't dare walk slowly.

When I got to the Big House, the adults were more serious than usual. "Go talk to Jimmy," someone said. "He's upstairs." I breathed a little easier. It couldn't be all that bad if it was Jimmy. They would never ask Jimmy to lay a heavy on me.

When I walked into the bedroom, he told me that my mother had left the Family the night before with FP. I was relieved, to be honest. I wasn't in trouble. I was scared for my mother and what would become of her but also disappointed in her, immediately judging her for it and for leaving with FP of all people. I couldn't muster up any real feelings. I'd been taught that people who left had never belonged with us in the first place. Those people were spoken of as traitors, if they were spoken of at all. I wondered if the stigma of her leaving would trickle down to me. I thought of Annalee and how she was forever saddled with the stigma of her father's suicide. I even started to think, "This could be good for me. Her low status was always threatening to take me down." For all the talk of selflessness I'd been raised with, what my environment had really taught me to think was: "How will this affect *me*?" Not in a cold, calculated way, more like the panicky thoughts of someone who wants to survive.

But there was more, and it was far scarier. As Jimmy explained, I would have to go join my mother, wherever she was. I was being sent away from the Family.

I was devastated. He hugged me. "Why?" I asked.

"Every kid here has at least one of their parents in the communities, and your father has never been a part of our Family," he said in a soothing tone. I didn't bother arguing—I just begged and sobbed, which made no difference. I was told to pack my things tonight because I was flying to Boston in the morning, where George would talk to me before I was shipped off to meet my mother and FP at my grandmother's in New Jersey. I would travel with Annalee, who was being sent away too.

Back at the Kids' House that night, I went into the room where all of our clothes were kept and pulled out a suitcase, but I couldn't quite make myself put things in it. I took in every detail of my surroundings, running my fingers down the bedpost, wondering if I'd ever be in this room again. I was a tragic heroine in a movie, and I was watching myself be the saddest girl in the world. I opened a wooden music box on the dresser—the little ballerina inside popped up, and I wound the key underneath and set it back down on the dresser. It plunked out a rudimentary version of "What Is a Youth?" from the film *Romeo and Juliet*, and I sang the melancholy lyrics to myself: ". . . so does a youth, so does the fairest maid . . ." No one could see me, but I felt this was a great cinematic moment, like the end of *Dark Victory*. I imagined a close-up of my face and the way my eyes would sparkle on the screen. I sat on the bed and willed tears to fall down my face until the music started to slow, the notes becoming so few and far between that they were no longer recognizable as a song. I didn't know if the tears were real. I mostly felt, "What is happening to me is very sad."

AUGUST 25, 04

Oh my God. I am totally stunned and heartbroken. I am speechless. My Mommy ran away with FP last night. How can that be? But do you know what is worse than that? I have to go with her. Never. I can't be away from everything I love. I can't sleep tonight. Anna is <u>*destroyed*</u>*. She is crying as much as me. But I swear to GOD I am coming back and I will be the same person. I will fight the World and get back to where I belong.*

I had been on the Farm for just three weeks.

CHAPTER 23

*"The sadness of this empty room. A room full of things. Things
that represent feelings I have known. Everywhere I cast my eyes
I find old feelings. Remember me all my things seem to say. Remember the tears you shed over me, remember the beautiful sun-
rises I showed you. How many people have I loved? Let me count
my things and see. My beautiful memories. Every one of you I
embrace, I hold you so dear to my heart, you all make up my heart
for without you I would have no feelings and without feelings I
would have no life."*

—MELVIN LYMAN

THE NEXT MORNING I WAS DRIVEN TO THE AIRPORT AND
put by myself on a plane to Boston. I stared out the window, marveling
at the clouds and thinking of Melvin's words. I was too nervous to ask
where the bathroom was or to eat the food the flight attendant put in
front of me. Everything was too unfamiliar, and I was sure I would get
something wrong. Plus the tragic heroine of this story wouldn't *eat.*
That's not what a sad person does.

I don't think I'd accepted that they were *really* going to send me
away. It didn't make sense. Why did I have to go live with this mother
I'd been raised to believe was an insignificant person, someone I barely
knew? Jessie had once proclaimed, to me, to the room, "Guinevere is
her mother's mother. It's the other way around in this lifetime, but
actually Guinevere is far older than her mother, and Bess has a lot to
learn from her." As with everything Jessie said, this was repeated over

phone calls and in letters among the communities and soon became common wisdom. I am positive it got back to my mother. When Jessie said it, I felt proud but also anxious. If I was my mother's mother and she had things to learn from me, what did I have to teach her, and why weren't we ever in the same place? Sitting on the plane, I wondered, "Am I being sent away to teach her something?" No matter what the scenario, my resentment toward my mother had begun.

On Fort Hill, I was taken to talk to George, who was waiting for me in the theater, a screening room that was set up in the basement with rows of actual movie-theater chairs. It was dimly lit, and he sat in one of the chairs, the smoke from his cigarette filling the room. I walked in hesitantly and stood there, nervous to be alone with him. "What do you understand about what's happening?" he asked.

"I have to leave because my mommy left, and she's in a bad place, and I'm in that same place so I have to go too."

"No." His voice was soft and kind. "No one is angry at you, and you aren't being thrown out. You are young, and a child should be where her mother is. Everyone is very sad to let you go."

I was so relieved to hear that I wasn't in trouble. I saw a glimmer of hope.

"I don't want to go!" I cried out.

"You have no choice. There is a big and painful decision you have to make—whether to live with your mother for the rest of your life or to live here, but you have to see her before you make that decision. I just talked to Jessie and she wants you to know that you are always welcome in her house and that if you choose to stay out there, no one will hate you. FP is a son of a bitch and a traitor, and we never want to see his face again, but if you decide you want to come back, just call me. It takes a certain kind of person to live with us, and you have to find out if you are that kind of person. You might know right away, but you should probably wait until you are a little older, like sixteen. You'll know when you get there."

There *was* hope. Jessie wasn't mad at me anymore! I just had to go out there and pretend to be thinking about a decision I had instantly made—to stay here with everything I knew. And Jessie had just said I would always be welcome in her house! This might all actually work out well for me. Maybe she still loved me after all. I figured I would spend a week out there, just to prove that I'd thought about it, and then come right back.

"And remember," George said, "never believe anyone or trust anyone. Just go by your heart."

I spent the night crying in an upstairs bedroom with Corrina and Samantha. I promised to write them letters, and I promised I would be back soon. Corrina drew a fairy princess on a page of my diary and wrote, "So you always remember home." Samantha said little as she gently tied a bracelet she'd made around my wrist—afraid, I think, to appear complicit in whatever I'd done wrong. "I'm *not* in trouble," I told them, probably more than once. "George said I'm not in trouble." But I could tell they didn't believe me and that, though they were genuinely sad to see me go, they might have been crying out of fear that this very thing could happen to them. It couldn't—they both had two parents in the Family, and pretty powerful ones at that.

My four-year-old sister, Annalee, was also being sent to join my mother. A wide-eyed kid with thick platinum-blond hair, she had barely lived with my mother either but was being shipped off to her nonetheless. We were driven to my grandmother's house the next afternoon. I helped Annalee into the tall van and held her hand for a while as we started our journey. I didn't know her at all, but I was used to taking care of little kids. She seemed in cheerful spirits as she watched the world go by out the window.

We said mostly nothing for the four-hour ride. It started to rain after an hour or so and I focused on the rhythm of the windshield wipers, a perfect soundtrack to the numbness I was feeling. The rain had just stopped when we finally pulled into the driveway of my grandmother's house, and my mother was sitting on the front steps waiting for us. I thought about how my world had turned upside down since I'd first walked up those steps only three months ago, but in a removed way, as if it was a funny story I'd heard. My mother's face was pulled into an anxious smile, and her shoulder-length brown hair was tucked behind her ears and looked dirty. Annalee ran toward her, and my mother folded her into her arms. I stood in front of them with my suitcase in one hand and my banjo case in the other. "I knew they'd send me Annalee," she said, her arms still enveloping my sister, "but I never thought I'd see *you* again." She said this with the tone of voice someone might use to say, "Fancy meeting you here" or "Well, look what the cat dragged in." She did not hug me. Had they even told her I was coming?

I looked up at the sky, where a brilliant rainbow was now sparkling over the roof of the house. "See?" my mother said. "It's all going to be OK."

Inside the house, my grandmother showed us the bedroom Annalee and I would be sharing, a small room with two single beds, the same beds my mother and her sister had grown up sleeping in. A crowded bookshelf lined one wall. "I've been using this as my sewing room all these years," my grandmother sighed. "I spent half the day clearing it all out for you girls." The resentment in her voice was my first inkling that our presence here was an imposition.

We followed my grandmother down the steep stairs to the basement, where my mother and FP would be staying. It was huge, the size of the whole upstairs, with a low ceiling, wood paneling, and a puffy brown leather chair with a lever you could pull to make it lean back and pop out a footrest. My late grandfather's framed paint by numbers hung on every available wall space. Annalee scampered ahead of us to the small pool table in the back, peering into the slots on the sides and reaching for the colorful balls. I wondered how she got this way, so fearless and inquisitive, especially after all the punishment I knew she'd endured over the last year, when adults had suddenly decided to treat her like she was possessed by the devil because of her father's suicide. I myself was hanging back, reluctant to embrace any of this, telling myself it was all irrelevant since I wouldn't be here for long. FP riffled through my uncle's record collection, chuckling to himself. "Uncle *Get Down*," he said in a mocking tone, holding up a Rolling

Stones record with an illustration of a giant tongue on its cover. My grandmother looked uncomfortable.

"Dennis usually spends his nights down here, watching TV and doing Lord knows what," my grandmother said. "But we'll all make do."

After she showed them the mattress she'd set up for them on the floor, she looked at her watch and said, "Better get that casserole in the oven. Dennis will be home from work soon," and she went up to the kitchen and got to work. My mother wordlessly joined her, taking plates out and setting the table as I imagined she'd done countless times when she was growing up. FP parked himself in the nearest armchair in the living room and picked up a newspaper. "That's Dennis's chair," my grandmother said, her eyebrows raised. "He'll want to sit in it to catch the end of the five o'clock news when he gets back." FP eyed her with barely concealed disdain and then got out of the chair with an exaggerated performance of horror.

"Can't upset Uncle Get Down," he said.

I was standing and staring out the bay window onto Summer Avenue, watching birds come and go from the bird feeder, not wanting to sit down or settle in this place in any way. Annalee sat on the couch, bored, kicking her feet up and down, which was making repetitive thuds. "Stop that," FP snapped across the room at her, and she made two more defiant thuds before she stopped. He came and stood next to me now, looking out the window with me. "Whatcha looking at?" he asked, and I shrugged, still staring forward. "You should try to be more cheerful," he said, his tone mean and a little ominous, and walked off to sit at the dining room table.

Soon Dennis's black Trans Am rumbled into the driveway and he walked through the front door. I guess I was expecting some kind of ogre, the way my grandmother was rushing around, but he came in with a shy smile and said, "Well, hello there," to me in an awkward but kind way. He was tall and a little chubby with a boyish swoop of brown hair across his forehead; he had a nervous gesture of carefully gathering it out of his eyes with both hands. He put his briefcase down next to his chair, and my grandmother handed him an open bottle of

Heineken beer. He took it and then shook FP's hand, saying, "I hear you'll be staying with us for a while."

"Oh, we'll be out of here just as soon as we can," FP said, and I marveled at how every single thing that came out of his mouth managed to be rude. "Son of a bitch and a traitor," I thought, remembering George's words.

Later that night I was sitting in bed in my nightgown, staring at my feet. Clotilde had painted my toenails a dark blue a few weeks before, and I vowed to myself that I would only change the color when I was back home, so I would always have a little piece of her with me while I endured this trial. Annalee was sound asleep on the bed across from me. My mother came in and sat down on my bed with a big sigh. "Just came to say good night and see how you're settling in," she said, speaking softly so as not to wake Annalee. "It's been quite a day."

I didn't know what to say to that. "You're ruining my life," I thought. "You are a traitor and I don't know you and you are ruining my life."

After a long moment where neither of us spoke, I said, "George said that I can go home anytime, and I probably will." She nodded and didn't say anything, looking forlorn. For the first time I felt a genuine glimmer of empathy for her—I'd just told her I was likely going to choose a life without her, and we both knew that would be a permanent break. But I hardened moments later. Just days ago, she'd left the communities thinking she'd never see me again. She couldn't keep me here. I waited until she left to pull out my diary, because I didn't want her to know where I kept it. I paused to cherish the purple ribbon Clotilde had made for me as a bookmark and carefully wrote on it, "Clotilde made this for me in January of 04."

AUGUST 27, 04

I don't think I am going to last long out here. I can't stand it. I don't know what to believe about what FP tells me. Oh yes, George said never believe anyone or trust anyone, just go by your heart. FP wants me to be cheerful. How can I? Would you be?

I found out what their plans are—to do a lot of work for my grandmother here and get some money, and then go to Vermont. I've never been to Vermont. I don't want to go there either. I want to go home. I hate FP for taking my Mommy and destroying both of our lives. I hate this so much. I miss Jessie. I don't ever want the world to change me. The days are so long and I am so lonely.

CHAPTER 24

"Loneliness is the sole motivation, the force that keeps man striving after the unattainable, the loneliness of man separated from his soul, man crying out into the void for God, man eternally seeking more of himself through every activity, filling that devouring need on whatever level the spirit is feeding. The only pain is separation and the only joy is break-through and the battle only really begins when man has finally, through exhaustion, worn out every tangible means, devoured everything in sight and arrived right back where he started."

—MELVIN LYMAN, *MIRROR AT THE END OF THE ROAD*

I HAD BEEN TAUGHT THAT LOSS AND LONELINESS WERE AN essential part of growth, and I thought of this new situation as a trial that I had something to learn from. Maybe this was what they were talking about when they said I had been on this planet too many times because there was a lesson I had to learn. I was alert and ready to learn it. But I was also shocked by how radically my reality had changed, and how quickly. Suddenly I lived in a three-bedroom house at the end of Summer Avenue in Dover, New Jersey, with five people I barely knew.

There was my mother, essentially a stranger, who was as surprised to have me in her life now as I was to be in hers. There was FP, previously utterly inconsequential to me and now somehow a central figure, especially because it quickly became clear that my mother did whatever he said. To me, they were both monsters. Yes, I was angry that their actions had upended my life, but mostly I seethed over their disloyalty and didn't want to be anywhere near it. In no uncertain terms, I felt they were beneath me and it was an indignity to be subject to their life choices. I was afraid that World People would rub off on me, starting with them. Then there was my grandmother, who grumbled a lot but was exceptionally kind to me, and Uncle Dennis, who I was predisposed to mistrust because of his love of evil rock'n'roll music but who I soon identified as a rare breed: a man who didn't think he could tell me what to do. I found him quietly charming and soon learned to listen for his understated asides—he was a witty man if you paid attention. And then there was Annalee.

Annalee hadn't had an easy time of it up to this point in her short life. Because of her father's suicide, she'd been branded "crazy" and lately often punished in the Boston community where she lived. The story went that Libes, as her father was known (because there were three Davids and he was a Libra), was playing poker with Melvin one night three years ago and simply got up, went into the other room, and shot himself in the head. Adults said that this kind of insanity was hereditary, and Annalee was treated as if his suicide was somehow her fault and she could be contagious. Her father had, after all, betrayed Melvin by leaving him, and in such a definitive way.

It didn't help at all that a few months ago she'd squeezed a hamster to death. Word got around that when asked why she did it, she simply said, "I just liked the way its eyes bulged and then popped out." I don't know if she really said this—I wasn't there—but it was the kind of story people liked to repeat. She'd spent at least a day locked in a closet because of it (probably not actually locked—it's not like we'd ever dared to try to get out, because, you know, then what?) and was thereafter spoken of as "possessed." I can't lie, I was a little spooked by her too, but maybe that's just because I knew the hamster.

But of all of us, she seemed to embrace the new situation with the most excitement and ease. Within days she'd made friends with some kids across the street in a family called the Bests. The Best family had a mother who stayed at home, a father who went to work every day, and two little kids about Annalee's age. I could see them out the front window, chasing each other around on the front lawn, and watched the father pull into the driveway at the same time every evening. Annalee came in from playing with them one afternoon, cheeks flushed, and asked my mother if she could eat dinner at the Bests' house. My mother opened her mouth to speak, then glanced at FP, who simply said, "No," barely looking up. "Go play in your room until dinner." Annalee stared at him, her eyes narrowing with unbridled hatred. My mother saw this and nervously ushered her out of the room before FP could notice.

When I'd visited my grandmother a few months before, I'd avoided calling her anything. "Grandma" seemed oddly familiar and "Grandmother" too formal. She'd never been called anything by her grandchildren, since all three of us had always been in the Lyman Family (my aunt Nell had my cousin, Pete, who was eight). But now we lived with her, and in what I would come to understand as his nature, FP dubbed her "Granny." I knew he meant it in a mean and dismissive way, but since none of us knew what to call her, it stuck.

I soon began to see FP as someone who took everything, left his paw print on everything, thought he deserved everything, thought every object in the world was his. This previously humbled and low-level man had become instantly emboldened out here in the World, and he took on the man-of-the-house role as if it had always been his. Even my grandmother, who'd been a widow for a decade, supporting herself and doing as she pleased, deferred to him, if a bit begrudgingly. She'd met him only days before, and now here he was living in her house with her daughter and two of her grandchildren, but she treated it all with a sort of resignation, as if she'd always known it was just a matter of time before another man came into her life and controlled everything.

He'd made himself at home, underlining every Lord's List movie in the *TV Guide* and placing his dog-eared copy of *Mirror at the End of the Road* beside their temporary bed in Granny's basement. I was surprised—he still cared about these things? After wandering aimlessly up and down the street one day, I came home to find him sitting on the couch, playing my banjo. He grinned at me when I came in. I felt nauseous just seeing his hands on it. He'd been painting a room for a neighbor down the street, and he was filthy. I could see what looked like grease marks on his hands from across the room. He had never played the banjo before, and he didn't play it even a little well. "See— you're not the only one who can play," he said. "It's not that hard." I couldn't bear the sound of his crude playing and went into my room to seethe. My banjo case was splayed open on the floor—and I closed it gently and thought that I'd rather light the banjo and its case on fire than ever have him touch it again. After a few minutes, I heard his playing stop and the front door open and close, and I came out to find the banjo thrown aside on the couch, in danger of falling to the floor. I picked it up gently and took it to my room, found a cloth inside my case for cleaning the strings, and got to work, hoping to wipe away any trace of him.

Within a few days, I'd made my decision. There was no way in hell I was staying here with these people.

SEPTEMBER 3, 04

Last night I had a dream that had Melvin and everyone in it and I don't quite remember what happened but it was a great dream, and I woke up missing everyone so much I was nearly in tears. I then re- alized that if I get this lonely in one week, I can never make it through 5 whole years. All day long I've been trying to tell Mommy. I can never find the right time. Tomorrow I promise you I will. I want to tell her so bad. I want her to know and I want to go home. I wonder where I'll go if I go home. Back to the Farm? I don't know.

And so I became consumed with how to tell my mother. I was sure she wouldn't fight me on it—how could she? She hadn't expected me to be here in the first place, so what was the big deal? I'd find her doing dishes in the kitchen with no one else around, and I would walk into the room filled with determination and then feel lead in my brain, a numbness in my limbs, almost like a paralysis. I would will myself to speak, but nothing would come out. I'd stare at the back of her head, study the pills on the stretched-out gray sweater she wore most days, and sometimes even clear my throat. Still nothing. This was going to be hard.

I started to think maybe it would be easier to tell FP. I didn't care about hurting his feelings at all, and in fact as the days wore on, I wanted to hurt him in some way. It was starting to become clear that he hated even the sight of Annalee, and he was always looking for reasons to punish her. He was cruel to Granny's cranky old cocker spaniel, King, insisting that he be confined in a small bedroom all day, until I begged to take him for a walk. He treated my mother like a disappointing servant. He joked around with me, trying to get me to laugh at Granny's shoes with him or make fun of something my mother said, and I tried to play along just enough not to make waves. What did it matter? I was leaving soon. But here's the thing: Granny did have really weird orthopedic shoes, and Mommy sometimes said goofy things. I never wanted to be on his side and certainly didn't want to make fun of them, but he wasn't always wrong. I struggled to find the balance.

One night FP told me that the Lord's List movie *How Green Was My Valley* would be on later, and he asked me if I wanted to watch it with him. "Don't look so shocked," he said. "I still love Melvin and Jessie, and just because we're not there anymore doesn't mean I don't still believe in the things they believe in."

"Then why in the world would you leave?" I thought but didn't ask. I knew they'd snuck out in the middle of the night, like cowards, and assumed it was because he was always getting in trouble and didn't like how little power he had in the Family. They left, and George had said he was a traitor, and that was all I needed to know.

But I'd never seen that movie and I was eager to keep all things Lyman Family alive while I was stuck out here. It was around midnight, and it was just FP and me—everyone else was asleep. FP was fully reclined in the La-Z-Boy in Dennis's den, footrest up, smoking Lucky Strikes, one after the other.

It had been about two weeks since I'd been sent away, and this story about a boy named Huw in a small Welsh mining town left me devastated and moved. It was about family, and home, and many times during the film the whole town sang beautiful Welsh songs together. It all made me wretchedly homesick. As the credits rolled, I tried to hide my tears, getting up to go to bed.

"Hey—where are you going?" he asked. "Let's talk about the movie. Why do you think Melvin put it on the Lord's List?" There was a tone in his voice like he was about to teach me a lesson. I'd learned he loved to hear himself talk, a kind of poor man's version of the already exhaustive rhetoric I'd grown up with but even more repetitive, contradictory, and just plain boring.

I really did not want to associate this film with him. Clotilde had read the book to me, a precious memory, and I was anxious to get away from him as quickly as possible to cherish the film privately. I didn't want him to know anything about my feelings. "Oh—" I said, and when my voice cracked, he pulled the lever on the La-Z-Boy and stood up, giving me a hug. If someone hugged me when I was crying, it usually made me cry harder, in a way that felt like relief; this hug hardened me. I hugged back long enough to be polite and then found a way to sigh that made it seem like the hug was over, disengaging and moving a few steps back. He kept one of my hands in his, sitting back down. I remained standing.

"Hey—your mother tells me you're thinking of going back to the communities." Oh, great! I wasn't going to have to bring it up. Here was my chance. I nodded, searching for words, realizing I could get my hand out of his by pretending to wipe away my tears, which were now dried up. But I didn't want to tell him what George said, or what George said Jessie said, because it wasn't his business and he didn't deserve to know.

"Yeah," I mustered up the courage to say, squaring my shoulders. "I'd actually like to go back tomorrow. George said I can call him anytime and someone will come pick me up."

"But didn't George also say that you should probably stay here until you are at least sixteen and know what is in your heart? Doesn't what he said sound like you should think about it for more than two weeks?"

Had my mother told FP about our conversation from the first

night I was here? Or had he read my diary? What exactly had I said to my mother? My words seemed twisted around; George said I had to leave but I could come back whenever I wanted—maybe sixteen, but not definitely sixteen. "Jessie wants you to know that you are always welcome in her house" was what I knew for certain George said, because I lived for these words and repeated them to myself many times a day for strength. "Jessie said I am always welcome in her house," I would tell myself. "Maybe that means when I go back I will live with her again." I wasn't welcome in her house just a month ago when she told me she didn't love me anymore, but it was possible she'd realized she still loved me after all, or else why would she say that to George?

"You can just leave your mommy like that?" he said then. I felt a wave of guilt and sadness—what kind of monster was I? He must have seen the conviction fading from my eyes and posture. He shook another cigarette from his pack, tapping it on his thumbnail before he lit it. A smug smile crept over his face. "I'll bet you never thought of the possibility that if you told Jessie you wanted to come back, she might say for you to think about it some more."

With his words, the dread set in. I knew that he was just saying it to mess with my head, because he didn't like that obviously I was still welcome in the communities and he wasn't, and I didn't believe him for a second. But I now realized they were not going to make this easy for me. But why did they want me to stay? It made no sense.

CHAPTER 25

AND SO AS THE LONG AUTUMN DAYS BEGAN, I WAS NEVER
not thinking about how to get back home. My grandmother and uncle
were at work all day, and my mother and FP were gone a lot, driving
to upstate New York to look at houses to rent or doing random painting jobs they found. I spent the days playing my banjo, working on my
bargello piece, and walking up and down Summer Avenue. I reread my
diary, cherishing every little note Clotilde, Daria, Samantha, and
Obray had scribbled in it.

One day I decided to peruse the bookshelves in the bedroom we
were sleeping in and pulled out a book called *The Group* by Mary
McCarthy. "A novel about eight Vassar graduates," it said on the front
cover, "that is a shocking, witty and almost continually brilliant social
document." I came out into the living room, where I found my mother
studying Granny's *Audubon Society Field Guide to North American Birds*
and looking out at the bird feeder.

"It's a nuthatch, I knew it!" she said, pointing to a glossy photo in
the book. "Look at its little white breast."

I politely glanced at bird and photo and then asked, "Mommy,
what's Vassar?"

She looked at me, amused, and said, "What on earth?" and then
saw the book in my hand and said, "Ah, I see. Vassar is a very fancy
women's college—if you do very well in school, maybe you can go

there someday." She went back to leafing through the bird photos, craning her neck to see another bird that had just landed on the lawn.

Did she hear herself? How could I do well in school if I wasn't *in* school? I wondered if the kind of school we had at home would be enough education to go to Vassar. I'd never thought about college until now.

"Did you go to college?" I asked her.

"Well, yeah, but only for a year, because then you came along." She ended this sentence on an oddly peppy note.

"Did Granny go to college?"

"Oh yes, she sure did, and I'm sure she will tell you *alllll* about it if you ask her." She was being sarcastic, a side of her I hadn't seen before.

"Did FP go to college?"

She snorted. "Hardly. He didn't even finish high school."

"You have to go to high school to go to college?"

"Child, enough with the twenty questions. You're eleven years old. You don't need to think about college. Why don't you think about getting the laundry out of the dryer and folding it before FP gets back? He doesn't like all the racket in the basement."

My wheels were turning as I went downstairs and started pulling things out of the dryer. If I wanted to go to college, I had to go to high school. But none of the teenagers I knew went to high school. Was Jessie against high school and college? You'd have to be out in the World to do it. But you'd have to be out in the World to be Miss America too, and she was excited for me to do that. I made a mental note that I would ask her about college when I saw her again, which I promised myself was very soon.

The Group had several words I didn't know, and when I went looking for a dictionary, I found a most amazing object. My grandmother had a giant dictionary with whisper-thin pages and words so small that you had to use a magnifying glass to read them. There were nine pages shrunken onto every page! *The Compact Oxford English Dictionary* would become an endless source of fascination to me. I looked up "lor-gnon" and then "enceinte," and when I discovered what the latter meant, I knew *The Group* was going to be a racy book and I was excited to escape into it, having very little else to do with my days except worry.

The young women in the book were sophisticated and rich, but I readily identified with their interpersonal dramas and intrigues. It was a book about complicated friendships, something I recognized and now yearned for. But they'd been to college and had exciting careers ahead of them as journalists and doctors and social workers. The only thought I'd had about my future was to become Miss America, which, while it looked very glamorous, was starting to seem less interesting.

Granny came home from work the next day and saw me cross-legged on the couch, well into Chapter Five of *The Group*. My mother was at the dining room table, the contents of Granny's sewing basket exploded around her as she mended the knee of a pair of FP's work pants. She'd been at it for some time, speaking only to mumble curse words to herself. Granny said hello in her oddly almost British way and then eyed what I was reading. She raised her eyebrows, which I had learned usually meant trouble. "Don't you think that's a bit of an adult book for an eleven-year-old?" she asked my mother. My mother looked up from her sewing and shrugged. "That was Nell's book." Granny shook her head and walked over to her own bookshelf, perus-ing titles and pulling out *Little Women*. She took *The Group* out of my hands and said, "Why don't you start with this one?" I made a note of where she put *The Group* back on the shelf, because of course now I *really* wanted to read the rest of it.

I begrudgingly started to read *Little Women*—I didn't appreciate being treated like I couldn't handle adult things—but was soon en-grossed in the lives of the March sisters. I had to admit that I didn't have to look up any words in the dictionary to understand it, and I was instantly in love with Jo March, the tomboy writer who wasn't afraid to speak her mind. I already thought of myself as a tomboy and a writer—if only I could speak my mind like Jo.

For the next month, we lived in this limbo of Granny's house while

FP and my mother took odd jobs and looked for places to live. I wrote in my diary nightly, truly feeling like Lavinia was my only friend.

SEPTEMBER 13, 04

I am so stupid and I am very angry at me because I didn't tell FP I've made my decision. If I don't tell him tomorrow . . . well I simply must. I wonder if I have learned the lesson that Jessie was trying to teach me about being self-involved, taking risks, and not making the same mistake over and over; to love. I want to live with Jessie so much. I shall go back by the end of this month, I promise you. For the love of Jessie. How sad it will be to tell Mommy that I've decided to never see her again. How sad.

SEPTEMBER 17, 04

Listen, if I tell FP my decision he's gonna ask me how and why I decided. I'll tell him it's because I know I can't live without Jessie. And then he'll say, "But you can live without your Mommy?" and I guess I will just have to say "Yes" because I can, and to tell you the truth, most of the people I know I know better than my Mommy. I don't even have any real relationship with her although I don't like to admit it.

SEPTEMBER 18, 04

Dearest Lavinia,

I am getting so lonely and there is no one to turn to. I feel so alone and lost in this big world. This is not the life I want. Not at all. It is not what I was made for. At least that's what I feel. I've had enough now and I want to go back to what I love. I have to admit that I will never ever forgive FP and my Mommy for leaving the community. Especially FP. It just makes me sad and angry, and confused. Life is an odd thing. Why does it have to be so hard?

Oh Lavinia,

How hard this day has been. So many times I've hated, been destroyed, and no one noticed. It started this morning when I woke up to find that FP has broken a string on my banjo. For a second time. For so long he's been treating my banjo like it's his, and like it is junk. He plucks and pulls at the strings like they were nothing. All day he's been so awful, just unbearable. After he had broken my banjo he started talking to Annalee about when she killed the hamster. She told the story like it was nothing. She calmly and cheerfully described it in detail, and he didn't even seem to care. He said how empty she was. He just laughed and I was nearly in tears.

Tonight we were watching the great Lord's List movie Jezebel, and FP hated the movie. Not even moved by it. He says he hates this and he hates that and he doesn't like Bette Davis and it destroys the movie and the whole feeling. Oh I don't know maybe I'm just a little brat full of judgments, but I know what I feel. And I know how I miss what I love.

SEPTEMBER 23, 04

Dear Lavinia Love,

We got on the road about 3:15 and I had a wonderful time reading Little Women during the trip. I didn't even notice the time fly by, and before I knew it, it was six o'clock and dinner and we stopped to eat somewhere. There was a beautiful sunset in rainbow colors and right in the middle a beautiful star and I asked that star with all my might to please help me get home because I can't do it myself. And somehow it seemed to twinkle.

SEPTEMBER 27, 04

Oh Lavinia,

What I'd give to hear a tape right now! Oh Lord knows what I'd give. I miss tapes. I don't think Mommy thought about what she was really leaving aside from the people. I feel like I've been stretched in all different directions today. I am trying to make my final decision for sure and I have, but telling is the hard part. Just put yourself in my place. Trying to tell your mother that you've decided to never see her again for your life. Painful, painful, but that's what all life is for me now.

SEPTEMBER 28, 04

My dear Lavinia,

FP is so mean to Annalee. He asked her a question and she wouldn't answer so he threw a ball right in her stomach. Ouch! That hurts. She can be a little brat no doubt, but he is just as bad as far as I'm concerned. I just wish Mommy would notice and put up a fight because FP thinks he's so great, and he has his own family. Well I'm __no__ part of his family. I don't think I've ever felt such through and through contempt for someone.

OCTOBER 1, 04

Oh I am a wretch! I just don't have the heart to tell Mommy. Sometimes I get a sudden strike of courage and feel certain that I will tell her when I get a chance, but when the chance comes I cowardly shy away. But oh, it seems like we're worlds apart. I'm such a coward. I fear I shall never get back home because of my sheer stupidity. Oh how I long to see familiar faces, with understanding. Last night I cried myself to sleep because of loneliness, longing and confusion. I think I'm liable to do the same tonight.

OCTOBER 2, 04

My Oh My Lavinia,

Oh how I long for music, Melvin's music. I can't stand the way FP says, "It's 3:00 o'clock Our Time." His time is the rest of the World! He has the audacity to say "Our Time." Our time is Melvin's time.

OCTOBER 4, 04

Last night I told Mommy finally very late at night. She said that she wanted me to stay longer, until I had something to choose from. But the feeling is so strong. I must go back. I know I can't bear to live without tapes and Jessie, not even for another month. She said we would talk more about it today but we didn't. Oh, this is not the life I want. No, and I must get back, and soon!

OCTOBER 8, 04

Ashamed as I may be, I am still here in this dreary place. But I got one step closer to Jessie. Tonight I felt so awful and I finally told Mommy I wanted to talk but when we got to sit down at first not a word came. Finally I told her that I couldn't be without Jessie and she said that Jessie would always be there. She just doesn't understand. I said that I just had to be there and so she said alright, but if I could just stay two weeks longer it would mean so much to her, but if I couldn't she wouldn't force me to. And I can't. I can't bear this for one week longer. Cruel as it may be, that's how it is. I know George will say I should stay longer, but I must be with Jessie. Now.

OCTOBER 12, 04

Today was just awful. When the morning started I was happy because Mommy quit her job and will be home now, and I thought we might have a good day. I went outside and just as I was about to come back in, I heard yelling and I didn't dare go in. Finally FP sent Mommy downstairs and gruffly told me to make breakfast. For half the day Mommy stayed downstairs and then finally came up to make dinner. She sat me down and told me that we had to talk about this stuff about me leaving. She said she stayed up nights worrying about me. She said it all seemed so unreal to her because in the day I was always so cheerful. That really hurt my feelings. I was just trying to be helpful and not bother her with my worries. She also said that one morning I would wake up and know where I wanted to be, and that this day had not come yet. But I know now that I have made up my mind. I told her I had doubts whenever she tells me that she doesn't want me to leave, but that it was only for her sake. Now I remember what George said, "It doesn't matter how anyone else feels, it's up to you." So now I know. How can I make her understand? It's all so confusing. When will I ever be done with it?

OCTOBER 16, 04

My Dearest One,

I must explain something to you. I want to tell Mommy I'm sure now, but I can't just go up and tell her. She said she would know when I was sure, but she doesn't. I don't want to have to act very sad so she'll ask me what is wrong—I want to tell her naturally and leave it at that. But how I don't know. I must find a way. To her, every time I laugh or joke it means I'm happy and I want to be here. But it's not so. I laugh because I can't be gloomy all the time. How I feel about it is if we only have a little time left together, why do we have to be sad? Why not be glad with our last moments?

OCTOBER 19, 04

I have got to get home somehow someway. I need help out here but there is nobody. My banjo is my only comfort and every time I hear FP playing it I want to go scream in my pillow. Sweet little girl, aren't I? Just your average little brat. I'm going nuts in this— whatever you call it. It's like living in a box. About a one sq inch box, if you ask me. Boy will I be glad to get out of it.

CHAPTER 26

"THE HAMSTER IS IN THE ZIGGURAT! THE HAMSTER IS IN the ziggurat!" These were the words that a girl was repeating frantically as she dashed out of the sixth-grade classroom, clutching a small plastic pony in each hand. We'd finally moved to a small town in upstate New York called Garrison, into a house with a nice lawn that wasn't so close to the other houses around it, like Granny's was. Compared to the houses I'd grown up in, it was small and unremarkable, but it was an improvement over being guests who had far outstayed their welcome in my grandmother's house.

Here at Garrison School, it was lunchtime, early November, and my much anticipated first day of Real School. I was about to meet my teacher, Mrs. Smith, but all I could think was "What in the world is a ziggurat and why is a hamster in it and why is a hamster even in a classroom? What do the horses in her hands have to do with it all? I will never make it in the World. There is already way too much I don't understand."

It had been more than two months since I left the Farm and I was finally, finally here. There were so many reasons to be excited: people my age, new books, actual structured learning. And getting away from this household, this man, this powder keg of a situation. Really, I wanted to be anywhere but in that house.

I'd spent the last week sewing the perfect outfit for my first day of school. Mommy said she'd "stashed aside some money" so I could buy fabrics and make something new. The night before, I ironed the blouse and pants carefully, then tried them on one last time, putting on my favorite boots to see if it all worked together. I studied myself in the mirror, flipping my waist-long hair behind each shoulder like I'd seen the lady do in the Breck shampoo ad, when I was home alone and sneakily left the sound on for commercials. Did my hair have "clean body" like that lady's?

My green velour bell-bottoms looked perfect. "Like store-bought pants," I thought. I was deeply enamored of the fabric I'd chosen for the top: giant purple flowers on a white background. The blouse had strings to make a little bow at the neck and I tied it, very pleased with how it looked—for a moment. Then I was seized with dread. What was happening to me? Had World People already gotten to me? Because I couldn't deny that I was curious about what they would be like. I had to admit to myself that I was looking forward to this experience. Nervous, yes, but also eager for something I'd never had before: the chance to meet a bunch of new people, the chance to show off my sewing skills and maybe for a minute be the center of attention. I felt ashamed of my vanity and how self-involved I was being. That's what Lou or Eve or Clotilde would say—I was being so self-involved. I got into my flannel nightgown and hung up the clothes carefully. I hated myself. I sat on the edge of my bed and braided my hair slowly as I tried not to cry. That night I wrote:

NOVEMBER 7, 04

My Only Lovely Lavinia,

Tomorrow morning is my first day of school. You know I can't decide whether to stay until the end of the month or what. Part of me wants to go and the other stay. I know I should stay if I'm not sure, but I feel like if I stay too long I won't be as close to everyone as I normally was. The sad thing is that I am really honestly much closer to any one at home than I am to Mommy or FP. For some reason I can't put my trust in their hands. I feel not at home around them. I

know that I will never feel like FP is my father, just because of
what he did to Mommy and me. God, I wish I had someone to talk
to and hear it all out and see clearly. Why am I in this situation? It
is very trying. I don't know what I want. I can't bear the thought
of leaving Jessie. I wish Faedra could talk to me somehow and
straighten my mind out. Anything. A dream, maybe. I don't know.
All I know is that I can't be in two places at once.

This step, the choice to go to public school instead of insisting on going back to Jessie, felt like a betrayal. And here I was excited to meet all these strangers, these World Kids, these people without souls. A couple of tears escaped as I whispered to myself, "I'm sorry Jessie I'm sorry Daria I'm sorry Clo I'm sorry George I'm sorry. I'm coming back. I'm just going to do this for a couple weeks to see what it's like and then I'm coming home. I promise." I couldn't allow myself to believe that I wasn't entirely sure my promise was real.

That morning I watched my mother carefully saw thick pieces off a loaf of bread she'd baked and then make me a peanut butter and jelly sandwich. She wrapped it in wax paper and hunted around for something to transport it in. She settled on a grocery-sized brown paper bag, folding it up to resemble something like a large clutch purse. Even I, who had never been to school, much less taken a properly sized bagged lunch to school, knew that this was not cool and that it was utterly embarrassing, especially for my first day. I slyly "forgot it" on the kitchen counter.

An hour later, we piled into the giant Suburban and drove the ten minutes to school. As we pulled into the parking lot, I admired the gleaming rows of yellow buses and couldn't shake the feeling that I was walking into a movie. I thought of Huw's terrible first day in a new school in *How Green Was My Valley* and wondered if the teacher would make fun of me the way the teacher did in the movie. But the small stone one-story school looked cozy and inviting, and I felt ready for the adventure.

I was relieved that I'd left the embarrassing lunch behind, until Mommy asked, "Where is your lunch?" When I said I'd forgotten it, she insisted that we go back to the house and get it. "We really don't have to," I said, trying to sound casual. "I'm not even hungry."

"Nonsense," she said, and my Big Moment was delayed another half hour. I secretly planned to throw it in the garbage the minute she left me at the school.

Finally walking down the hall to the principal's office, I was overwhelmed by the many unfamiliar aromas. Did I smell sour milk? Windex? Dirty sneakers? It smelled impersonal and somehow populated, clean but not really clean. I glanced through the windows of classroom doors, catching glimpses of the tops of students' heads, fascinated by the fact that there were people—lots of people—behind each door, and I imagined they would soon pour into these quiet halls.

In the principal's office, I sat nervously in a chair next to the secretary's desk as Mommy answered questions. "And where can we send for her school records?" the stern woman asked, pen poised for the information.

"Oh, the school burned down," Mommy said. I pictured our schoolhouse in Los Angeles in flames, shuddering at the thought. It felt like bad luck even to pretend this happened. I marveled at how easily my mother lied. Had she anticipated this question?

The secretary raised an eyebrow. "Oh, that's terrible. Hmm—well, what grade is she in? Do you have her birth certificate? I can make a ditto of it for our files."

"The hospital where she was born burned down too," Mommy said, and this fact I knew to be true. "But I have her birth certificate somewhere—I just didn't bring it today."

The secretary, incredulous, looked Mommy up and down and then gave me a brief but intense once-over. I smiled and fiddled with the barrette in my hair. There was some commotion outside the office door, and I looked up to see faces crowded in the small window, apparently straining to get a look at me. Now seeming a bit irritated, the secretary got up and opened the door. "Girls, it's not polite to stare," she said. "Go eat your lunch—you'll meet her soon enough." One of them waved to me excitedly before they all dissipated. The secretary smiled at me. "Looks like you're big news around here!" she said. I was big news! My heart beat a little faster. The secretary sighed and sat back down.

"OK, so I think what we're going to need to do here is give her an IQ test to see which grade to place her in. How old is she?"

My mother paused for a moment, which felt like a very long moment, because it was clear she was searching for the number. "Eleven," she said, and without thinking I blurted out, "I will be twelve in May." I wanted to be in the highest grade possible. After all, Jessie had dubbed me the little forty-four-year-old. I could obviously handle it. Wasn't I, after all, my mother's mother?

"Can you come in Saturday to do the test?" the secretary asked, running her finger down the calendar on her desk and tapping her nail on the Saturday square.

My mother looked anxiously at me and back at the woman. "I'll have to check with my husband," she said, "but I think so, yes." Husband! If she made up any more lies, I was going to have to start writing things down.

"In the meantime, I'm going to bring you in to meet Mrs. Smith, who will likely end up being your teacher. We can't just keep you out of school until we get your test results!"

She motioned for us to follow her down the hall and to the classroom, where the girl was yelling about the mysterious ziggurat. Mrs. Smith was a round and tough-looking lady with frosted short hair and large glasses that rested on a chain on her bosom. She was wearing a woolly jacket-and-skirt suit and sensible tan loafers. She reminded me of one of the scary nurses in *The Snake Pit* who'd given Olivia de Havilland shock treatments against her will. But Mrs. Smith smiled warmly, shaking her head at the hysterical girl with the horses in her hands. "You see what I have to put up with?" She chuckled. "I don't know how that hamster is going to ever get out of there." She gestured toward a two-foot miniature of a sprawling brick and clay building, which sat on a nearby table. "Poor thing. Anyway, hello, I'm Mrs. Smith; welcome to my classroom." I nodded. "What's your name?" she asked, in a tone that sounded to me like she thought I was stupid because I didn't know that when someone told you their name, you should then tell them yours.

Mommy interjected, "It's Gwen—short for Guinevere." I'd noticed recently that she pronounced my name wrong, which struck me as odd because she was the one who gave me the name in the first place. She pronounced it "Gwen," when clearly it was "Guin." I started to wonder: If your mother mispronounces your name, is that your name now? I decided in this case, no. My name was pronounced the way my real family pronounced it. I wasn't going to correct her, but I wasn't going to say it that way when I said it either.

Mrs. Smith made a light clap with her hands and said, "OK, Mom, I think I can take it from here." Mom? No one I knew ever called their mother Mom. It seemed so impersonal. Mommy gave a wan smile and looked at me somewhat wistfully. "God, just *go,*" I thought. "Let me throw this awkward lunch bag away and get on with it." This new arena had suddenly started to smell a little bit like freedom to me, and I didn't want her to be in it for another second. I wanted it to be mine.

CHAPTER 27

"Ok—HAVE FUN . . ." MY MOTHER SAID, SPEAKING IN HER meek high-pitched kind of breathy voice that always felt utterly false to me. She walked out and Mrs. Smith turned to me with a dazzling smile.

"So! Boston! It gets cold up there, right?" Why was she talking about Boston? Oh, right. That's where I was "from." I thought about Fort Hill and a giant snowstorm a few years before, where I put my leg into a snowbank and the snow pushed up my pants so my entire leg was just naked in snow. That had been somehow thrilling but very cold. Yes, it was cold in Boston, I determined, not wanting to lie about things, hoping she wouldn't ask me about how my school burned down. I'd been raised to tell the truth and yet also raised to figure out what an adult needed to hear and to say it.

"Yes, it's cold there," I said, and then, desperate to change the subject, I summoned up the courage to ask, "What's a ziggurat?"

"Oh—we've been studying Mesopotamia, and this was a couple of students' class project. Pretty cool, right?" My face must have looked blank or panicked because she said, "Mesopotamia was an ancient civilization. Don't sweat it, kid. You'll get caught up."

I didn't have time to "sweat it," because students came rushing into the classroom, rosy-cheeked from being outside, hanging up coats on hooks with their names on them, laughing and chattering, falling into their assigned desks. I stood awkwardly next to Mrs. Smith's desk at the front of the room. "Quiet down now," she said. No one seemed to even hear her. I was shocked by this disobedience—wasn't she the teacher? In *How Green Was My Valley,* Huw had been whipped for nothing on his first day, and Lou had told me stories about how the nuns in her school would smack kids' knuckles with a ruler just for bad penmanship. Why weren't these kids afraid of punishment?

Mrs. Smith raised her voice. "Quiet down!" she bellowed, and then they all did, and all eyes were on me. "This is our new student, Guinevere. She's from Boston. Let's make her feel welcome." She pointed to an empty desk close to the front of the room. "You will sit next to Keith. But be careful, he smells." The class tittered knowingly. I looked over at Keith, an awkward, overweight kid with a hint of a mustache. He shrugged and smiled at me. I really thought that World People were going to be nicer to each other, even if it was all fake. I took my seat next to him and subtly took a whiff. I couldn't smell anything in particular.

As the last bell rang, I was dreading figuring out how to find the bus, which one to take, and where to get off. I had decided in the last half hour that I would just call Mommy and hope she'd be able to come get me. I'd memorized our phone number and I had several dimes. Or I could go to the office and ask to use their phone? Was that allowed? My fears of doing something wrong in the eyes of the school (asking to use the phone), finding a pay phone and using it (I'd never used one, but I'd seen it in movies), or getting on the wrong bus (how would I even know?) were all swirling around in an anxiety soup when my classmates Clare and Mary came up to me, all energy and questions and excitement.

We quickly determined that they both lived near me. I was so relieved and grateful. I had a giant stack of textbooks on my desk and struggled to get them all in my arms. I didn't know I'd need a school bag. "Just put them in your cubby," said Mary.

What the heck was a cubby?

"I didn't bring a cubby," I said, feeling I could admit this to these girls and they wouldn't make fun of me. They looked baffled, then smiled. Clare pointed to the back of the room, where boxy wood squares were built into the wall, and I could see that each box had a student's name on it.

"We call those cubbies. What did you call them in your school?"

"Cubby," I thought. "Those are called cubbies," making a mental note to start a list of new things I was about to learn. "We didn't have those," I said.

"Ohhhhh," they both said, and then Clare said, "You probably had those desks where they open and you keep stuff inside them, right?"

I nodded. I hated lying, I really did, but saying, "Oh, we didn't really have school, and when we did, we didn't really have books. I mean, we didn't have our *own* books. We shared books, and we wrote on pieces of paper when we had assignments," was just way too much for the moment. They were already bubbling over with questions, and though I loved how friendly they were (unexpected!), I could barely answer one before they asked another.

They offered to help me carry my books after I told them I wanted to take every book home so I could catch up. "You're going to try to, like, learn everything we learned since September tonight?" asked Clare, and I couldn't tell if she thought I was really stupid or a total genius. I told them I just wanted to look at the books for now. I'd never had a social studies book before. Well, actually I didn't even know what "social studies" meant, so I wanted to at least try to figure that one thing out. I didn't say all that; I just laughed. A new skill was developing—if you don't know what the hell is going on, laugh like you are in on the joke.

We got on the bus, and it was utter mayhem. Or certainly exponentially more mayhem than I'd ever seen firsthand. Kids were standing, throwing things, yelling, hanging out the window to talk to somebody outside, changing seats. There was music coming from a boom box on the back seat, and a kid who looked like he was too old to be in this school was standing up in his seat, doing what I didn't yet know was air guitar. The faces he made were repulsive, and I was taken aback.

Clare and Mary saw my shock. Mary leaned in, lowering her voice. "That's Tino Yanitelli. He's actually a nice kid. Just don't ever sit next to him on the bus or he will tell you dirty jokes so fast you can't even understand them."

"Total gross-out," Clare added.

Noted. I knew a lot about hearing dirty jokes I didn't understand. Adults back home told dirty jokes all the time, and I'd laugh nervously, hoping they would just talk about something else next. Clare and Mary and I found a seat and they squeezed in on either side of me, firing a new string of questions at me as I turned my head rapidly from left to right.

"Did you know you look exactly like Laura Ingalls on *Little House on the Prairie*?"

"So who do you think is the cutest boy in our class?"

"Have you ever kissed a boy?"

"How many pairs of Jordache do you have?"

"Do you know anyone who's gotten their period yet?"

"Did you notice Karen wears a bra?"

"Why did you move in the middle of the school year?"

"What does your dad do?"

I answered all of these the best I could—some lies, lots of laughing it off, all of it kind of a blur. But the last one I know I answered in no uncertain terms. "He's *not* my father."

CHAPTER 28

THAT NIGHT AFTER DINNER, MOMMY SAT CROSS-LEGGED ON the purple shag rug in the living room, rummaging through a cardboard box, looking for my birth certificate. Annalee was upstairs in our room, and FP was out finishing some painting job, and when he wasn't around, Mommy was more relaxed and a lot chattier. I was sitting on the floor next to her, eager to see this document and wondering: If it was so important and she didn't think she'd ever see me again, why did she take it with her when she left the communities? She pulled out a photo and cooed, "Aww—look at this. That's you on Fort Hill when you were four." The photo was a little blurry, but I was smiling big and recognized the outdoor space between the Kids' House and the Big House there. Mommy sighed. "That's the only photo I have of you when you were little. I put all the baby photos of you in an envelope and then lost it somewhere along the way."

I thought about how that meant that there was an envelope of baby photos of me floating around in the world. Then I thought about the old diary I'd stashed on a very high shelf in the Kids' House in L.A. in April, knowing I'd be back for it in November, and how it was November now. Was the Caravan on the move? Did anyone talk about me?

Mommy let out a dramatic gasp and said, "Here it is!" She unfolded the weathered piece of paper in her hand and smiled at it for what seemed like a long time. "I remember when I was pregnant with you, I used to smoke reefer until I couldn't figure out which end of my cigarette to light, take a bunch of downers, and pass out until I woke up and did it all over again," she said wistfully. I scooted next to her and looked at the document. There it was: "Guinevere Jane Turner, May 23, 1968." I was oddly excited at the sight of it, as if I'd never realized I was legally and legitimately a person until this point. Where it had a space for "father," there was simply a squiggled line. When I asked her about the squiggle, she said, "I wasn't going to tell them your father's name!" When I asked why, she said, "In those days you just didn't tell people stuff that was none of their business."

Still on the floor, she leaned back on the end of the couch now, looking off and shaking her head. "Boy, was I scared. I thought I could handle it and didn't go to doctors or anything, and even when I was in labor I was feeling real cool, like this was going to be fine. I just got myself to the hospital and they laid me down on a gurney and I was ready. But then they wheeled in this girl who must have been thirteen, and she was in labor too and screaming the most bloodcurdling scream, like a maniac." She paused a moment to shudder. "And right then I realized that what was about to happen to me was terrifying and was going to be very painful, and I started screaming too."

I briefly considered asking more questions about my father, but I didn't want to break the spell. This was possibly the most real and personal way my mother had ever spoken to me, and I held my breath, hoping she would keep going. She wasn't even looking at me as she spoke—she had that look in her eyes like she was watching a movie of her life somewhere in her mind.

"Hoo boy! The doctors did not like having two screaming teenagers on their hands. The last thing I remember is some nurses holding me down and a big needle in a doctor's hand, and then I woke up three days later, and they handed me you! I was planning to give you up for adoption, but I just wanted to see you before I did, and then there you were, and I just couldn't. I decided I would figure out a way to keep you."

She smiled at me, a big beaming smile, and for a moment I was lost in the romance of the story, forgetting how it had turned out, choosing not to notice that ditching me had been a pattern for her since before I was born.

"I need a cigarette," she said, and I followed her as she got up and walked into the dining room, grabbing her pack of Marlboro Reds off the table, taking a cigarette out, putting it in her mouth, and sitting down in one fluid motion. She shook the box of kitchen matches on the table and pulled one out, lighting her smoke and exhaling deeply. I sat down in a chair next to her. She wasn't done spinning her yarn.

"When I was giving birth to you, I had a vision of a queen, all in white, and that's why I decided to name you Guinevere." She smiled to herself and dreamily looked out the window onto our front lawn, but it was dark, so she could only see her reflection. Headlights flared through the kitchen window and into the dining room, accompanied by the sound of the gravel in the driveway under tires. She stamped out her cigarette quickly, her dreamy expression snapping into an anxious one, the moment gone. "Didn't know he was gonna be home this early," she said, crossing the room to fluff up a tattered throw pillow. "He's gonna be hungry, and the lasagna isn't even in the oven yet." She walked over to the full-length mirror on the other wall and looked at herself but didn't fix her hair or center her necklace. She just stared for a second and then rushed into the kitchen.

I wanted to go upstairs—he'd inevitably come in grumpy and demanding, and depending on his mood, that might be aimed at me. But I also knew that he might be angered if I wasn't there, and he'd take it out on her. So I stayed at the dining room table until I saw the dirty ashtray that Mommy had left there, which I also knew could set him off. I quickly swiped it from the table and put the box of matches back in its place. Every single object in the house had a place, down to the centimeter, and keeping that order was another way we might avoid his wrath. FP came through the front door now, the long-johns shirt he wore covered in dust and a fresh rip on one leg of his worn Levi's. He put his metal toolbox on top of the washing machine with a loud clang, and when he walked into the kitchen, he was holding a bottle of Asti Spumante in one hand and had a huge smile on his face.

"The Doyles love my work so much, they want me to paint a couple of other rooms in their house. Cha-ching!" he said.

"Oh, great, that's great," my mother said. He put the bottle down with another bang and walked past her and up to me, putting a hand on each of my shoulders and shaking me playfully.

"Did ya hear that?" he said. "We're gonna be rich!" I managed a smile.

"Let's celebrate!" he said, peeling the foil off the bottle, then opened the cabinet and peered inside. "Of course we don't have any fucking fancy glasses," he muttered to himself, but pulled out three regular glasses, carefully pouring precisely the same amount of liquid into each one.

He handed one to each of us and took a big slug of his, ending with a theatrical "aahhhh," followed by a loud burp. Mommy looked over at me. "Oh, I don't know if she should have that. It's a school night and everything—"

"Oh, it's a *school night*," he said in a mocking tone, looking at me when he said it. Take a sip and make Mommy look stupid? Don't take a sip and risk him flying into a rage? I took a sip, the bubbles tickling my nose.

He put his fingers through the new rip in his jeans and peered up at my mother. "What do ya think, Bess? Can you fix this one?"

She furrowed her brow and said, "They're getting pretty threadbare on the front."

"Well, then I guess it's time to retire the side!" he said, and yanked on them, ripping the leg apart down to his shin. He laughed uproariously, and I saw my mother's eyes glance upstairs quickly—she didn't want him to wake Annalee but didn't dare say that.

"Oh my," she said with a nervous giggle, and with that he dug into another rip in his pants and left them in shreds hanging from his belt, now standing mostly in the long-johns bottoms he wore underneath.

He walked dramatically into the dining room, lifting his legs high so the shreds of his pants would flail around him.

"You gotta get a picture of this, Bess. Get your camera," he said as my mother followed him, laughing, and then crouched to reach into the cabinet where she kept the camera. For a fleeting moment you might have thought this was a happy family. I came into the room, hoping to slip upstairs, but he grabbed me as I passed him and said,

"Where do you think you're going, young lady? You gotta be in this picture too," and sat down, pulling me into his lap.

I resisted, in a joking way—"No, I don't want to be in the picture, I look ugly"—but he play-wrestled with me and said, "Come here, you little ugly duckling," and my mother kept laughing and took the picture.

He reached for a cigarette from the table with one arm, and I made the most minute of movements to get out of his lap, but his other arm was wrapped tightly around my waist, holding me there, and now his muscles tensed to hold me tighter. "You aren't going anywhere until I'm ready to let you," his arm said, while his voice said, "I think we should get a dog! Let's go look for one this weekend." He turned his face toward me, and it was inches from mine. He bounced his knee up and down underneath me. "What do you say to that? You want a puppy?" I really did want a puppy with all my heart, but his arm around me felt like it was made of steel, reminding me of who he was.

"There's ads for puppies in the PennySaver," I said. "I'm gonna go get it so we can look—" And his arm muscle clenched around me one last time before he let me go.

CHAPTER 29

WHEN WE ARRIVED AT THE SCHOOL THAT SATURDAY FOR the IQ test, Mrs. Smith met us at the front door with a giant set of keys and chattered away excitedly as she led us to her classroom. She was wearing a burgundy velour sweat suit, and because I was already feeling an immense amount of pressure, it made me uncomfortable that she wasn't dressed in her usual sensible jacket and skirt. This was a very serious day to me, and I was determined to prove that I was smart. I'd learned that my age dictated that I land in the sixth grade, but I really wanted to be placed ahead into seventh grade and dared to dream that I might be so smart as to be put in eighth grade. Now more than ever I needed to live up to what Jessie said I was, the little forty-four-year-old, who surely belonged in the highest grade possible.

"This is exciting!" Mrs. Smith said, dropping her bulging purse on top of her desk with a thud. "I've never actually seen an IQ test done before."

"Should be interesting," my mother said. "I took one when I was in college. I have an IQ of 145." Mrs. Smith nodded politely, her eyes scanning the classroom, and I could see this reaction wouldn't do for my mother. "That's considered pretty high," she said, but Mrs. Smith didn't hear her, because she'd started dragging desks around, pulling three together, and motioned for me to sit behind what now seemed like an imposing table.

"The proctor said you'll need lots of elbow room," Mrs. Smith said, slightly out of breath, and my anxiety mounted as I quickly glanced at my elbows. Why did I need a big table if this test was about my brain, and what did my elbows have to do with it? What was about to happen to me?

My mother stood awkwardly near the chalkboard. "Please, take your seat," Mrs. Smith said to me, glancing up at the clock. "He should be here any sec." My mother wriggled her way into a nearby student desk. Mrs. Smith chuckled nervously. "Sorry, Mom, no parents allowed while we administer the test. Just the teacher and the proctor." My mother looked surprised, then disappointed, and then eyed me like I'd kicked her out of a party.

"Well, enjoy," she said in a vaguely haughty tone. "I guess I'll wait in the car."

"Nonsense. Let me let you into the office and you can hang out in there. At least they have some comfortable chairs, and it's nice and toasty," she said. "I'm pretty sure it will take at least an hour—well, depending on how long it takes her to get through it, right?" My eyes widened as she glanced over at me, and she quickly added, "I mean, take your time, kid; don't worry about the outcome. It's only to help us understand where you belong. It's not like a *test* test."

"What is she talking about?" I thought. "Then why would they call it a test?" But there was no time to dwell, and she clearly knew the stakes were high and was doing a terrible job of pretending they weren't. It was something I'd started to notice about adults in the World. They talked to you like you couldn't see for yourself what was going on, and what came out of their mouths was often so obviously a lie. It was different from the adults I knew. They didn't lie—they just told you truths you couldn't understand yet.

But now my mind raced. So: fast equaled smart. I needed to be fast to do well. I could crochet fast, and recite poems fast, and do three-finger picking on the banjo pretty fast. I'd seen an episode of *The Bionic Woman* where Jaime Sommers cleaned up the kitchen really fast with her bionic powers. I willed my mind to be bionic like that.

Mrs. Smith hustled my mother out the door and I dared to really take in the room, leaning down to peer into one of the ziggurat tunnels to catch a glimpse of the hamster inside. I noticed a cloudy old mirror hanging on one wall in the back of the room and strained to see myself in it, smoothing my hair and trying on faces I thought looked smart.

A throat cleared behind me and I flew out of my skin, yelping as I whipped around. Standing there was a smallish man with thinning hair and a half smile that made me think he'd been practicing it just before he walked into this room. He was holding the handle of a gray plastic box that looked like ones I'd seen used for fishing tackle.

"Hello, Guinevere. I'm your proctor, Mr. Rennetti," he said. "Where is your teacher?" I said I thought she'd be right back, and he said he guessed he'd start setting up. As I watched him open the box and pull out folders, some mysterious little containers, and a timer, I felt embarrassed that he might have seen me making faces in the mirror. I wondered if the test had secretly already begun. If so, what could I do to look smart? Right before we left Granny's house a week ago, I'd found a copy of E. L. Doctorow's *Ragtime*. I'd read enough of it to know it was an adult book and kept it hidden so no one could take it from me. I had it with me because I'd planned to stash it in my newly acquired cubby.

I sat down and made a show of taking out a pencil and an eraser, casually putting the book on the desk too. Mr. Rennetti didn't look up, only said calmly, "Nothing on the desk, please. We are about to begin." I put the book away quickly and sat with my hands folded in front of me. Mrs. Smith was hovering behind him now, watching him set up, and he turned to her. "We'll need to ask you to sit down and let the student take the test without the added pressure of watchful eyes," he said in an oddly soothing voice.

Mrs. Smith seemed a bit flustered by this order but also mildly thrilled by the formality of it all. She dutifully settled behind her desk, rummaging through her bag and pulling out a paperback with the cover torn off. She opened it, taking out the tattered bookmark and putting on a serious reading face. But she couldn't help herself—she stole a look across the room at me, and when our eyes met, she gave a quick reassuring wink, then went back to reading her book. I'd only known her for a few days, and I didn't know how to interpret this wink. I thought winks were a flirty thing, or maybe it meant you were just kidding or had some kind of a secret joke? Mr. Rennetti was done arranging all of his tools in front of me and was clearly ready to begin. He let out a sharp huff and gave me what I think he thought was a soothing smile. I struggled to keep my heartbeat normal. I was ready to use all my might to excel.

Mr. Rennetti began, his tone slightly altered to the same calming one he'd used with Mrs. Smith. There were pictures to point to, patterns to identify, and word sequences to remember. The time flew by. A headiness was creeping in, because it wasn't turning out to be as hard as I'd dreaded. Some things were a little challenging but the fun kind of challenging, like puzzles. A few times he said, "Good," and then "*Very* good," sounding as if he was genuinely impressed. Yes, the back of my neck had tiny beads of sweat on it, but I was daring to feel like I might be doing OK at this.

"Last one," he said, and pulled out six blocks that were each divided diagonally into a red half and a white half. He put a stack of cards in front of me that had geometric red and white images on them. Not photographs of the blocks, just abstract red and white shapes. "Recreate the pattern you see on the card with the blocks, and then hit the button on top of the timer when you are done with each one. Ready?" His hand was hovering over the timer.

I had no idea what he meant. To me, the word "pattern" meant the patterns I had grown up with—white envelopes with ladies drawn on them; inside was tissue paper marked with how to cut fabric to sew clothes. A pattern was also whatever kind of flowers were on fabric. What did any of that have to do with these blocks? I was stupid. I was stupid after all because this didn't make sense to me. I was panicked.

"Here, let me demonstrate," he said, coming over to my side of the desk. He arranged the blocks in a way that represented what I saw on the card, and I thought he was nothing short of a magician. I knew there was no way I could do that. Those objects, that image, what? "Ready?" he said again, and I nodded, maybe a little too quickly.

For the rest of the test I was crying, the timer ticking, the blocks slipping out of my hands and clattering onto the desktop because my palms were sweaty. I never made it past the first card, and eventually Mr. Rennetti said, "OK, OK, it's OK. I think we're done here."

The results were supposed to come in the mail "in a week to ten business days." I rushed to the mailbox daily in expectation of the envelope, dreading the inevitable confirmation of my shortcomings. I'd replayed the blocks nightmare over and over, especially in bed at night, the sad circus of being unable to complete this seemingly simple task haunting me. Had all these kids I'd just met done it without even thinking? What was wrong with me? I shuddered to think I might be demoted to the fifth grade.

CHAPTER 30

BY MONDAY I WAS FEELING LIKE I HAD A HANDLE ON THINGS—
I'd begged my mother to buy regular-sized lunch bags, I understood
that social studies was essentially like the history classes I'd had but
with no astrology, and all of the girls in my class were being nice to me,
especially Mary and Clare. The boys were mostly standoffish, but it
didn't bother me. I studied every detail around me in an effort to understand how things worked, hoping to blend in, and thought I was
doing a good job of it until the morning when Clare whispered to me,
"You can't just stare at people all the time. It's not polite. No offense,
but it makes you seem kinda weird."

I was staring at people? Over the next hour or so I observed what
other kids did with their eyes when they talked to me. I saw that they
looked you in the eye, but then looked away for a quick second, and
then looked back, over and over again. I'd never noticed that before.
Was that what people did with their eyes in movies too? Back home
I'd been taught that looking someone directly in the eye when they
were speaking to you was a sign of respect and showed that you were
in the moment. "The eyes are windows to the soul" were words I'd
grown up with, and I'd been slapped for looking away when an adult
was talking to me.

Sitting at my desk, I tried it a couple of times, but it felt unnatural,
like the kind of thing you would do with your eyes if you were lying—
trying to keep whatever was in your soul hidden. Ah, I thought, but

maybe it's because World People always *were* lying. Or were they trying to hide that their souls were empty by never letting you look in their eyes for too long? No matter what it was, I made a mental note to practice in the mirror at home, since my goal here was to fit in. Well, no, I reminded myself, not to "fit in"—I didn't want to become one of them, God forbid! It was more that I needed to learn how not to stand out.

The first time we had "gym," I followed the rest of the class into the hall, ready for the next new thing. I knew where the gymnasium was, because you had to walk past it to get to Mrs. Smith's classroom, so I was confused when everyone walked in the opposite direction. "Where are we going?" I whispered to Clare.

"Oh, bathrooms—to change," she said nonchalantly. Like the answers to many of my questions, her words only created more mystery. I nodded and followed.

In the girls' bathroom (which I'd never been in, afraid of navigating an unfamiliar space), there were lockers, and the girls opened them and started taking off their clothes. What the hell was going on? I wanted to stare and understand, but I was also now hyperconscious of my staring. I decided to wash my hands so I could slyly observe where this was all going. Out of the corner of my eye, I watched them put on T-shirts and shorts, like it was no big deal to be practically naked in front of each other in the middle of the school day.

I followed them to the gym, where a stout and stern man waited for us. "Mr. Chadwick is super mean," Clare warned me, and he blew on the whistle around his neck so loud it echoed sharply around the gym and rang in my ears. The class shut up and stood at attention. He barked out everyone's last name and made check marks on a clipboard, then said, "New girl, Turner, why aren't you changed?"

All eyes were on me. "I—didn't—"

"T-shirt and shorts, Monday Wednesday Friday," he said, and went on to explain that we were starting our gymnastics unit today. "Your routines are due in four weeks," he said. "Three minutes each, and it's ninety percent of your grade, so get to work!"

Everyone scattered, one girl leaping on top of a balance beam and gracefully walking on it, dipping her leg on the left, then the right. A few other girls did cartwheels on the giant mat in the center of the room. The boys gathered around the rings hanging from the ceiling on ropes, showing off for each other. When Clare explained to me that a "routine" meant a performance, a gymnastics performance in front of the whole class, a knot formed in my stomach that would be right there where I left it every Monday, Wednesday, and Friday morning for the next few weeks. "But I don't know how to do gymnastics!" I whispered urgently. I'd seen Nadia Comaneci do her incredible routines at the Olympics and was in awe of her, but me? In front of *these* people?

"I'll show you," she said cheerfully, and then, "You can do a forward roll, right?" She dropped to the mat and did an effortless somersault, standing up again in one fluid motion. I could do a somersault, but was I just going to do somersaults all over the mat for three whole minutes? I was mortified by this idea. "Try it," she said. "Mr. Chadwick will come over here and yell at you if you don't look like you're practicing." I kneeled on the mat, glanced around the room hoping no one was watching, and did a very slow somersault, trying to get up at the end like she did but stumbling a bit. I saw the look on her face when I regained my balance. It said she was embarrassed for me, and maybe a little worried. "I like the balance beam," she said. "Let's try that."

"WHERE AM I GONNA find a T-shirt and shorts for you in the middle of November?" my mother asked when I got home and told her about it. "That's ridiculous." I felt a sliver of hope—if she wouldn't buy me the clothes, then maybe I could get out of the whole thing. She was spraying Pledge on the dining room table and started rubbing it in, getting worked up. "A gymnastics routine," she muttered to herself, shaking her head. She looked up at me and said, "No one is good at athletics in our family, so don't be disappointed when you realize you can't do the things the other girls can do. It's just not in our genes."

Within about two weeks, I'd become the boys' favorite person to make fun of. They'd huddle and whisper, stealing glances at me, and then burst into laughter. They mocked me for wearing skirts and for the fact that in gym class I now wore the only shorts I had, which weren't athletic shorts, and a T-shirt I'd borrowed from my mother, which was too big and had the words HAPPINESS IS A COLLIE on the front. I was "dog-faced" and a "scuz," and one day one of the girls asked me, "Does it bother you that none of the boys in this school think you're pretty?"

But I held my head high. Jessie had said I was beautiful and going to be Miss America (but was I still?), and the boys always wanted to cheat off my tests. I let them: Even though they pretended it was because they were too cool to study, we all knew it really meant that I was smarter than them. (Didn't we?) I told myself I didn't care about the things they said, but I was on edge. Some mornings I dreaded going to school, but nothing could be worse than what life was like when I got back to the house I lived in.

NOVEMBER 14, 04

School was just horrible. The boys are getting worse. I've told myself, promised myself, that I won't have anything to do with them. I can't stand any of them. Oh what does it matter? I can feel myself being slowly but surely pulled into this outside world which I don't like at all. I keep wanting and needing help from someone or something. But I guess it's a job I have to complete myself.

At home, my mother and FP fought every night—fights that escalated into him yelling at her, her crying, him in their bedroom with the door closed for hours, her sleeping on the couch. They argued about the right way to cook bacon or whose faces were on Mount Rushmore. One time he said he didn't want the last meatball on his plate because he was full, and when she fed it to our dog, he flew into a rage about what a waste that was. He screamed at me for being slow on the clicker that muted the commercials but didn't want to take over the job himself. The coffee was too cold, the soup was too hot, the sideboard had dust on it, and what the fuck was Annalee's doll doing on the couch? It felt like cooking, cleaning, and keeping things exactly where he wanted them was all I did when I was home. But even when all of that was done perfectly, he'd ask a seemingly normal question, in a tone that you knew meant he was looking for something to be angry about.

Dinner was always just me, FP, and my mother; Annalee wasn't allowed to eat with us. FP usually held court, talking and talking about himself—the softball team he'd started playing on ("What a bunch of morons"), or the rich people he was working for ("I'd smack those kids across the room if they were mine"), or the neighbors who had two cars up on blocks in their front yard ("Fucking white trash").

"This spaghetti sauce is burned," he said one night as he shoveled it into his face, only pausing to wipe the sauce off his mouth every third or fourth bite. "My dingbat mother makes it better and she isn't even Italian." (He was very proud of the Italian heritage on his father's side.)

"I know, sorry," my mother said. "I guess I heated it up too fast." She barely looked up and didn't sound particularly upset about it, or particularly present for that matter. She was starting to perfect the art of underreacting.

He turned to me. "So, you've been in school a week. How's that going?"

I thought three things, all at once: "1. Don't take the bait, whatever he is doing right now, 2. Figure out something to say that downplays anything good so he doesn't feel threatened, but 3. Don't seem so blasé about it that he starts to drone on about how he does everything for us and we don't appreciate it."

I'd been lost in my own thoughts, though, because earlier in the day I'd learned I had a new nickname: Guinaqueer. When we came back from lunch, Mrs. Smith had placed the composition papers we'd written that morning on our desks. Mine had a big red A on it, circled for effect, which pleased me, until I noticed that at the top of the page my name had been scratched out and "Guinaqueer" written in its place. I pretended not to notice, because I could hear the usual group of boys snickering in anticipation of my reaction. I sat down and calmly tucked the piece of paper into my notebook. Guinaqueer. Everybody in this school called each other "queer" and "fag" as an insult on a regular basis, and I'd figured out that it didn't have anything to do with the homosexuals I'd been raised to believe were disgusting freaks of nature. It was more like calling someone a loser. So the sentiment was no surprise to me, and I had to admit the turn of phrase was particularly inventive.

But there was no way I was telling that story here at the dinner table. FP was likely to either laugh along with the boys or threaten to beat them up, and I didn't like either option. I had to think of something to say. "I got an A on my composition," I said, instantly regretting it. That was exactly the kind of thing that could set him off. Too braggy. I'd learned it was dangerous to seem smarter than him. "There was a food fight in the cafeteria, and a bunch of kids got sent to the principal's office," I quickly added, which I think I'd seen in a movie and wasn't the slightest bit true, but it sounded like the kind of thing he'd like.

"Oh yeah?" he said, seemingly intrigued, and then added, "I bet you were Miss Goody Two Shoes in the corner the whole time, right?"

I ignored the jab, trying to make a joke. "Well, I was hungry and didn't want to throw my lunch across the room."

He laughed, genuinely amused. "Anybody you know get in trouble?"

"My friend Mary got hit with one of those little milk cartons, so she got kinda mad and threw something back, but my friend Clare just picked up her tray and went to eat in the hall." Where was this coming from? Look how quickly this man was turning me into a liar. I hated myself for it and hated him more.

I hadn't even eaten in the cafeteria, pretending I had a stomachache and spending lunchtime with the school nurse, a strategic move because her office was off the cafeteria: If she left the door open, I could see where everyone was sitting and try to understand how things worked. Besides, my lunch was embarrassing. Other kids had sandwiches with store-bought white bread and slices of baloney, or they bought the school lunch—cool things like sloppy joes or macaroni and cheese. My lunch was always thick brown slices of homemade bread with peanut butter and jelly. It was dense and ugly and if I threw it at someone it would probably kill them.

FP was quiet for a minute, scraping bits of food out of his teeth with a toothpick, and I could see his mood turning dark. He snapped the toothpick in half and tossed it onto his plate.

"So ... you have little friends now? Guess you won't be whining about writing a letter to Jessie anymore. That was fast."

This stung. A month ago, I'd said I wanted to write Jessie a letter and asked how I could mail it to her. I knew the addresses of all the communities—they were carefully written in the address section in the front of my diary—but I didn't know how to get a stamp and how to get it in the mail. At home I'd written letters all the time to my friends in other communities, but I would give them to adults to mail and had never seen that part of the process. "Don't you think Jessie would have written you by now if she wanted to hear from you?" he'd said, and the subject was dropped.

FP grabbed the *TV Guide* and got up from the table after his mean words, and I watched him bitterly, frustrated that I didn't have a snappy comeback. My silence made it feel like he was right.

As I cleared the dishes off the table, I worried: What *would* I say to Jessie if I wrote her? I told myself that I was only going to stay until the end of 04, just to prove to everyone that I'd tried to see what it was like out here. Six more weeks. Surely that was enough time for people in the communities to understand that I'd really tried. I would write to Jessie then, and I would finally be able to go home. I quietly resolved not to get too attached to anyone in school, because in six weeks I would never see them again.

Two Saturdays later I came downstairs, combing my waist-length wet hair and feeling the joy of how relaxed the house was when it was only me, my mother, and Annalee. FP was visiting his father in Vermont and wouldn't be back until the next night. He'd begun to regulate when I could wash my hair—he said he didn't like how long I took in the shower—so if he was away, I would jump at the chance to take my time in the bathroom, staying until the hot water ran out.

The house was filled with the smell of the bread my mother always baked on the weekends, and while her bread embarrassed me at school, I never missed a chance to eat a slice of it fresh from the oven, slathered with butter. It reminded me of home—I liked that my mother still baked bread every week like the ladies did in the communities. I found her cleaning up the kitchen, the front of her sweater dusted in flour, the timer she set ticking away on the counter. "It'll be out in ten minutes," she said, "but you know we have to let it cool for at least a half hour, so don't start licking those chops yet." I bent and peered into the window of the oven, where two golden loaves were bursting from their pans. "I made two," she said, "so you girls can eat an entire loaf today if you want. It's just us chickens." She was quoting the film *Rebel Without a Cause,* which we had watched for the millionth time a few days before. I'd cried again when Plato died but hidden my tears from them. Though his death was sad and unfair, I was crying more because the Lord's List movie reminded me of home, but I didn't want them to see that. My mother wiped her wet hands on the thighs of her paint-splattered jeans and said, "I'm going to get the mail."

Annalee was sprawled on the dining room rug, surrounded by a messy array of her toys—something she'd never be allowed to do if FP was home. Even my cat, a gray-and-white-striped diminutive girl I'd named Wuz, wasn't hiding under the refrigerator like she usually did. I picked her up off a dining room chair and sat down, putting her in my lap and petting her, her tentative little purr an endless source of delight to me. I felt sad that I would have to leave her soon and hoped they would treat her well when I was gone. She was a difficult cat who hissed at everyone but me, and I loved that about her. Annalee came over to pet her too. "Be very gentle," I whispered. "We don't want to scare her away." I whisper-laughed as Annalee moved her hand almost in slow motion to pet Wuz's silky fur.

"Let's curl your hair!" I said to her. "I want to see how big we can make it." Wuz fled out of my lap, alarmed at my sudden enthusiasm, but Annalee was excited by this idea. I ran upstairs to get my mother's curling iron, plugging it in and sitting on the floor to get to work. Annalee scooted herself against my crossed legs, and I marveled at the impossible thickness of her blond tresses as I untangled them. My mother came back inside with a stack of mail and sat down at the dining room table to open it. "FP's gonna go through the roof when he sees this electric bill," she said, her voice tinged with anxiety. She'd been known to say, "Close the refrigerator, for God sakes!" if I ever stood with it open longer than a few seconds. "What, do you have stock in General Electric?"

I was testing the heat of the curling iron against my hand when she said, "Looks like the IQ test results are here," and I glanced up to see her roughly opening the top of the envelope with her thumb. I wanted to jump up and snatch it out of her hands—it was mine, wasn't it?— but I resisted the urge, deciding to play it cool. I was watching her out of the corner of my eye as I wrapped a section of Annalee's hair around the barrel of the curling iron. "It doesn't matter if I get put back into the fifth grade," I told myself. "Who cares? I'm not going to be here much longer."

"Huh," she said finally, keeping her eyes on the piece of paper in front of her. "Your IQ is 125. I always thought you were smarter than me, but it turns out you're actually not."

CHAPTER 31

NOVEMBER 16, 04

Today after school Mary told me that Scott said I was a lesbiend for trying to hold Mary's hand. I don't even remember trying to hold her hand, but tomorrow I am going to show that stupid faggy Scott a thing or two. Horrible kid. I don't see what's wrong with holding Mary's hand anyway. Mommy and FP are out grocery shopping. I hate it when they leave me here all alone. It makes me feel so lonely. All alone in a quiet house with just the animals and one sleeping girl. I don't like it at all.

NOVEMBER 23, 04

When we went to the grocery store fat creephead said "My, you're enthusiastic," and I said "So are you." Then he kicked me and said "I don't want none of this shit from you no more!" I glared at him and walked away. Needless to say, I can't stand his fat guts. I am getting tired of this life and wish terribly that I could go back to the life I love.

NOVEMBER 25, 04

It's been nearly three months since I've been gone. I miss the tapes so much. I would be so grateful just to hear one song. Anything even

close makes me so happy I just want to fly. Pretty soon is Daria's
birthday. I wish I could be home by then. It gets later and later every
time I say that. I don't understand quite why. I think just to be with
my Mommy, but why? I'm not happy here in the least. I confuse myself very much sometimes. My best friend is my little Persian kitty.

DECEMBER 2, 04

I worked and slaved all day to clean this house. I really sparkled it
clean. I went up and down the stairs and really scrubbed. I kept remembering the days cleaning the schoolhouse. How grumpy we used
to all get with each other and fight over the vacuum cleaner. It's odd
how you can think you're having such a good time, as I did in those
days, and then look back on them and laugh and think of them as "the
good old days". I know one thing for sure, I will never look back on
these days as the "good old days". I miss Daria, Jessie, Clotilde, Frida,
Delia, Lou, Henry, Luka, Cybele, Samantha, Gabriel, Obray, Anthony, George, and everyone else I can think of, as you well know.

DECEMBER 3, 04

I'm God Oh so lonely. Today more than usual. I feel like I'm missing a part of my life sitting over here in dead, boring New York.
Everything that means anything to me is there with Jessie. It's my
life and myself. What is holding me back? A strong pull is telling
me to stay and live with Mommy for a while. But the other half is
saying that a while will be too long and I will get used to this way
of life and not want to go back. But why am I staying? That's the
real question. (I'm going nuts).

DECEMBER 11, 04

Lavy Lavy,

What a day. I'm getting so lonely. In this horrible outside world truth
doesn't pay off at all. If you're honest everyone else hates you. All day

during lunch period I just sat there, wanting to go home, and hoping this was all a long, horrible nightmare. I could have cried all day and all night out of loneliness and longing. I love you Jessie.

DECEMBER 22, 04

What an awful day this turned out to be. This morning I was awoken by the sounds of FP getting mad at Mommy. Oh God, you wouldn't believe what he was saying. He said Mommy was committing the ultimate crime (and he kept using the word "ultimate" because he thought it was so great) by not hating Annalee because of her brattiness. So Mommy felt awful all day and I was so infuriated by what he said that I had to clean the house from top to bottom very thoroughly so I didn't start screaming. I wrapped the presents all day, and Mommy just slept. I was wanting Daria so badly to tell my feelings to today. Telling your feelings to her is like putting yourself into the gentlest hands.

DECEMBER 26, 04

Last night Annalee kept waking up and crying and crying, and when I'd ask her what was wrong, she'd say "nothing." She tosses and turns all night.

DECEMBER 27, 04

Last night Mommy came into my room and said that I had hurt FP so much that he wouldn't even talk to her. She said that she has seen for quite a while that I hate him, and she's tried to ignore it, but it can't go on. She said I either have to learn to live with him or leave. My heart leapt into my throat. It was a good chance to tell her. Boy, I'm dumb. Whenever personal subjects come up, I turn mute. I couldn't say anything. Mommy sighed. The reason I hurt him last night was because I was standing there when he came home from work and he made a face and I said "Oh don't make faces at me" and walked away upstairs. I'm wondering all day if this is the right time to leave. I certainly can't hide my feelings about him. Mommy said that if I'm blaming FP for being here, I should blame her. I said, "No, it isn't your fault." I will not blame her because I know for one thing that she always puts the blame on herself for everything. This may be my last day here. I'm really not sure.

DECEMBER 31, 04

Farewell My Lavinia,

Today was a very weird day. First in the morning FP said he was going to leave us and he went out the door and got in the car and Mommy had to beg him not to leave. God! If he's going to do that every time he isn't the center of attention then that's dangerous. Then I just stayed in my room until breakfast. When we came down FP was sitting there. When Mommy came up before to tell me he almost left, I told her that I wanted to go back. She said she thought there was no stopping me now. So when I went downstairs FP laid this whole heavy on me about how it was a crime to leave and hardly have a relationship with Mommy. He argues with every-thing George told me. I was so positive and clear about my decision and all he did was mess it all up and make me confused again. George said not to listen or trust anyone but to go by my heart and by God I'm trying. But all the while FP is telling me that he <u>had</u> to leave. But it seems to me that just because he wasn't outstanding in the crowd he had to make himself be Mr. Terrific. He said he wants to get rich and give all of his money to Jessie. Jessie hates his guts and never wants to see him again! So utterly stupid of him to ruin my life and Mommy's life just because he isn't the most wonderful amazing person in the world. Tonight he is perfectly regular just like nothing happened. I still want to go back. He blurred it a lot, but I've almost got it straight again. Now I have to tell Mommy all over again because she thinks I changed my mind. She just can't let me go, so every time I tell her (and it's been three times) it somehow *messes up so I have to do it over. And it's hard, I tell you, very hard. Good Bye, dear 04, you were a rough road to ride, but I've managed this far, and it gets easier to get used to all the time. And good bye to you too, Lavinia. You have been of much comfort.*

Los Angeles-
-Caravan-
-Farm-
-Caravan-
-Boston-
-Martha's Vineyard-
-Boston-
-New York-
-Boston-
-Martha's Vineyard-
-Boston-
-Farm-
-Boston-
-New Jersey-
-Upstate New York-
-New Jersey-
-Upstate New York-
-New Jersey-
-Upstate New York-
-New Jersey-
-Upstate New York-
-New Jersey-
-Upstate New York-
-New Jersey-
-Upstate New York-

CHAPTER 32

JANUARY 1, 05

My Dearest. . . . Hmm what shall I call you? Margaret? No, not Margaret. Meg. Meg is a good name. After Meg from A Wrinkle in Time.

My Dearest Meg,

I'm very glad to meet you. You seem like quite a nice diary and I hope you will comfort me in times of crisis. You are just like the kind of diary that all the boys had in LA. Now let's get down to the day.

Good-Bye 04, Hello 05!!!
I simply did nothing all day. I made another patchwork pillow for FP and Mommy's rocking chair up in their room. Everyone seemed right on edge today, just ready to fall off. I was trying to be cheerful, but something is wrong. I don't know, but I just feel some heavy hearted sadness creeping over me.

JANUARY 4, 05

My My Meg,

I can't take this world. The hamster that the class owns died of starvation because everyone forgot about her over Christmas vaca-

tion. That is so cruel. But the worst part is that everyone laughed and jeered and screamed, "Oh, the hamster died!" It's so terrible. Just thinking about it makes me want to go back and punch every one of those kids, which I nearly did. It ruined my day completely. I was angry, sad and confused all at the same time. That adds up to frustration. I'm trying to get along with FP and be nice to him but each day it gets a little bit harder. He doesn't really care about us at all.

JANUARY 5, 05

Darling Meg—

It's January 5, that day that we were supposed to leave this trying Earth and go to Venus. Tonight I was wondering what Jessie was doing for January 5. It's a sort of holiday. Last year we celebrated so wonderfully. Oh God . . . I can't think about all of this anymore or I'll cry.

JANUARY 25, 05

Oh. My precious Meg,

Since this was just your average Friday (except for the fact that Andy Saunders, the boy who sits next to me, shot rubber bands at me and stole my pencils all day), I shall tell you a few feelings of mine. Especially this one I have been fighting for a while. It's letting the World change me. I struggle not to get involved with anything like rock music, boys, tight jeans and high heel boots, and I'm doing a pretty good job of it. Except it's hard not to be left alone if you don't join in these things. (I'll tell ya this, you'll never catch me in those disgusting jeans). Sometimes I am very tempted to tell some of these girls what my real life story is, but I don't think I can trust them not to tell. If I just tell them (like I did, I told them FP wasn't my real father) they will talk to you out loud about it. I don't know, maybe my story wouldn't even interest them. I just somehow have to get it out of my system, and I don't know how.

JANUARY 27, 05

My Darling,

*Last night I had the most horrifying dream. I dreamt that I went
back to everything, and Jessie said I couldn't come, and that she
wouldn't accept me because I had turned into a person of the World.
I woke up crying.*

FEBRUARY 4, 05

My My Meg,

*How everyone at school raved about my haircut. I was ooooohed
and aaahed over all day long. I've noticed that if I'm going to be
out in the World and not be thought of as a "weird dimwit whose
hair is mile long and wears skirts all of the time," I have to do
what they call "modernize." In other words wear clogs, jeans, and
velour shirts and get my hair cut. That's the only way. That's the
only way you are going to be more than a dodo bird with no
friends. It's not too great, but them's the breaks.*

MARCH 10, 05

Dear Girly Meg,

*As you know I'm the ugly, dogfaced oddball of the class. You should
hear some of the things they call me. It's annoying after a while. In
fact it's annoying from the beginning. Sometimes I think I could
commit suicide and nobody would be any the least bit affected by it.
I'm in that same stupid spot where I wonder if I'm just being plain
old self-involved, then I think that I'm being selfish to wonder about
it and it just goes around in circles til it's too silly to think about.*

MARCH I-P2.637, 05

Megooshi,

*Today . . . ummmm . . . well all I can remember is tonight, because
Mommy made stuffed veal and FP and I didn't like it. But FP*

was being so awful, he said, "It's like having a baby calf on your plate, see how it's so hard, it's just like it's still alive." He was going on and on and getting more and more gross each time. It was just awful. It gets worse and worse with him each day. If he had to live with himself he'd be beaten up every day. Why am I wasting my page on him? The creep.

MARCH 18, 05

Y'all,

I don't even know what to say except each day I miss everyone so goddamned much and I'm so lonely just someone to talk to is a comfort. I think that maybe I'm not quite ready to go back yet. Although I don't know why I think that, because I'd give anything to be at this moment hugging Jessie. Sometimes I just don't know what I am or where I'm heading for. I just try to make the most of it, because somewhere in all of this new life I'm living there's a lesson to be learned by me.

MARCH 19, 05

Meg,

Today it was just gorgeous outside. I know what day this is, but I'm not supposed to know so I'll forget it, and pretend I don't know. Ummm . . . let's see. Not much is going on around here. I felt just a little bit happy today for the first time. I don't know why. Isn't it strange? This is certainly not a day to be happy about. I keep having dreams about going back, some that nobody wants me there anymore and that I'm stuck out here, and some so wonderful that I just cry with joy through the whole thing.

MARCH 26, 05

Meg My Dear Girl,

One thing I just realized is isn't a house supposed to be happy when the father comes home? Yes, but it isn't like that in our house. As soon

as FP comes home, everything is very quiet, Annalee has to go up-
stairs, all of the neighbor kids go out of the yard, it's like darkness
comes over the neighborhood, all because of him. God sometimes I
think I really, really hate him. It drives me crazy the way we live.

MARCH 29, 05

I'm rather grumpy today because everyone in this house has at least
three pairs of pants. Including Annalee (not to mention all of her
velour shirts and other gorgeous clothes.) Yet I'm only entitled to
one pair of jeans. Mommy and FP say that girls should wear skirts
to school, and FP says that if in LA school I had to wear skirts, I
should here too. But he doesn't understand that in this school wear-
ing skirts is very odd, and I'm teased all the time because I almost
always wear skirts. He's such a drag. Mommy says she would get
me a pair if he would let her.

APRIL 20, 05

Dear Meg,

This is awful and gross but FP keeps making me sit in his lap and
then he puts his hand down my shirt. I keep trying to edge away
from him but he pulls me with his hands back again. Ugh, it just
gets me sick!!!!!!!!!!!!!!!!!!

MAY 6, 05

OH Meg,

Boy what a jerk I am to look forward to getting braces. It kills!!! I
hated every minute of the four long hours of the appointment—it
was torture. Tomorrow we get our individual class pictures and
isn't that a nice little coincidence that I got my braces the day be-
fore? I have a horrible night brace, too. When FP saw me wearing
it and heard that I have to wear it a couple hours around the house
he goes "Yuck—I don't want to look at that all night!" Boy does he
know how to encourage someone to wear what's good for you!

MAY 13, 1980

Dear Meg,

There is something that Mom said today that has kept coming to my mind. I asked her, half jokingly, "How can you stand to live with FP?" She replied "I've got no choice, there's nobody else." I said "What?" she replied with a sigh, "He's all there is." All that makes me feel like is that she is just being nice to him and bearing with him because of the support. If she doesn't love him, what the hell did she leave the Communities for?! I sometimes feel like I'm being pushed and pulled in and out of different worlds just for the heck of it! I'm lonely tonight.

MAY 17, 1980

Mommy and Annalee went shopping and me and FP mowed the lawn. I can't stand when I am alone in the house with him he is always hugging me and picking me up, and I hate it.

MAY 21, 1980

Mommy just gets me so mad sometimes how she lets FP boss her around and tell her what to do. I know it sounds like women's liberation, but she should stand up for her rights. She is like a slave. How can she stand him much less love him?

JUNE 22, 1980

Hello Meggie,

Boy you'll never believe what Mom said to me! She said that she was considering just calling it quits with FP and going back to Granny's. But I don't believe she'd do that after all of this! After taking herself and her kids out of the communities for this one man, and then deciding to forget it.

I'm so lonely, all I can think about tonight is home, <u>real</u> home. With all the people who really mean something to me. I can only think of small things I am missing, like Henry's first birthday, and Luka is already going on two. Jessie's birthday is soon. Oh God, I miss them all so much. Mom is such a mess, FP is just bossy and mean, Annalee is a prisoner, and I just want to go home. I miss you Jessie.

JULY 31, 1980

Dearest and Kind Meg,

Mommy just doesn't understand me one bit. For one thing she doesn't understand that I'm not capable of having something happen (like a fight, or being yelled at) and just forgetting. She calls it pouting, just because I am quiet and solemn after something like that happens. She is not an understanding Mother at all, and believe me, it's hard to live with someone who yells at you when you're sad, screams at you for not expressing yourself, while if you come up to her and ask what's wrong she'll say "Nothing!" and grab a cigarette which she will proceed to smoke in one drag. She never expresses herself! And after all of this she will say (yelling of course) "Yelling, who's yelling?!!" I really hope that we can learn to trust each other more, and know each other better. I wish we could've known each other a little better, a little sooner.

AUGUST 1, 1980

My Sincere Meg,

Well, it's been almost an entire year since I saw Jessie. The last time I saw her was August 2nd around 9:30 at night. I cannot begin to tell you how much I miss her and wish I could somehow see her. I am so afraid to decide to go back, because once I'm there I can't change my mind, and I know I will miss Mommy. The longer I stay the more I get attached to this place and everything about it. But if Mom ever left FP and went back to Granny's I would tell her then and there that I couldn't stay. It seems kind of cruel now

that I think of it because that would be the time she most needed
me. Oh, why am I thinking about this? It hasn't happened!

All I want to say is, I will get back to you one day Jessie, and I
hope our love is still strong and that the world hasn't changed me
into a stranger.

AUGUST 3, 1980

Meg Meg Meg,

What a Dreadful Day. The morning began with FP in a grumpy
state (as usual) and then Mommy and FP going up in their room
for two hours, only to come back out and Mom said to me "FP
wants only me and him to go grocery shopping." So they did, and
when they came home we put the groceries away and they went
back upstairs. After a few minutes they came back down again and
I was just standing in the kitchen and Mom said "What do you
want?" which told me she was mad. Then I went upstairs and I
heard FP say "Get out of here!" and when I came back down Mom
was gone and Annalee said she went for a walk. She came back
after an hour and they went back in their room. I was in the
kitchen and Mom came down and said "Why do you stand around?
I can usually count on you when I'm sad, but now you are just a
burden!" She called me selfish and gave me a long talk, and I just
couldn't stop crying because she doesn't understand me and I can't
talk to her but I want to. I'm so lonely and I just can't stop crying.

AUGUST 16, 1980

My Darling,

To renew you on the political front, Carter won the Democratic
nomination and a while ago Reagan won the Republican nomi-
nation. The hostages are in their 290th (or around there) day, and
the Shah of Iran died. Some think the person buried in L.H. Os-
wald's grave isn't Oswald, but his brother won't let them dig him
up to find out.

SEPTEMBER 18, 1980

Deary Poo Meg—

What happened today is all above and beyond me. I came home from school and Mom is nowhere to be seen. I looked everywhere and then FP came home and he looked. We were so scared (at least I was). FP walked up South Mountain Pass and to the Appalachian Trail, all across 9D and up to Anthony's Nose. I was so nervous thinking of all the horrible things that could have happened. I mean, you name it, I thought of it. Snake bites, broken legs. Anyway at 9:05 her and FP came walking in and she said she was up hiding behind the house the whole time. You see, her and FP got into a fight so she left. Boy did she give me a scare!

NOVEMBER 5, 1980

Oooh Meg,

Tonight I had to fix dinner and do all the dishes all day because Mom lay abed. Doing that for a day makes me say positively, I'll never be just a plain old housewife. That's a promise. If I am I will change immediately. I think I am slowly turning into a Women's Libber, but boy, I'll never slave for a man the way Mom does. No man could be worth wasting your life and career.

DECEMBER 1, 1980

Daria. Happy Birthday. I've missed you a lot this past year and I hope that I will see you soon. I will never forget you as long as I live and I hope you will always remember me. I almost got the nerve to call and I want to write you a letter. I love you and I always will.

CHAPTER 33

MY SEVENTH-GRADE TEACHER WAS MR. WEEKS, AND I INstantly had a crush on him. The other teachers in the school struck me as old and deeply adult—the women wore thick pantyhose, and the men seemed vaguely sad. But not Mr. Weeks. Mr. Weeks had hair that hung just above his shoulders, and a mustache and short beard. I'd never seen a man with long hair before—was he a hippie? I'd been raised to believe that hippies were dead inside, but Mr. Weeks seemed very alive to me. Tall and thin, he always wore brown corduroy pants and cool shirts with no tie and the sleeves rolled up. If students used aggressive language or playfully hit each other, he would say, "Violence is not the way," in a serene tone. Kids laughed at this behind his back, but it somehow worked to make everyone behave a little better when we were in his classroom. He was a science and health teacher, and we soon had jade leaves planted in little cups to demonstrate how you could grow some plants from just one leaf; he'd also helped us collect crickets, which then lived in a tank in our classroom so we could observe their behavior.

A few weeks into the school year, we came into class to find the words "Sex Education" written on the board. The class was quieter than usual when we settled into our seats, and there was a nervous energy in the air. I felt a little embarrassed but also interested to learn about sex and happy that it was Mr. Weeks who was going to teach it to us, since his calm presence made it less scary.

He pulled down diagrams of the anatomy of reproductive organs and explained how the vagina was an "elastic muscular canal" and the penis consisted of "three cylindrical sponges that filled with blood when a man gets an erection." He explained "intercourse" and "semen," and even the most smart-ass boys stayed quiet while he talked. Finally, when he was done with his lesson, he asked if anyone had questions. "No question is too embarrassing," he reassured us. "The human body is a beautiful thing, and there is no reason to be shy about it." There was a very long pause now, where he looked hopefully around the room at us all, and no one said a word. He seemed utterly comfortable as he stood in front of the wordless class. "Any question at all?" he said kindly. "I know some of you *must* have questions." Of course we had questions! But no one spoke.

Eventually he shrugged, as if to say, "Well, I tried," and glanced up at the clock—we were all keenly aware that the bell was going to ring in a few minutes. He was about to speak when a girl sitting in front of me named Pam shot her arm up into the air. Pam was a stocky girl and had big breasts. The few of us who already had breasts tried to down-play them, but not Pam. She wore designer jeans and tight sweaters, and sometimes high school boys in cool cars would pick her up in the parking lot while we were all getting on our buses to go home. She wasn't popular—she wasn't good in school, or particularly pretty—but I was secretly impressed with her because it seemed like she had a whole other life outside school that wasn't her family.

When she raised her hand, Mr. Weeks looked very pleased. "Yes, Pam?" he asked.

"Can you get pregnant from swallowing semen?" she asked. There was a stunned silence, and then the class exploded in shocked groans. "Class, class," said Mr. Weeks, never raising his voice as his hands pressed slowly downward toward the floor. He waited until the room was quiet again and addressed the whole class, not just Pam. "No, a woman cannot get pregnant from swallowing semen. Fertilization only occurs when the sperm meets the egg, and for that it has to travel through the vaginal canal." The bell rang, and the kids couldn't get out of the class fast enough.

On the bus ride home, while Mary and Clare chattered around me, I wondered over and over, "Why would anyone swallow semen?" and contemplated what Pam's life was like. When the class had exploded, she'd just shrugged one shoulder and seemed annoyed at how juvenile they all were. I was impressed. I wondered if I would have been brave enough to ask my follow-up question if the bell hadn't rung, imagining myself raising my hand and asking, "Mr. Weeks, why would anyone swallow semen?" No, I knew I wouldn't have, because right now my biggest goal in life was not to draw attention to myself.

CHAPTER 34

MY MOTHER NOW HAD A JOB AS THE SECRETARY AT MY
school, and she sat on the other side of the same desk that we'd stood
in front of a year ago when she claimed the school I came from burned
down. Earlier in the week she'd learned that her job wanted her to
start attending school-board meetings every Monday night from seven
to ten. Tonight was the first Monday and the first time I would be
home alone with FP at night for such a long period of time. He was a
different person when it was just the two of us—playful, grabby, encouraging me to make fun of the way my mother dressed or wore her
hair, or teasing me about my new braces.

The week before, the school had held an "international luncheon,"
where each class learned dances and songs from different countries
and performed them for parents. Our class chose Ireland and had to
learn an Irish jig. My mom was already at school because she worked
there, but FP showed up for the event. He was late, and I saw him arrive and take his seat just as we were lining up on the stage to do our
dance. At thirty-one, FP was significantly younger than the other parents, and his jean jacket, work boots, and shaggy hair stood out among
a sea of polo shirts and boat shoes. I'd really hoped he'd be working and
wouldn't be able to come—I didn't like having him in this world that
was mine and immediately felt self-conscious about how much he
stood out. "Hey," he'd said the night before, "maybe it'll get me a job
with one of these rich people." It was already embarrassing enough

that my mom worked at the school—nobody else's mom even worked. To have him there trying to drum up a gig on top of it was mortifying.

While people mingled afterward, I bit into a piece of Irish soda bread someone's mother had made and stood with the other girls, agonizing over the mistakes we'd made onstage. I kept one eye on FP, who was talking with a group of the boys, and I saw him play-punch Scott, making him laugh. Clare noticed where I was looking and said, "Your dad is so cool," and then, "Sorry, stepdad, I mean stepdad," but even that was too much for me. The fact that he got to pose as a parental figure at all was such a joke.

He walked over to us now and said, "Good job, girls," as he took a theatrical bite of the soda bread in my hand, making the girls giggle. "Gotta get back to work, just came over to say bye," and he leaned in close to my ear and whispered, "You were looking a little jiggly up there—might be time for a bra," then said, "Bye, ladies," and walked off. I crossed my arms tightly around my chest as I watched him saunter through the crowd.

"He kinda looks like Robert Redford," one girl said, and then sighed. She was wearing a T-shirt with KISS ME, I'M IRISH on the front, and I focused on the shamrock on her shirt to calm myself. "My parents are so bogus," she said then, wistfully looking after him. I shrugged and smiled, on the verge of throwing up.

So when my mother told me that next Monday she'd be gone for three hours, I tried to find all kinds of ways to make her bring me with her to the school for the meeting: I could take the minutes! ("That's the only purpose for me being there," she said.) I could help her organize the minutes from the last meeting, then hand them out to people? She admitted that if I wanted to do that for her during lunch, it would actually be a big help, and she'd consider taking me with her to the meeting. When lunch period came, I hurried to the office, and she handed me several tall stacks of paper, organized crosswise to distinguish the pages.

They were double-sided pages, dense with boring words, but I thought I could figure out how to do it. I laid each section on chairs in the office, on the floor, and on a side table, creating an assembly line for myself as I made my way around the room, enjoying the definitive stamp of the stapler at the end. But people were coming and going from the office, asking me what I was doing, and soon I became completely discombobulated, losing track of where I was. My mother was busy talking on the phone, and when she hung up she came over from behind her desk and picked up one of my completed sets, thumbing through it. "Oh no—no no," she said, panicky. "This is—these are—" She flipped frantically through a few more. "Jesus, it's going to take me all afternoon to sort this out."

"I got confused," I said, "but I can fix it."

"No more of *your* help," she said, reaching for the staple remover on her desk and yanking the staples out of my work.

"But—" I said. "Well, can I help you take out the staples at least?" She looked up at me like she felt sorry for how useless I was. At least she wasn't angry.

"I don't know what I was thinking, asking you to make sense of all this nonsense. Thank you for trying, though, I guess." She licked her thumb and started to separate the pages into her own piles. I was sweaty and nervous, still trying to figure out how to prove myself so I could go to this meeting with her tonight.

"You should go eat your lunch with what's left of the period," she said, glancing up at the clock on the wall. "Wouldn't have been a good idea for you to come anyway—the meeting is supposed to go till ten, but for all I know they'll yammer on and on and I won't be home till all hours, and you have school tomorrow."

"OK," I said, and took a long time gathering my bag and looking around for nothing.

"No need to mope—it's not the end of the world!" she said, trying to make light of the situation. I managed a small smile.

I walked out of the office and slowly down the hall, pausing to contemplate the construction-paper turkey art that lined one wall, with a sign that read MISS TINTLE, 1ST GRADE. GOBBLE GOBBLE! Tonight Mom would leave at six-thirty, and I usually went to bed at ten-thirty but could maybe say I was tired and make it ten. Three and a half hours. An eternity. I thought I'd strategically mention before she left tonight that I had a research paper due next week, and I'd go upstairs and bury myself in that. Or I'd jump up from the table in the middle of dinner and rush to the bathroom, pretending to have a stomachache so I could go directly to bed. Maybe the car wouldn't start tonight, so Mom couldn't leave, or there would be a freak snowstorm that kept her home.

That night, I waited a very long time to go downstairs after Mom left at six-thirty as planned. I'd successfully performed anxiety about my research paper at dinner, so I'd been in my room since then, index cards and notes spread around on my desk to indicate how busy I was. Annalee's little bedroom was a dressing room off mine, and I'd chatted with her before she went to sleep, checking in on her monster problem: In the ceiling above her bed was a door that led to the attic, and when we first moved in, she'd told me she was afraid of the monster that would surely be creeping out of it while she slept. I'd told her that if she saw it, she should jump toward it and grab at it, saying, "Aha! I got you!" and that would scare it away. She liked this idea, letting me know that it hadn't happened yet but she was ready, and she didn't feel scared anymore. I turned off the light for her and said good night. But I'd been too stressed at dinner to eat much, and now I was hungry and wanted to get something from the kitchen.

In the year I'd been out here in the World and living with these people, I'd learned the art of avoidance, deflection, and de-escalation. Act happy, but not too happy. Laugh at his jokes. Make jokes too sometimes, but be sure they aren't too clever or that he can't construe them as making fun of him. If he starts to give a long boring lecture, find a face to make that looks like you aren't dying inside. Don't stand up for the dogs if you don't like how he's treating them; same for Annalee—it doesn't make it better for them. If he starts to yell at Mom, get out of the room as quickly and quietly as possible, because you're next. If he punches a wall or throws something across the room, that usually means no one is going to get hit tonight. That's him trying to control himself.

I'd grown accustomed to avoiding eye contact with him—as much as I could get away with—so I could hide my hatred, because I knew from experience that if he caught a glimpse of what I really felt, he would kick me or slap me or take it out on Mom or Annalee, and he was so much more violent toward them. The key was not to engage him much at all, while remaining pleasantly present.

I figured he was watching TV, though I realized I couldn't hear it like I usually could from my bedroom. Whatever he was doing, he would be in the living room, and I knew that he could sometimes get so focused on things that if I tiptoed down from my bedroom, he might not even notice me passing by to get something from the kitchen. He and my mother had started to point out to me that I was fat and that, since I had come to live with them, I'd gotten fatter. "Hey, Porky," he would greet me when I came home, putting his hands around my waist. I didn't need him to point out the new body I was quietly dealing with, now that I had braces and breasts. I also didn't particularly want to deal with his reaction to me getting food. The re-frigerator would make noise if I opened it, but there was a plate of chocolate chip cookies on the kitchen counter. I'd quickly eat one and go back upstairs.

I successfully slipped past him through the dining room, not even turning my head in his direction. I inhaled the cookie, making sure not to leave a crumb, and was creeping through the dining room on my way back up.

When my foot made it to that first stair, I dared to glance in his direction and saw that his back was to me. He was facing the TV, but now I noticed that the TV wasn't on and he was sitting in the dark, one of his feet oddly visible on the side of the chair. I quickly averted my eyes and took another step up—whatever this was couldn't be good. I heard the familiar squeaky swivel of the chair as he turned around. No one was allowed to use that chair except him, so when he wasn't home, I would sit in it and grab the side table next to it to propel myself around and around as fast as I could go, inviting Annalee to get in and come for a spin. She loved it.

When I looked around at the sound of the swivel, he was sitting there facing me, legs spread wide, in the light-blue shorts he wore to coach the Little League team, slouched far down in the chair as if he'd been asleep. He was smiling the way I'd seen drunk people smile in movies, eyes with heavy lids, not all there. I was unnerved by this look on his face—I'd never seen it before—and then my eyes went to his hand, which was resting on a bulge in his shorts.

"Hey, do you want to come talk to me for a minute?" He was vulnerable in a way that I'd also never seen before, and my feet walked backward down the stairs and toward him. I stood in front of him, a foot away, and he started to stroke the bulge in his shorts. It was magnetic somehow, repulsion and curiosity mingling in such a confusing way. He reached his arm out to me, not getting up, and said, "You should feel this. It feels really good. It means I've been thinking about you."

I was struck by how he seemed like he wasn't in control, like he needed something from me, and I liked that fleeting feeling of power. "Come here," he said. "It's OK to touch it," and I kneeled down between his spread legs and let him take my hand and put it on top of the shorts. He put his hand over mine and moved it slowly up and down, his breath quickening while I held mine. "Do you understand what this is?" he asked, moving my hand more quickly up and down as he spoke. I was so outside my body, watching this happen to me. I'd been on this planet too many times before, and it seemed likely I'd be here many times again—did any of this really matter?

"It's three cylindrical sponges that fill with blood," I said, and I was surprised that my voice was calm and somehow like Mr. Weeks's.

FP let out a languid laugh, then said, "Well, I guess if you know all that—then you must be ready. I thought so."

"I don't know why I said that I don't know why I said that," I thought, "why did I say that?" I snapped into the reality of what was happening. It was true that when I felt his penis, I understood how it could be made of sponges. FP got up and walked the short distance to the couch, pulling off his shorts before he lay down on it, adjusting the throw pillow behind him with some ceremony, as he did with every single object in his world. His erection was out in the open now, and he was stroking it. "Sit down with me," he said, as my trance dissipated. This was disgusting, he was disgusting, and if I was going to be with a man who was going to teach me things, it wasn't going to be him. How humiliating. All the girls I loved and missed had had better, more important men.

I sat down on the couch as far away as I could from him, but his legs were spread wide on the back and the side of it, and he wrapped his hand around my wrist to pull me toward him. I knew that resisting would just make him violent, so I let myself be pulled forward. Once I got close enough, he put his hand on the back of my neck. The gesture was a more tender one than I'd ever felt in my life. Here was someone who wanted me—until his hand crawled up the base of my skull and he was forcing my face even closer to the erection in his other hand. That didn't feel tender at all. "Go on, put it in your mouth," he said. "I've been thinking about what this would be like with your braces. Be careful with those."

I froze, and my head filled with static and fluff all at once.

He said, "I promise I won't shove it down your throat." It had never occurred to me that a penis could be forced into my mouth, or anyone's. So while he led me there and I tentatively put my tongue out, licking it like it was covered in poison, I was very nervous that he would shove it in my mouth, because he was a violent man who rarely kept promises. This fear snapped me out of my haze, and the indignity of what was happening started to creep in as he guided it into my mouth.

He thrust his hips into my face a few times, which scared me, and when I choked, he took his penis out of my mouth and chuckled softly. "Sorry, sorry," he said. "I'm getting a little carried away. I guess you've never done this before."

I shook my head no as I sat up, wiping my mouth with the back of my hand. I couldn't believe he thought I'd done this before. I didn't even know that this was a thing people did. Was it? Was this what Frida was doing to George, what Clotilde was doing to Melvin? Did it feel less disgusting if you knew the man was important, powerful, wise? I was sure that if Jessie knew about this, she would be furious. He would never have been allowed to do this to me if we were in the communities.

"That wasn't bad," he said, his voice encouraging. "I didn't feel your braces at all. So that's good news."

The static was back in my brain, and I was only partially aware of taking out the barrette that held back a front piece of my hair, the familiar texture of the yellow flowers on it comforting as I clicked it into place again.

"OK, your mom is coming home soon. You should probably go upstairs," he said, reaching to the floor for his shorts and methodically turning them right side out. I didn't want to move. I thought about how if you leave a moment, then it's over, and then it exists as a thing that happened, and you can't take it back, and what you did is forever. If I did what he said and went upstairs, it seemed like I was OK with it all and we now had a secret together. I didn't move. "Don't worry," he said, standing up to pull on his shorts. "I'm not gonna tell your mother about this—she wouldn't understand, and she'll probably just get jealous."

He walked over to the TV and pulled out the knob to turn it on. I slinked away while his back was turned, feeling like a ghost.

Upstairs, I brushed my teeth for a long time. His words "that's good news" were echoing in my head—it sounded like he intended for it to happen again. I was getting angrier and angrier at myself for not fighting him, intentionally gagging myself with the toothbrush until my eyes watered.

I threw the toothbrush in the trash, and then, realizing I wouldn't have any way of explaining that, I took it back out again, scheming to find a way to ask for a new one that didn't seem suspicious. The orthodontist! He'd given me a spare toothbrush after my last appointment. I rummaged in the bathroom cabinet until I found it, then threw the old one away again.

In my bedroom, I put on my nightgown and sat on the edge of my bed. My limbs felt heavy, so heavy that I could barely pick up my diary. I opened it, wrote "Dear Meg," and stared at the page for a long time. Finally I willed myself to write about what had physically happened, in the plainest way I could think of, and then wrote about how I hated him and how he didn't deserve me. I wrote how much I wished I could talk to Jessie about it. I wondered if this was part of the lesson I had to learn so that I never had to come back to earth again. I thought that if this had been some kind of test, I hadn't done very well. I felt relief that at least he hadn't touched me at all except for the back of my head. But I hadn't fought him. I hadn't fought him or said very much at all. I'd done it, and it was dawning on me that I'd crossed a line that couldn't be uncrossed.

As I lay down in bed, I briefly wondered if this had been his master plan all along—to leave the communities so he could "have" me. I quickly realized that this couldn't be the case: They hadn't expected for me to be sent to them. But that meant him doing this to me was an afterthought, which then made me wonder if something I'd said or done had made it seem like I wanted it. I'd pressed down my hatred and tried to be nice to him after my mother begged me to, almost a year ago. "If you aren't nice, he will leave us," she'd said, tears streaming down her face, "and then what will we do?" And this was where being pleasantly present had gotten me. Did he think it meant I liked him, felt romantic toward him? I shuddered, rage mounting at the trap they had set for me, though I was pretty sure it hadn't been intentional on my mother's part.

I was about to turn out the light when I heard my mother come home. Now she was talking to FP; now her footsteps were on the stairs. When we first left the communities, she'd come into my room every night after I got into bed to ask me how I was and to say good night. I'd protested when she called it "tucking me in," because that was for kids and I wasn't a kid. She hadn't done that in a long time, but tonight she stopped in my doorway and smiled. "Hi, just thought I'd come say good night." I felt relieved at the sight of her.

She was still wearing her work clothes—a corduroy suit jacket and skirt—and I thought about how she looked nice and that she seemed a little bit happier now that she wasn't helping FP prep rooms for painting at his various jobs.

She sat down on my bed and asked how the research paper was going. I wondered if I looked different. I wanted to look different. I wanted to scream, to hug her, to tell her what had just happened to me, to beg her for us to leave right now, to apologize to her, any of it. All of it. But I shrugged, only able to give a slight indication that something was wrong, feeling a chasm between me and the words. All I could think to say was the word "help," but the static took over in my brain and I couldn't even say that. I wished I could cry so she would see that something was wrong, very wrong, but the static wouldn't let me cry. The static wouldn't even let me think.

"Hey, kiddo—what's going on?" she said, putting her hand on my knee and shaking it gently. Far, far away somewhere, a thin voice was saying, "This is it. The time is now. It's not a secret if you tell her. Tell her and everything will change. Tell her tell her tell her tell her . . ." The voice got smaller and smaller, as if it were being dragged away from me, until it was gone.

She got up, saying, "Well, if it makes you feel any better, you would have *hated* the board meeting." She reached down to turn off the lamp on my bedside table, shaking her head. "So consider yourself lucky. You would have died of boredom. Can't believe I have to live through that every Monday night until May."

CHAPTER 35

I'D GOTTEN SO USED TO PRETENDING TO BE SOMEONE ELSE that I didn't really feel any different the next day at school. I was already a fabrication; what was another layer? I simply put it out of my mind. As much as I was ridiculed at school, I loved being there, mostly because it was the only thing I'd ever had that was utterly mine. Yes, Mom worked at the school now, but I wasn't the kind of kid who got sent to the office, so I rarely saw her during the day. I was Guinaqueer— I'd even graduated to Rentaqueer, which I also thought was hilarious, but those boys didn't scare me. Some of them were even nice to me when no one was looking.

The dread at the sound of the final bell and the walk to the bus was the same as it had always been. I hated going home, but I relished the hour or two before FP and Mom got there, when I would play the radio and not even feel guilty about liking Hall & Oates or Pat Benatar. Annalee and I would dance around and eat a few Mallomars—but not so many that FP would notice, since we weren't allowed. That afternoon I sang Leo Sayer's "More Than I Can Say" into my hairbrush in front of the mirror, Annalee imitating my dramatic moves behind me and laughing. The next Monday night was a million years away.

As the week went by, though, tension was mounting in the house. I'd been avoiding FP as much as possible, and though I knew this was a dangerous game, I couldn't manage to make myself behave any other way. I knew I didn't want to be alone in a room with him or anywhere near him. I also knew this would cause strife for all of us, but I had ceased to think about the big picture, because I couldn't let myself. For now it was minute to minute and every man for himself. At dinner I spoke as little as possible, and I went up to my bedroom afterward instead of watching TV like we usually did. FP's dark moods escalated, and he took it out on Annalee and Mom, as I knew he would. One night he stormed into Annalee's room, declaring it a pigsty, and threw every toy that wasn't in its place into a garbage bag, taking it all the way down the driveway and putting it in the trash. He screamed at Mom for hours about how Annalee was a psycho robot kid and she was a terrible mother. When she finally burst into tears and got up to leave the room, he punched her in the back, and she sat down.

When the weekend came, my mother was making pancakes, a joyless ritual we had in which we played a normal family who had "Pancake Saturdays." When we got everything arranged on the table—butter, syrup, napkins just so, plates for the three of us—Mom came in with the stack of pancakes on a warm plate, and FP was stabbing at the pancakes with his fork before she could even put the plate on the table. She sat down with a heaving sigh, not serving herself, just watching us with a vacant stare. I noticed that she had a clump of pancake batter in her hair and thought about how to tell her without making a big deal out of it. It was only a matter of time before he noticed, but I decided to stay quiet—he could easily turn it into the two of us making fun of her if I said anything. He was slicing the butter and putting each slice carefully between the pancakes on his plate, then deliberately pouring the syrup in a precise swirl on top. I watched him cut a perfect triangle out of the stack and stuff it in his mouth. He was licking the syrup off the back of his fork when he looked up finally, and he jabbed it in Mom's direction. "Bess, what the fuck is in your hair?" he said, and she looked confused. He thrust the fork closer to her, pointing with it. "Is that pancake batter? What are you doing in that kitchen that you get batter in your hair?"

She reached up to where he was pointing and felt the sticky gob, then picked up her napkin and dipped it into her glass of water, halfheartedly raking it over the strand of hair, effectively spreading the batter around more.

He slammed his fist on the table. "You're a fucking slob!" he screamed. I stared at the flower pattern on the tablecloth. Mom started crying and then said, "What do you want me to do?" She got up to go to the kitchen, but he jumped up and backed her against the dining room wall, screaming into her face about how disgusting she was. I knew he was mad at me, not her. There was a long moment of stillness, where he was panting, inches away from her, and Mom was whimpering. I was still staring at the tablecloth. Mercifully, he then grabbed his keys and stormed out the front door, and we heard the car start and back down the driveway.

Mom sat at the table and cried for hours. She asked me what we should do, what had she done, how could she make it better? "He's not good for you, he's not good for Annalee, we have to get out of here," she mumbled quickly to herself. Eventually she calmed down and decided we were going to Granny's—for good this time. "I hope you can forgive me," she said as she haphazardly stuffed Annalee's clothes into a pillowcase. "Please don't be mad at me, but I just don't want to do this to us anymore." I wasn't mad at all, I was elated, packing as quickly as I could because there was no way of knowing when he would return.

Mom got on the phone and called our neighbor Linda to see if she could give us a ride to the train station. She hung up and said Linda would be here in fifteen minutes. I ran upstairs and snatched my banjo case from under the bed, then hurried downstairs to take the banjo off the wall. Mom saw me and said, "We have to travel light, we can come back for stuff later," but I ignored her, because there was no way I was leaving my banjo behind and there was definitely no way I was ever coming back to this house.

When my suitcase and banjo were by the front door, I ran upstairs to get Annalee. "Can I take 1234?" she asked, holding up the ratty doll she'd named that series of numbers.

"Yes, but here, put her in my purse—Mom is freaking out that we're taking too much stuff." Mom was walking past the door when I said this, and she poked her head in. "Awww, come on, of course she can take 1234. You don't have to hide stuff from me."

"It's 1, 2, *three*, 4," Annalee grumbled under her breath, perpetually disappointed in us for not getting the emphasis right on her beloved doll's name.

I took her hand and we hurried down to the dining room and waited for Mom, listening to the sound of drawers opening and slamming shut. It was really happening. I started to clear the plates and half-eaten pancakes from the table, then stopped. Let him clean up after himself for once. I poured syrup on a pancake instead, handing it to Annalee. "Handcakes!" I said, and she gleefully scarfed it down, enjoying the mayhem of it all. I grabbed our coats from the rack, and we put them on. I took Mom's coat off the hook and held it over my arm.

I was pacing, trying not to look at the clock and peering out the kitchen window at the driveway every two seconds, when Mom finally appeared with her suitcase, frantic but determined. "About five more minutes and she'll be here," she said as she nervously cleared away the dishes, scraping food into the garbage, also checking the driveway every few seconds. I decided I should fill up the bird feeder quickly—he'd never do it, and those birds had come to depend on us for food. I was outside pouring seed into the feeder when I heard the familiar tire-on-gravel sound and dropped the bag where I stood, rushing inside. Mom was physically pushing Annalee up the stairs, saying, "Go go go!" and she seized the suitcases from the front door and thrust them into my hands, saying, "Hide these under your bed!" I knew this meant it wasn't Linda in the driveway, it was FP. "I'm gonna go outside and talk to him—call Linda right now and tell her not to come. God, I hope she's not on her way." She fled out the front door like a maniac.

As I shoved the suitcases under the bed, I told myself there was still hope. When I rushed downstairs, I heard the car door slam and peeked outside enough to see that Mom had gotten in the passenger seat of his car; they were just sitting there. I picked up the phone, and my hand hovered over the rotary dial for a long minute. What if I *didn't* call Linda? If Linda showed up, I'd grab Annalee and the suitcases and get in her car, saying, "Come on, Mom!" in a cheerful tone. One thing I knew about FP: He was a *completely* different person when anyone else was around. He would never make a scene. But what would Mom do?

I panicked and did what she told me to, and when Linda asked, "Is everything all right?" I put on a breezy tone and said, "Oh yeah, fine—my granny called and said there was a fire at her work today and she had to stay longer to take care of some things, so we're gonna take a later train." I don't know why I said that. Maybe because somewhere in the back of my head I wondered if it would solve everything if I just lit this house on fire and Annalee and I ran for the woods.

They sat in his car for hours. I hoped it was because Mom was holding her ground, but I knew how his droning on and on and twisting of words could wear you down.

I hated hated hated this. I hated being stuck. I hated waiting for their drama to unfold. As the hours ticked by, I was more and more sure that he would talk her into staying. I was in despair. It was a full hour before I took off my coat.

Finally, Mom came in, and her face was a crazy unfamiliar shade of pale.

"Go sit down in the living room right now," she said, and went quickly up the stairs. I walked slowly, my mind racing—what was happening? Mom was often sad and dramatic, sometimes irritable and snappy, but right now there was conviction in her voice—an intensity that I didn't recognize. I sat on the couch, on the farthest end, away from where the thing had happened, letting it flicker in my mind for a second and then shutting out the images with all my might.

I stared at the purple shag rug, at the hook on the wall where my banjo usually hung, at my beloved collection of Funk & Wagnalls encyclopedias. There was my bargello pillow on one chair; there was the clicker on the small table next to FP's chair, the cord that came out of it meticulously stapled to the baseboard all the way to where it connected to the TV. Melvin's face stared back at me from the wall above the record player, which was a giant console they'd bought at a yard sale. I thought about the time that FP's brother Shep had given me Michael Jackson's album *Off the Wall* for my birthday. The minute Shep left, FP spit out some hateful words about how we had to return that "disgusting music" immediately, but in the small window between having it and returning it, Annalee and I had played it when no one was home and I read the lyrics off the sleeve, singing along like I already knew them. I'd felt a little guilty loving music that wasn't from Melvin, but I thought it was some of the best music I'd ever heard and told myself that maybe if Melvin was alive when it was made, he would have liked it too. I thought about the party for my twelfth birthday a few months ago, where we'd pushed the furniture against the walls and slept in sleeping bags on the floor, until FP got enraged because he wanted to watch a movie and made us all go upstairs, and three of the five girls at my party had called their parents and gone home.

Eventually I heard my mother's footsteps on the stairs, and I braced myself. When she came into the room, tears were streaming down her face, and she was clutching my diary tightly in one hand. I hated that she was holding it—why was she holding it? It was mine, it was the one thing that kept me connected to my real home, where I dreamed that Clotilde was faithfully writing in hers too, that we were essentially writing to each other and we would share it all one day and I would have every detail of my life to share with Daria and Jessie and all my real family and it would all seem like a terrible nightmare. My mother sat on the chair next to the couch and said, "So it's true. I didn't want to believe it, but it's true." She sounded very sad.

FP came in behind her, oddly sheepish, and sat on a footstool.

"I told her," he said. I looked from him to her and back to him. What was he talking about? "I told her what you did to me," FP said, "what we did together."

I could feel the blood run out of my face. What on earth would make him tell her that? I'd managed to make it not real until now, but suddenly it was, and I was filled with terror and I wanted to run out of the room and the house and down the driveway and maybe to the road where I would stand in the middle of it and wave my hands to make someone stop and take me away and if they didn't stop I would be dead or injured and that was what would be happening and not this.

And then, inside my terror, a tiny tendril of relief. My diary had saved me. I hadn't had the courage to say it, but Meg did. Now it was out in the open, and we would finally leave here and be rid of him for good. I sat there, wheels turning, thinking about how it was great that we were already packed, thinking once Mom and Annalee were safely at Granny's, I could go back to the communities at last. I didn't say anything. In my mind I was running up the hill to Jessie's House on the Vineyard and everyone was on the front steps to greet me.

My mother jumped up from her chair, throwing my diary on the coffee table and standing over me, her face twisted in rage.

"Don't you play innocent!" she screamed at me. "Don't you sit there like you don't know *exactly* what's going on. How could you let me spend this whole day packing and getting ready to leave him for good, when all along you knew the problem was *you*?"

I was stunned, barely able to piece together what was happening— terrified because I'd never seen my mother anything like this. Her eyes were teeming with hate, and that hate was all for me.

Seemingly out of nowhere, she slapped me hard across the face. She had never even come close to hitting me before. "Of course you're going to be Miss America!" she hissed. "You'll sleep your way to the top."

And it was as if I wasn't there—I was just a spectator in what was happening to me. I thought of Humphrey Bogart in *The Maltese Falcon* saying, "When you're slapped, you'll take it and like it," and then re-lived her words: "You'll sleep your way to the top." What? I took a moment to be amused at what a prude she was. She couldn't bring herself to say "fuck your way to the top," because she would never say "fuck" or even "sex." Here she was, slapping me about something she couldn't even say the words for. I imagined what sleeping my way to the top would look like. Just taking naps in people's offices or being rolled out on a cot to accept an award? I purposely didn't touch my cheek where she slapped me, though it stung. I stared at her blankly, pretending she was see-through and that I was looking at the wall behind her.

She looked scared now, and her voice was shaky as she sat back down. "This can never happen again," she said.

"No duh," I thought, a phrase I had recently learned and found quite useful. I glanced at FP, and his eyes were cast toward the floor.

"Just get out of my sight," my mother said, and I got up deliberately, eyeing my diary there on the table, wanting to take it with me but not daring to do anything but get out of that room.

In my room, I sat on my bed, reeling at the new development.

OK, so it was all my fault, and she thought I was trying to steal her man? Gross. I would have killed that man in his sleep if I thought I could get away with it. I mean, I really thought I was capable of killing him. No, not in his sleep—the only way that would be satisfying would be to duct-tape him to a chair and stab him over and over so he died slowly and knew it was me killing him. I was devastated that we weren't leaving and anxious about how life would be now that this had come to light. How had I become the monster in this house of monsters? But at least Mom had stood up for herself for once, even if it was against me, and I'd seen FP act humble for the first time ever. Most important, this would never happen again. It was over. No more wriggling away from his rough hands, no more dreading being left alone in the house with him. I didn't care that they hated me—I hated them first anyway. I'd hated them from the moment I was dropped off at Granny's a year ago. No, that wasn't even right. I'd hated them since they left the communities, before I even knew I'd have to go with them.

I could hear Annalee humming in her bedroom, blissfully unaware of what was happening. I thought it was mean that she always had to stay in her room when FP was home, but, also, she was lucky. Maybe now I could always stay in my room too. I would go to school, work as hard as I could to have perfect grades, live through the next six years as a shunned person in this household, and finally escape to college. I could do this.

Around dinnertime, my mother walked through my room and into Annalee's room without looking at me. "Come have dinner," she said, and she led Annalee by the hand through my room again. As they passed, Annalee stared at me with nervous eyes—even at five years old, she could tell that the balance had been upset somehow and was clearly wondering what it would mean for her. I tried to look back at her with reassurance that she wasn't in trouble, and as I listened to them descend the stairs, I felt jealous that Mom loved her so much more than she loved me. In fact, now I was pretty sure that she didn't love me at all.

I decided to get into my homework—homework was suddenly the most important thing in the world. My ticket to freedom. I sat at the small desk in my room and took out the notebook I had for my research paper. A few weeks ago, inspired by an afternoon in the school library—where we'd been shown how the Dewey decimal system works and how to find things in the magazine archive—I'd chosen to write about the so-called Jim Jones Massacre. I'd found a *Newsweek* from two years ago, the words CULT OF DEATH emblazoned on its cover, and I thought the story was fascinating. Who were these crazy people who would blindly follow a man and then commit suicide together? I was putting "salient facts" on index cards, as I'd been instructed to do as part of the process. "Jim Jones went to Indiana University," I wrote, "and then transferred to Butler University in Indianapolis, Indiana, where he matriculated in 1961." I wasn't sure what "matriculated" meant, but the dictionary was downstairs and I'd look it up later.

Eventually Annalee came upstairs and went to sleep. I was listening carefully to what was going on in the house, waiting for them to go to bed so I could go get my diary. It was making me anxious to think of it out there for all to read. I couldn't remember exactly what I'd written and was dying to revisit the words that had set all of this in motion. I could hear the TV now; they were watching the *CBS Evening News,* the house sporadically quiet as FP muted the commercials. I heard the familiar sound of Walter Cronkite's voice, ending the broadcast with "And that's the way it is . . ." They would be in bed soon.

When I heard them go into their room and peered down the hall to see the light go out under the door, I tiptoed down the stairs, skipping the third one for Ratso, of course. My diary wasn't on the coffee table anymore, and I had a moment of panic. Had they thrown it away? I looked in the garbage can in the kitchen, and it wasn't there. This object was so precious to me—I hadn't realized how precious until now, and I was not sure what I would do if I couldn't have it anymore. But how would I write in it after this? I'd spent the last year and a half enjoying the fact that for the first time in my life I was truly writing just for me—no audience, no haunting awareness of the people who might read it. And they'd taken that away from me too. But I wanted it, if only to destroy it myself. Finally I found it in the living room, placed neatly on the bookshelf next to books that were its size. I had a fleeting moment of fear that taking it would lead to more trouble but then decided I didn't care.

Everything in this room scared me now, and I practically leapt into the dining room to escape from it. I sat at the dining room table to read what I'd written. It was last Monday, November 10. There was November 8, there was 9, there was 12? I flipped back over the pages. Was I losing my mind? No, there was no November 10 page. Its absence made me shudder. I brought the diary close to my face, peering into the binding, where I could see the slightest, tiniest remnants of the page that had been carefully sliced out.

CHAPTER 36

ONE OF THE BEST THINGS THAT HAPPENED THAT YEAR WAS
that the new library the town had been building was finally done. The
Alice and Hamilton Fish Library was surrounded by plush lawns and
had big windows and little reading rooms that smelled of carpet glue
and varnish. But most important, it was a place I was allowed to go and
be away. Away from them, away from kids at school, anonymous and
free. On weekends I would get up early and do my chores as quickly as
possible and then beg for Mom or FP to drop me off there, promising
that I would walk the long way back home if I had to.

When I was very young, I'd become obsessed with finding four-leaf
clovers on Fort Hill. Some adult had told me they were good luck but
didn't exist in real life, and for some reason this made me determined
to prove that they did. I'd spend hours lying in patches of clover, quietly staring and searching for one. Other kids would join me once they
realized what I was doing, ripping out fistfuls of clover and then tossing them aside when they didn't see one with four leaves, soon getting
bored with the endeavor and wandering off. I felt sure this was the
wrong approach, that the elusive four-leaf clover would only make itself known if you patiently stared at the patches but didn't touch them.
Eventually I developed a technique: I focused on a patch of clover and
then let my eyes go a little fuzzy, imprinting the pattern of three onto
the back of my brain, and voilà! A four-leaf clover would stand out to
me as if it were a different color. Once I figured this out, I found four-

leaf clovers all the time, usually within minutes of looking at a patch. I'd gently pick them and press them into the pages of books to dry, then give them as gifts.

By the time I was thirteen, my mother had at least three small framed four-leaf clovers I'd given her, and now her response when I would find one was "There she goes again," no longer impressed. During my precious hours at the Hamilton Fish Library, I'd wander out onto the lawn and find four-leaf clovers, then press them carefully into the pages of random books inside, imagining people I'd never met discovering these little emissaries of hope as they read.

There was a blue U.S. mailbox in front of the library, which meant I could write to Jessie and send the letter without anyone knowing. I sat in my favorite place in the library, a window seat in the children's section, and thought for a long time about what to say. I'd stolen a stamp and an envelope from the house; now all I had to do was write. I considered telling her what was really happening, but no. Why? It was too embarrassing to admit that this lowly man had gotten the better of me. I didn't want her to know that. Instead, I wrote about my daily life, that I was getting good grades in school, that Annalee had gotten much taller, that I hoped I hadn't become too much of a World Person to come back someday, and I missed her and everyone and thought about them every single day. Standing in front of the mailbox, I kissed the envelope, then put it inside, feeling a rush as the metal chute slammed shut. It was done and couldn't be undone, and there was nothing FP could do about it.

I raced to our mailbox every day after, desperate to see if she wrote me back and, if she did, to get the letter before anyone saw it. But Jessie's answer came on a Saturday, and when FP sauntered in that afternoon with the pile of mail in his hands, I was sitting at the dining room table, deeply engrossed in Ann Landers's advice column in the newspaper. He tossed the letter onto the table in front of me and walked away. There it was, "Miss Guinevere Turner" in her handwriting, the return address from the Vineyard, saying simply that it was from "JBL." My heart soared. I knew that FP had seen that it was from her and something bad would happen because of it, but right now I

didn't care. I hurried upstairs to my room, sitting on my bed and staring at her handwriting on the envelope for a while before I got the
letter opener from my desk and carefully opened it. It read:

JULY 14

My dearest Guinevere,

*I am so glad to hear from you. Your letter arrived just when I had
been thinking about you. I have done that often, and FP too; and I
miss you. I don't think people change that much, at least not on the
inside, and the love you feel for your friends doesn't change either.
You will always be my beautiful Guin and I will always love you
and care for you, no matter where you are. Everyone has duties, you
know that word, and some are easy and some are very hard. Your
duty at your age is that you must do what your mother wants you to
do, no matter how hard it is. Your mother and FP made a choice.
Now they must follow it. You are too young to make choices and it is
not the same. There is such a deep dark chasm between you out there
and us here and only you can cross it because only you did not make
the choice.*

I paused here and reread that last sentence several times, not understanding it at first. "Only you can cross it because only you did not
make the choice." But then I got it: She was acknowledging that my
mother and FP weren't allowed to come back, but I was, because I
hadn't made the choice for myself. To see these words, two years after
I'd been sent away, was a huge relief to me. I kept reading.

*It seems hard, doesn't it? So many times I have wanted to write to
FP and so many times I have wanted to know how you were, but
it is a long complicated sensitive story that has not ended. I want
you to know that you are always welcome here and that everyone
misses you too, especially Daria. The children have been through a
lot of hard times and hard lessons lately because you are all grow-*

ing up and must take more responsibility for yourselves and what kind of people you are going to be. I think that most of the children understand a great deal more now than they did, and they talk about you often; you must never be afraid of what I think about you. I don't think, I am just so happy to have heard from you and grateful that you still think of me.

You know I've been talking to the kids about "world people" and how they are not bad. We have lots of friends here on the Vineyard who don't live with us and they are all fine people. It's just that there is a big difference in the way that we live with each other and the way most people live with each other. We work at it, striving for inner consciousness, self development on the inside instead of on the outside. This life we live is not for everyone, only if you have Mel inside of you and believe in the life. I do, I always have; I love it. Some of the children will leave perhaps and some will stay together and keep living this way. But I still feel like there is an end to this road. Just don't know where or when.

Anyway darling life is what you make it no matter where you are. Don't worry about it, just live it as hard as you can.

Daria has braces and just went off to Boston for her monthly appointment. And we have a new baby named Justine, who is the most precious thing in the world. I adore her and dote on her like an old granny. Cybele is almost taller than me, enormous. Irene is a knock out. All the kids are good. We are all into embroidery. I love you and write to me. I want to know all about you.
Love, Jessie.

I read and reread the letter a dozen times before I finally put it back in its envelope, treasuring the postmark it had from my beloved Vineyard. They missed me. They talked about me. I was always welcome. And then this sentence: "Your duty at your age is that you must do what your mother wants you to do, no matter how hard it is." This was a good thing—it meant that Jessie would *want* me to stay out here, and she understood it as doing my duty and not as betrayal. I did a few celebratory twirls in the middle of the room.

Of course, I didn't bother hiding the letter—I didn't want them to read it but knew that they would. So I left it on my bedside table, waiting for the inevitable bullshit that would rain down on me. I wasn't "allowed" to write to Jessie—and now I felt disappointed in myself that it had taken me this long to figure out how—but what was he going to say? I was Jessie's beautiful Guin and she would always love me. It was there, in her handwriting. Even he couldn't find a way to take that away from me.

That night and for the next few days, I braced myself for whatever was going to happen, knowing this was a win for me and that FP would find a way to get back at me for it. But there was nothing. He was chipper and friendly and didn't even mention the letter, much less ask what it said or if he could read it. But I knew he had. I'd developed such an elaborate system for knowing if one of them read my diary that it was impossible for them to even touch it without me finding out. I would put it on a shelf as if it was placed there casually—part of it hanging off, and at an angle, and in a different spot every morning. Then I would measure the distance between the diary and the back of the shelf, then put a piece of thread on it in a way that looked accidental, but I would know that it was placed over the letter Y in the word "Year" on the cover, exactly splitting the Y down the center. I'd write the coordinates down in an old school notebook, upside down on the back of a page of boring notes.

It was always moved. Yes, the cat could have done it or the wind could have done it, and I knew Annalee liked to rummage around in my stuff, but I also knew in my bones that it was them. Not together, and possibly checking up on each other in the process, but they were reading it like the news, and I was writing in it like I didn't know that. I stopped writing feelings and just wrote facts, quoting their words and describing their behaviors in a way that I hoped would chill them when they read it. So far it didn't seem to be having any effect.

But with Jessie's letter, I didn't bother with any elaborate system to see if they'd read it. I left it front and center on my nightstand—no measuring, no piece of thread. I wanted them to read it, because I was dancing inside, giddy that Jessie still loved me. I felt alive and well and realigned. Jessie was grateful that I still thought of her. Jessie, grateful, for something from *me*. There was nowhere to put this joy—no one in my life knew where I came from, and I wasn't even sure if Annalee remembered. So I told Wuz that Jessie loved us, and that I was sure she would love Wuz too when she met her, and that everything was going to be OK.

And on top of that happiness, I'd been invited to a statewide spelling bee! In May, I'd won first place in the spelling bee we had at school, and then a very fancy-looking letter came that invited me to Albany to compete to represent the state in a national spelling bee. It was a whole weekend, with a special dinner and awards ceremony, and FP had begrudgingly said I could take the two-and-a-half-hour train ride on my own in a couple of weeks. I was living for it. My triumphant word had been "acknowledgment," a challenge because of its tricky silent d. I imagined there would be great ballrooms and I worried over the words I might not be able to spell, annoying my mother by spelling out any word she said that I thought might be a challenge. I was excited to meet all the kids, who would probably be able to spell better than I could, and by the luxurious idea of sharing a hotel room with other smart girls. I had the letter from Jessie, and I had this big, exciting thing to look forward to, away from this place. I dreamed and dreamed. I would be a national champion, and I would get into college, and all of this would be behind me.

How I dreamed. I wanted to be Emily Dickinson and Jaime Sommers, or Lindsay Wagner, who played her as the Bionic Woman on TV. I wanted to be Hot Lips from *M*A*S*H* and Jo from *Little Women* and Lakey from *The Group*. I was feeling the hope of a life after this, and I was high on it. Jessie would be so proud of me. I would be a huge success and return to her, doing our family justice by proving that I could hold my own out in the World and thus that our way of living was a good way to live.

Several days had passed since I got the letter from Jessie, and the unspoken tension was palpable as I waited for FP's jealousy to rear its ugly head. Then one night FP was on the phone for a long time. This wasn't unusual—he was always talking on the phone at night, to one of his brothers, to his mother or father, to a client or potential client. We were all relieved when he was engaged. As long as we could hear the familiar drone of his voice talking to someone, we were briefly free. I was always disturbed at how fun and casual he sounded when he talked on the phone—not like a man who would punch a woman for leaving a shelf dusty or choke a twelve-year-old with his penis. But I also understood how easy it was to be someone else outside this household—it came naturally to all three of us. We were fake people— the people who lived here and then the other people, the ones who went out into the World. We were the people who were from a place we never spoke about and who everyone thought they knew but most definitely did not.

I was brushing my hair that night—a girl at school had told me to brush it for one hundred strokes every night to make it truly shine— and I had counted to seventy-two when I heard him hang up and his heavy footsteps on the stairs. Only he was allowed to walk like a normal person—the rest of us tiptoed by instinct. I'd been gabbing away with Annalee, because the mirror was in her bedroom, and when we heard his footsteps I threw the brush onto her bed and she dashed under the covers, pretending to be asleep. It was crucial that he didn't see me brushing my hair—acts of vanity could throw him into a rage—so I quickly sat down at my desk and picked up a pen before he got to the top of the stairs. He stood in my doorway.

"I just got off the phone with Jessie," he said casually, then paused dramatically to wait for my reaction. Though my stomach flipped, my face gave him nothing. "Anyway, I'm going to visit the Vineyard next week. She said everyone has been dying to see me."

My heart sank with his words. He could. He could take every single thing away from me. My diary, my body, my mother, my real home. Why did I think it would ever be any different?

"She told me about the letter she wrote you. She said she feels sorry for you but you're better off out here and that it's obvious that you belong with us and not in the communities. When I told her about you, how you are now, she agreed with me that you should stay out here."

Nothing. No feelings, no words, no anything. I just wanted to die. Was everything in the letter from Jessie a lie? Why would she write that they weren't allowed to come back but I was, and then invite him to visit? He droned on and on about how he'd been right all the time and I didn't know anything and Jessie didn't really hate him or love me, but I wasn't listening. I was too busy falling apart and then hardening. Hardening a piece of me that had been alive for a moment when I read her letter. I thought she still loved me, and now nothing was true. Adults were full of shit. I couldn't even understand what they wanted anymore. My fury at the injustice of it all congealed into hate and resignation. Absolutely nothing was true or safe.

"So you're not going to that spelling bee thing in Albany. With this trip, we can't afford it, and your mother will need your help while I'm on the Vineyard."

When he came back the following week, he was unbearably pleased with himself, telling long stories about what a great time he had and how welcoming everyone was. "Nobody talked about you," he told me. "Nobody even said your name once."

CHAPTER 37

This is my last diary entry. I've decided no diary because it causes too much trouble. It's like it's always there for Mom to read—so what's to stop her? She promised me once that she'd never do it again and she did it again so every time she gets a bad feeling she'll just read it. It's not fair. I can't trust anyone. I know that a diary is really good for many reasons. It helps you write your feelings and realize and think about what is going on. It is very disciplinarian and it helps writing skills. Also, it's a historical document to look back on and be remembered. I've recorded every day of my life since I was nine and it really helps me. But diaries always seem to get you in the end, just like Frida. It's a shame. It really is. But that's the way it has to be, or I will always wonder whether she read my diary, and she will always have access to all my secrets. I wish she kept a diary. Anyhow, it's going to be hard to adjust to not writing about things. I'm really so used to it.

Just before I sign off, I'd like to tell you what's been going on in my life. A survey was done for the yearbook and a lot of people said they voted me for Best Dressed, Smartest, Most Likely to Succeed, Wittiest and Class Politician. I still have a broken jaw, but no bandage. I can't chew—just liquids and squishy things. This morning Mom blew up at me and said that I was hanging all over FP yesterday and that I'm asking for trouble and I was really hurt because it's not that she's trying to protect me, it's that she's jealous, and that hurts. She has nothing to be jealous of—I wasn't doing anything. You know, I really hate her. She's in it for herself—she really is. She likes to pretend she loves FP or anybody, but she doesn't. She loves herself, and ultimately everything she does is for Numero Uno. She hurts me so much—she will never know how much. If my heart were visible there would be scars all over it from her. She's put a streak of hatred in me. I mean I really hate her. I probably won't hate her this much always, but I do know that I can never love her. She's not my mother, she's a superior officer at some times, and just a woman to woman bitch at other times and I don't have any relationship with her at all. I can go through my mind and think of so many things she's said that have hurt, really hurt me so much I could scream. Sometimes I wish I could just once hurt her that much so she knows what it's like. So, I conclude my life volume. It's sad, and it makes me feel guilty, and I really don't want to because I've gotten so used to it, but I have to. It's part of life . . . I just have to.

GUINEVERE JANE TURNER
MAY 23, 1968
12:01 ♊ ♈
8TH GRADE
ELIZABETH TURNER JOHN SNYDER
LONELY PERSON.

CHAPTER 38

By the time I started high school later that year, things were different, at least externally. My mother had discovered that she was pregnant, and we'd moved to a new house, not far from our old one. They didn't buy it—we could still only afford to rent—but this house was much roomier, with a kitchen big enough for a table and chairs, a separate living room and dining room, and three bedrooms, so I finally had one all to myself. Also, there was a garage, which meant a whole new place for FP to spend time that wasn't in the house. Everyone was excited about the new baby, and when my brother, Benjamin, was born, the mood felt lighter for a little while. FP was making more money, and he was so focused on having a boy to mold that he wasn't paying much attention to me and was being less violent toward all of us. I was foolish enough to think that maybe everything was going to be better.

O'Neill High School was across the Hudson River, in a town called Highland Falls, which was the town that shared a border with West Point, the U.S. Military Academy. This meant that more than half of the kids at O'Neill had parents in the military, and many of them had moved every two years for as long as they could remember. Being from a lot of places wasn't unusual to them at all, and I discovered that it also meant most of them were deeply driven overachievers like me.

I walked into O'Neill on the first day feeling the exciting possibility that I could reinvent myself. I'd erased all the "weird" things about me,

I thought. Here, nobody had seen Guinaqueer in action. Yes, the boys who taunted me would be there—but there would be about three hundred more students, and new teachers. Our small eighth-grade class was integrated into a much bigger student body, which meant soon we all started to gravitate toward our groups: athletes, smart kids, and "burnouts" who hung out on the smoking patio and wore heavy-metal T-shirts.

The previous February, I'd broken my jaw. It happened at the icy bus stop at the end of our driveway, where the neighborhood kids gathered and waited for the bus. One kid, who was a year younger than me and the only nice boy in the neighborhood, would sled down his steep driveway to get to the bus stop, and one morning he accidentally slammed into me and I fell face-first on the ice, my metal braces cutting through my lower lip. The irony that I lived in such a violent household but my jaw was broken by accident was not lost on me. "Don't go telling people I did that to you," FP had joked when I got back from the hospital. His tone was confusing, like he didn't realize he'd almost done something like this to one of us a million times.

Since it was only a hairline fracture, I didn't have to have my jaw wired shut, which I almost thought would be cool. Instead, Dr. Lewis wrapped a bandage tightly around my head—with haphazard clumps of hair poking out at various points—and I had to stay like that for a month. Dr. Lewis said I was lucky, that getting your jaw wired shut was painful and took much longer, but I would have endured any amount of pain not to look like a mummy with greasy hair. But because I could only get food from a straw, I lost a significant amount of weight, and once it was over and the bandages were off, I felt pretty for the first time in my life. I basked in all the compliments I got for being thin and vowed to never weigh any more than this again. And, of course, FP had left me alone while the bandage was on, a brief but merciful respite from his repulsive touch.

Now, as I started high school, I was thin, my hair was feathered, and I'd saved enough money from babysitting to buy a few pairs of Calvins and a pair of Sergio Valentes, with purple stitching on the back pockets. I desperately wanted to be in the drama club, to work on the school newspaper, and to go to football games and the parties I heard about every weekend, but I was not allowed. No after-school activities, no social life. I couldn't even talk on the phone. I'd devised a system with a few of my friends: If they wanted to talk, they should call, let it ring once, hang up, wait a minute, and do it again. If I was home alone, I would just guess who it was and call them back.

But this wasn't foolproof. FP would sometimes call the house when he and my mom went out, and if he got a busy signal, he would come home furious and demand to know who I was talking to and why. "Clients could be calling me," he'd say. "I could lose a fucking job because you're bullshitting with friends you see every day anyway."

Now and then I'd be allowed to sleep over at Clare's house—but only Clare's—and on those rare occasions I'd devise elaborate plots to sneak off and do other things, but all of that worked only if her parents were away, which wasn't that often. I spent a lot of nights pining for everything I was missing; I felt it even more on Monday mornings, when everyone would be gossiping about who made out with who at a party or how someone got wasted and wiped out on the dance floor in front of everyone.

Later that fall, I brought home school pictures from a few of my friends. They were wallet-sized photos, two of them of senior boys who were genuinely my friends and nothing more—among the only people who were willing to use my elaborate system to talk on the phone with me sometimes and were OK with being friends with someone they could never see outside school. I did have a crush on one of them, Brian, but he was a senior anyway and out of my league. Plus, how could I possibly date someone? What guy would put up with all that?

On the backs of the photos, my friends had written benign things—jokes about how they looked in the photos, a dig at a teacher. "I'll miss us watching Mr. Ponchak pig out in study hall," Brian wrote. "You better come visit me in college—it's only an hour away!" wrote Michael. I'd asked them to keep whatever they wrote very innocuous, because I knew that nothing I brought into this house would escape FP's eye.

Two days later, the photos had disappeared. They just weren't in my wallet. I casually asked my mother, Annalee, and then him if they'd seen these photos of my friends. No one had. But this was ridiculous. All of us had been in the house the whole time. Less than forty-eight hours had passed. He had taken them—that was clear to me.

Later, when he and my mother went out to the grocery store, the hunt began. I searched the dresser drawers in their bedroom; I lifted the edges of rug that were under furniture. I looked in the pages of books, in the jackets of records. I knew they were somewhere in this house. My heart was pounding. What would I do if I actually found them hidden somewhere? I would have to openly accuse him or pretend I hadn't found them. They would be home soon too.

After looking for about an hour, I sat down on my bed and went into a meditative state. The thing is, I fucking *knew* him. I knew how he thought. I'd spent the last three years trying to anticipate his moods, circumvent his violence, his sexual advances, and the combination of the two. It was my job to be one step ahead of him.

I imagined he'd snooped in my wallet and then compulsively taken the photos in a fit of jealousy, not really thinking through the act. But hiding things in our house was near impossible, by his design. Every object had its place, and we kept the house psychotically clean for fear of his wrath. Nothing was not in his control. There was grape juice in the refrigerator that only he was allowed to drink. When the *TV Guide* came in the mail, he would sit down with a cup of coffee and spend at least an hour with a red pen, underlining what he intended to watch, making notes in the margins, and creating a schedule of what we would watch on a separate piece of paper. He always wrote with a ballpoint pen, in deliberate block letters, pressing so hard on the page that the words would be etched in layers of pages beneath it. We weren't allowed to touch the TV or the record player, and I don't even know why we had a radio, because we certainly weren't allowed to play it and listen to modern music, and he never did. He regularly burst into my sister's room and made her throw out any toys that weren't put away to his liking. On more than one occasion I thanked my lucky stars that, as I had learned since we'd left the communities, it was illegal to keep us out of school. I knew he couldn't stand that he didn't have control over that.

But where would he hide these photos? There was nowhere we weren't required to clean. And what was his logic? What do grown men who compulsively steal high school photos from fourteen-year-old girls tell themselves? I chastised myself for even showing him the photos in the first place, but I also knew in my heart of hearts that I did it because he would hate it, and these small acts of resistance were all I had.

And then it came to me in a flash. He had this suit, his only suit, which I'd seen him wear just once, to his father's funeral. His life rarely required a suit. To him, this suit was like another country, an out-of-commission player, a no-man's-land. I scrambled to their bedroom and into the closet, finding the suit way in the back, covered in a plastic sheath. I reached into the inside pocket of the jacket, and there they were, the awkwardly smiling faces of Brian and Michael, wearing their Picture Day best. I shuddered. I shuddered because it was disturbing and undeniable that he and no one else had put them there but also because I was repulsed by the fact that I knew him well enough to think like him and to know where they were. I didn't want to know him that well, but I did. I heard the unmistakable sound of his giant blue Suburban's tires hitting the gravel of our driveway. They were home.

The thing was, I was putting us all in jeopardy by finding these two-by-three-inch objects. These little things, these nonsense things, two wallet-sized photos hidden in the inside pocket of a suit, would leave none of us unscathed. If one of us was in trouble, we all were. And whatever it was, it would last for days. There would be violence; there would be endless droning speeches. I would be allowed to do even less than I already was; my mother would cry. I considered putting the photos back, but my indignance wouldn't let me. I was nearing a point where anything that upset the status quo was a welcome relief. I was also perversely curious to see how he would justify this. I walked to my room and put the photos into my wallet, my hands shaking. Then I imagined the way his hands must have touched this object, surreptitiously slipping out these photos, and I recoiled. He ruined everything.

I helped Mom put the groceries away, my fear commingling with something close to smugness. He came into the kitchen a few minutes later. On the surface we might have looked like a normal family. There were running jokes, and I talked about making turkey tetrazzini for dinner, a specialty of mine. Annalee was, as she always was when he was home, alone in her room. We all knew he was too jealous of her dead father to stand the sight of her. But if you walked through that house in that moment, on that sunny Sunday afternoon, you would see a mother and her teenage daughter making a game of reimagining lines from Edgar Allan Poe, laughing. There would be a seven-year-old playing happily in her room, while the man of the house likely installed a dimmer on a light switch or sat at the kitchen table smoking and scouring the PennySaver for a good deal on a new dining room table.

He looked up from that PennySaver and casually said, "Oh—did you find those school pictures you were looking for?"

I turned my back to him, needlessly straightening things on the counter as I said, "Yes, I did, actually." I surprised myself with my own boldness—almost regretted it—but there it was, hanging in the air. A thick silence, and with it an adrenaline rush that I fucking loved. My mother must have known he took the photos when I was asking about them earlier. Or did she? What my mother knew at any given point was always a mystery. But I did understand that allowing herself to be aware of everything that was happening around her, every day, was clearly not an option. She knew what she could handle knowing, which was not much at all.

In the silent deadlock, I could feel his wheels turning behind me. For a fleeting moment, I had all the power. It was his move. "Where did you find them?" he said finally, his voice so tightly wound that my bravado was in danger of failing. But there was no going back.

"In your closet," I said, and turned around to face him. "In the pocket of that suit you have." I heard my mother's sharp intake of breath and was glad she was here in the room. I wanted her to witness what he did to me, what he was doing to me, even though this was a laughably tiny thing.

He stood up from his chair and said, "See, that just proves my point. You snoop around in my stuff when I'm not here. I knew it." It was nonsense, but you can say any kind of nonsense when the threat of violence behind it is real and in everyone's recent memory. Inside, I laughed. How pathetic. He left the room calmly. My mother avoided my gaze. I put his beloved frozen grape juice concentrate into the freezer, tucked the box of number-9 spaghetti exactly where it had to be, and went to my room.

CHAPTER 39

A TORTUROUS TWENTY MINUTES LATER, HE WAS STANDING in my doorway. There was no door on my bedroom. Why would there be? "Come talk to me in my room," he said, walking away. I followed.

The next three hours behind the closed door of his room were the familiar cocktail of big speeches about things, followed by the unspoken offer of forgiveness and peace in the house if I would suck his fucking dick. I had made the choice between the two before. I guess giving those speeches and watching my face go dull as I said nothing for hours on end was exciting for him, because as his tone softened, his erect penis came out of his pants for the millionth time. Was it the sound of his own voice that got him hard? I suppose it was my perceived submission, since I had long ago stopped bothering to argue with him, or reason with him, or even talk. I was mostly just dealing with the mounting anxiety once his voice lowered. It wasn't even the dread of the sexual part, though that was there; it was the fact that when he was yelling, my mother would be able to hear that what was happening behind the door wasn't sexual. When she couldn't hear anything, she could fill in the blanks. She was having her own little uptick in bravery that day, though, because at that moment she knocked on the door, and the knock was bold, urgent and unlike her.

He sighed deeply, annoyed. He got up from the bed and barely bothered to zip up his pants before he opened the door. "What?" he said to her. "What do *you* want?" His emphasis made him sound like he was exhausted from the three of us always wanting something from him. I think we all just wanted him to die. My mom's voice was high, and trembling, but in that determined Victorian way of speaking she and my grandmother both had from time to time. "I'm taking Annalee and going out," she said in her shaky yet defiant voice. She peered over his shoulder at me, where I sat on the bed. I was looking right at her with all the hate I could muster, because I knew she hadn't come to save me. "I'm going to leave you two to make love or whatever it is you're doing in here." She said those words: "make love." He shrugged and slammed the door in her face.

He sat down on the bed next to me, shaking his head as if we were partners in being annoyed with her. He smiled a little as he put his hand on my shoulder. "See what I mean about her?" he said. What had he said about her in the last three hours? I didn't know. His voice had long ago ceased to register to me as anything but static. He was nothing but an endurance test. I heard the jingling of my mother's keys and the slam of the front door as she left. He put his other hand on my thigh, rubbing and chuckling to himself softly. "She'll be back. Where's she gonna go?"

What followed was a white-hot rage. I gave it to him, and he gave it right back. In my mind, I screamed and pushed him away with all my might. But in reality it was only the smallest, involuntary sound of disgust and a weak attempt to shrug his hand off my shoulder. In a flash, he slammed my head against the headboard, over and over, and I relished the pain. There was no sexual contact after that. He always knew how to turn anger into something sexual, but he didn't know how to get from violence back to sex. I knew that about him. If I got him to be violent, I was safe.

I walked out of that room a few minutes later, triumphant. I went to my room and sat on my bed in an altered state, my head throbbing. The few tears I cried once I was alone stung the scrapes on my cheekbone, and in seconds I willed them to stop. I hated myself for crying. I summoned the strength to look in the mirror and saw that the side of my face was scraped and swollen and knew that bruises would form by morning. I leaned in, studying my skin closely, and saw hundreds of tiny red dots that seemed to be spreading. I stared out the window and watched the sun go down. I sat in the dark. I heard my mother come home and the sounds of them talking in low tones. I heard her laugh weakly.

On this day, my rage at her was bigger than my rage at him. I'd won this round, but the last words I'd heard her say gnawed a hole in me. I'd learned to tune out his words, but in daily life she said very little, and when she spoke it was often a series of tiny falsehoods—her part in the performance of us being a group of people that we were not. Today she had chosen to be brave, but only to speak out against me. She had summoned her courage to knock on that door for no other reason than to one-up me as her competitor. She had used the words "make love." I was the Other Woman in her mind. I was the enemy. Not this man, who turned us against each other, who beat us, isolated us, told us daily that we were worthless. "You think you're so smart," he'd said to me once, in the middle of the night, in the middle of that dining room, stroking his dick. "You and your mother and your creepy little sister think you're so damn smart."

I heard the house quiet down. I had barely moved except to look in the mirror, and hours had passed. I didn't want them to hear me. I didn't want them to talk to me. I wanted them to wonder if I was dead. I lay in wait on my bed, against the farthest corner, one you couldn't see if you walked by my doorless bedroom. When I heard him go into the shower (only he was allowed to shower at night, and I was allowed to shower only every three days), I shot up like a feral creature, storming to the room I knew my mother would be in.

She jumped when I came in, but these were jumpy times. I pulled back my hair to show my swollen, beaten face and said, "Just so you know, this—THIS—is all the 'love' we were making." The lights were dim in the room, and she looked confused. "This, Mom," I said, half-lunging toward her so she could see what I was talking about. Her nervous eyes surveyed my face.

"Oh," she said sadly. And then nothing, looking back down at her book. "I didn't know."

I wish I'd said, "So what the fuck are we going to do? How long are we going to let it go on like this? Who are we? What's happening to us?" But I didn't. I stood there. She sighed. Finally, she spoke: "You probably shouldn't go to school tomorrow." Then I hadn't won anymore. He had. I wouldn't go to school, maybe for a few days. Tomorrow we'd joke around in the kitchen. The things that happened today wouldn't have ever happened.

The thing about violence is that it's not something that can be happening every second. Lives have to be lived. Houses of cards have to be reconstructed. I imagine they both told themselves lies to get up the next morning. I imagine I told myself a few as well. "Who will I call to get the homework assignment while I miss school?" was an easier question than "What's to become of us?"

The deep undercurrent of my defiance informed every moment inside the house after that. I knew I'd upset the balance, but I still didn't know how to escape. I want to say there was no more sexual abuse, but that would be a lie. I probably did what I was coerced into doing because, though the violence saved me from sexual abuse, it kept me from school, and school was my only portal to freedom. I had to go to school. A few days later I was allowed to wear makeup for the first time, to cover up what was left of the bruises.

CHAPTER 40

IT WAS ALMOST A YEAR LATER WHEN I STORMED ACROSS THE two-lane highway near our house with a death wish, not only not looking both ways but staring straight ahead. I knew cars always sped around the bend, driving way over the speed limit, and I dared them to fucking kill me. Instinct told me I would be spared such a mercy—the hell I was living in was far from done with me. I should be so lucky to be hit by a car. I approached the familiar entrance to the Appalachian Trail and charged into the woods, up the steep incline, satisfied at the angry crunch the branches made under my feet, happy for the power of disruption in the dusk of the quiet woods.

My hand still clutched the kitchen matches I'd grabbed before I walked out of the house. I shoved them into my pocket, marching up the trail as if my life depended on it. FP's words echoed in my head, insidious and accusing: "Then why are you still wearing the ring I gave you?" My ring finger was scratched where I'd torn the inappropriate gift off my finger and thrown it across the room in disgust. I heard it clatter against the washing machine and land somewhere behind it. Why indeed had I kept the ring on my finger? Because it was easier than making a scene by not wearing it? Because it was actually pretty—a gold ring with an emerald stone, my birthstone? Because I'd chosen not to think about what it meant—I didn't have a choice anyway, so why not just wear it? No one in tenth grade needed to know anything except I had a very fancy ring on my fifteen-year-old finger.

"It's hard having a girlfriend who's a virgin," he'd said to me a week before, his erection pressing against my foot as I lay on the dining room floor, naked from the waist down. My sweatshirt was still on the upper half of my body, a tiny act of resistance. He'd lifted his head from between my legs to say this, after having said, "Don't you like this? Women usually make noises to let the man know that they like it." I made no sound. I could hear my mother wandering around in the kitchen, a ghost in the middle of the night, and didn't know what was more terrifying—the fact that this was happening or the fact that she might walk in on this happening and see me as complicit. Mostly I was terrified that he had just used the word "girlfriend." We'd been here on this floor several times before, but he'd never used that word. He thought of me as his *girlfriend*? The permanence of this, the distorted reality of this, was a revelation to me. In his mind, he had my mother and he had a girlfriend. Were we starcrossed lovers?

In the woods, I replayed some of this in my head as I continued to rush up the trail, figuring out what my next move would be. I'd stay in the woods overnight. I'd scare them. I'd show them I was serious. I had no endgame—only that I would find a place to lie down and I'd light a fire and sleep there. I was out of breath now, leaning into the sharp pain squeezing my chest.

In my daily life I wasn't allowed to go anywhere except school, but I was allowed to walk on this trail, through these woods. I'd come up here many times with my mother and my sister—loving the white rectangles painted on the trees that guided hikers to where the trail continued; one painted on top of another indicated a turn. It felt like a secret conversation between the woods and the countless weary strangers who hiked the trail. The marks always felt to me like they had been made by the trees themselves, an exciting invitation if you could find the next mark, which in the summer would sometimes be difficult because of the lush new foliage obscuring them. I often dreamed of taking the trail all the way up to Maine or all the way down to Georgia. The Appalachian Trail had been there since the

1920s, a response to growing urban sprawl, a utopian experiment. We'd run into hikers of all kinds—the day hikers like us or the really impressive people who'd come from Georgia and were now in New York State, the relative closeness of Maine fueling their exhausted bodies. I admired them. Wanted to be them. They seemed so free.

My mother always brought her binoculars and *The Audubon Society Field Guide to North American Birds,* and we'd find a log to sit on when we got tired, poring over the book and getting excited about seeing a pileated woodpecker or a scarlet tanager. I'd marvel at how in the world of birds, the male was the showy one. The crimson cardinals we'd see at our bird feeder shone in glorious relief against the white snow, and their mates, the females, would peck at the suet at a safe distance, their drab gray-green no match for their scene-stealing male companions. I always wondered at this: Didn't being such flashy fools make the males more likely to be killed by predators? Perhaps, which meant that nature understood that the females were more important, their understated plumage the key to their survival.

Now, on the trail, the sun was setting, and I hurried to make my way to a clearing I knew at the top of the mountain, where I could perhaps actually see the sun sink below the horizon instead of dappled through the leaves. I congratulated myself for the foresight to put on long pants on this muggy September night.

I'd thrown the ring at him, then there was stillness. He stood there, somewhat shocked, I noted with satisfaction, though I was terrified of what would happen next. My mother's righteous stance across the room, arms folded, had turned slightly less so. She was also on high alert for which one of us he would turn on, and how. I willed my face not to look scared while my heart pounded in my chest. "Let them see a blank expression," I thought. "Don't give them the satisfaction of a single emotion crossing your face." I braced myself for the violence that was likely seconds away. It's possible that a full five minutes may have passed. This kind of deadlock wasn't unfamiliar.

I'd learned when I was very young what it felt like to be stuck like this, to know that any action could be as punishable as no action, and any answer could be as dangerous as the wrong answer. There was a very particular static that would happen in my head, accompanied by a heaviness of limbs, a semiconscious state. A familiar boredom combined with high alert. An irritation because nothing was *happening*—no one was doing anything. Because the situation was impossible, because it was volatile and mundane all at once. Because it was pointless. I'd learned to wait it out.

There in the kitchen, after I threw the ring across the room, his question still hung in the air: "Then why are you still wearing the ring I gave you?" I'd changed the conversation, at least—I wasn't wearing it anymore. I was seething at the trap he'd created. I hadn't fully admitted it to myself, but I knew what it meant to him. I knew that wearing the ring meant that I was accepting that I was his "girlfriend" and that it was OK. Not to wear it would also have given it value and meaning and would have most definitely resulted in any number of punishments and manipulations on his part. It wasn't that hard to wear a ring. I had chosen the easier path. I was disgusted with that choice now.

I made it to the clearing at the top of the mountain before sunset and started to gather branches for a fire. I felt pride, resistance, independence, fury, conviction. And serenity. They couldn't find me here, and they wouldn't. I didn't let myself think about the wrath that was raining down on my mother and sister. Instinctively I had known for some time that his sexual focus on me somehow protected them, and tonight I had taken that away. This would not be an easy night for them.

I gathered some pine branches and some leaves and tried to fashion a kind of mattress, though it resembled something more like a nest. I lay down, testing it, feeling where sticks were still poking me. I got up and rearranged things. I fantasized about college, about a new life, about burning down the house I'd just run from. I was exhausted and ready to settle in and light my fire. I pulled the matches from my pocket, but they wouldn't light. I tried striking them on rocks, on hard pieces of bark, on the bottom of my shoe. Nothing worked. It took me a while to realize that they were safety matches. The "safety" was that one strip on the side of the damn box that you needed to light them, so you wouldn't accidentally set things on fire in your home. They didn't even count as matches anymore.

It was much colder in the woods at night than I expected. In the dark, I finally curled up in my little nest, my defiance not so fierce now that I was still. For all the time I'd spent in these woods, this safe haven, I'd never thought about what it would feel like at night. It was not quiet. The rustling of creatures was everywhere around me. They were not the familiar and sometimes rare birds I'd spent the days looking for through my mother's binoculars. They were just here with me, alone in the woods, and I did not know them.

Lying in the dark there, listening to these sounds, my mind went to Lizzie and Wayne. Lizzie was one of the women assigned to take care of the kids at the Farm, and though we instinctively knew that like most women who had the lowly job, she didn't have much power among adults, we still behaved. She was a diminutive woman—some of the older boys were taller than her—but this didn't mean we weren't a little afraid of her. We were afraid of most adults; one report of our bad behavior could lead to all kinds of punishments. We sometimes curried favor by hoarding packs of cigarettes from the cartons they bought, so that when there were no more cigarettes they would say, "OK you kids, which one of you has stashed a pack of smokes for us?" The nearest town was an hour drive away, and there was usually only one trip to the grocery store every few weeks, so cigarettes were a precious commodity, and every single adult smoked—Marlboro Reds for the women, Lucky Strikes for the men. There were always cans of Bugler tobacco around, and at night we rolled cigarettes and put them in canisters, but the "store-bought" ones were the favorites.

But I had my own reasons for feeling anxious around Lizzie. I knew things that she didn't know I knew—or did she? A few months before, a bunch of us kids were sleeping on the floor of her bedroom because the Caravan was visiting, and those kids got the beds in the Spring House, where we usually slept. I woke up in what seemed like the middle of the night to the sounds of grunting and heavy breathing and realized that there was a man in her bed, and they were—did I understand what sex was?

I tried to remember what my eight-year-old self knew about sex. I had known that there was a thing that adults did, that adults joked about and fought about, and that got people pregnant. I'd seen people kiss in some of the movies we watched, but those were films from the forties and fifties, and those people never did more than kiss, and even those kisses were simply lips pressed urgently together. I'd read and reread that passage in *Mirror at the End of the Road* where Melvin wrote, "I want to cut off my leg and fuck the bloody stump," and because of that, sex was also somehow tied up with amputation and frustration. There was the thing that happened with that one older boy when I was five, but I hadn't thought about that in a long time, and I didn't want to think about it now either.

As I lay on Lizzie's floor, I could hear her crying out occasionally, and then she murmured, "Oh, Wayne . . ." It was Wayne, who was actually my mother's "husband" at the time! I was mortified—I understood the concept of cheating, and I knew he was cheating on my mom. And, if it wasn't clear already, he suddenly gasped, "Bess would kill me if she knew," and kept going, and then underlined it, panting, "She'd kill me . . ."

Lizzie and my mommy were friends. I'd seen them smoking on the porch together and laughing. They were both women with very little status—no one asked them their opinions, and they did what they were told and went to the community they were sent to. I felt mad at Lizzie because of this, but more important, I was terrified that Wayne and Lizzie would know I was awake. I squeezed my eyes closed, pretending to be asleep, but opened them seconds later to see if anyone else was awake. No, just me. How could the other kids sleep through this? How could Wayne and Lizzie think that anyone could sleep through this?

The next morning I woke up very early, stressed about the night before, nervous that I would be found out and somehow punished. I don't know what my logic was, because the only crime I'd committed was being a light sleeper, but I *knew* something, and I was sure this illicit knowledge was somehow evident on my face.

I came into the kitchen and saw Wayne sitting there, smoking as he cleaned the round wire-framed glasses he wore, chatting like it was any other morning. I suddenly felt like I needed to remind him of my mommy and how she was special. I wanted him to feel guilty. So I decided simply to be wonderful, which in this case meant cooking for him. "I learned how to make battered eggplant," I boasted, apropos of nothing. This was indeed something I was proud of at eight years old. I could cook like a grown-up.

He chuckled at me. "Is that so?"

"Yeah. Yvonne taught me and I made it and all the kids said it was really delicious. Do you want me to make you some?"

"Well, sure, OK, have at it, kid."

I scrambled to gather the ingredients, dragging a kitchen chair to the cupboards to reach the flour from a high shelf. "I can't wait to be old enough to be able to reach the food," I thought, eyeing a bag of chocolate chips. "When I am older, I'm going to eat whatever I want whenever I want." As I sliced the eggplant and beat the eggs, I was picturing myself well over six feet tall, stuffing my mouth with cookies, a real adult! But I kept one eye on Wayne. Could he tell that I knew?

Wayne went outside and came in with an armful of wood, expertly feeding it into the giant woodstove at the center of the kitchen. I dragged the kitchen chair over to the stove now and stood on it as I placed the first slices of eggplant into the oil and heard the satisfying sizzle of it cooking. "Bess would kill me if she knew." These words were rattling around in my brain. Was he saying that to Lizzie to make sure she didn't tell? Everyone knew that Wayne and my mother were together. Would Lizzie feel guilty and confess? I imagined her telling one of the more powerful adults and them not believing her and her pointing to me: "She was there, she heard it all—tell them, Jenny!" And how I'd have to stammer and pretend I didn't know what sex was or pretend I didn't hear. Or maybe someone would say, "Why didn't you stop them? Don't you love your mother?" What would I say to that? Then I'd also have to pretend to love my mother—a whole other complicated performance, made more difficult by the fact that I barely knew her.

I was getting more and more nervous as I gamed out all these scenarios, and I got flustered. I flipped the eggplant nonetheless, but as I reached for the plate to put the crispy slices on, the chair I was standing on lurched and I fell forward, putting my full weight on both hands on the searing-hot top of the woodstove. I screamed and fell backward onto the floor.

I couldn't remember much about what happened after my hands were maimed by the stove. I remembered that they had giant burn blisters and were bandaged for weeks. Of course we didn't go to a hospital when it happened.

I wasn't really able to sleep on this forest floor, on the top of this mountain, sticks poking into my back, arms out of the sleeves of my sweatshirt and curled around my body for warmth. Lying here in my makeshift bed, I tried to simply enjoy the power of being gone and not think about tomorrow or the future. I put my arms back through the sleeves and stretched them out, studying my hands against the starry night sky, and wondered how I didn't have scars from that accident. For years I'd felt guilty about not telling my mother that Wayne was cheating on her, certain that I had been burned as punishment. Now I just thought about how unsafe it was to let an eight-year-old cook over a woodstove.

I woke up with the first light of dawn (Had I been sleeping? Had I been dreaming about burning my hands?) and formulated a vague plan. I'd wander along the trail for as long as I could, then maybe I would go to Clare's house.

That first day I met Clare, when I got off the bus at my stop, she'd exclaimed, "Oh, you live right down the mountain from me—I live up South Mountain Pass. You should come over someday!" At the time I knew I wouldn't be allowed to but made a mental note.

Days later, I'd dragged my bike up South Mountain Pass, a very steep and winding country road, hoping that I'd somehow magically run into her. I got all the way to where the road started to go downhill and figured I should turn around and go home, feeling stupid about my optimistic plan. "Hey!" I heard, from way up high somewhere. "Hey! New girl!" And I looked up the winding driveway and saw her, small at the top, waving her arms. "Come up here!" I was thrilled and a little nervous. I'd never been in someone's house before, a normal person, with a normal family.

I pulled my bike up the driveway, and she was blaring a song called "We Don't Talk Anymore" so loud that I could hear it as I got closer to her house. She was dancing, pointing at me and belting out the lyrics: "Well, I hope you know which way to go/You're on your own again . . ." She stopped singing as I got to the top. "Don't you *love* this song?" she said. I didn't know it, but I liked it, and I felt guilty about liking this song, and making this new friend, and the World People of it all. Inside her house, no one was home, and we ate Ritz crackers with peanut butter spread on them. We sang "We Don't Talk Anymore" over and over as she put the needle back to the outer groove of the 45. I wandered around her house, marveling at all the framed family photos hanging on the walls. She had three sisters and one brother, and a mom and a dad, and they smiled at me from ski vacations and annual Christmas photos, growing older in each one. I thought about what was hanging on the walls at our new house—a painting Mom bought at a yard sale of a field and some trees, a framed photo of Melvin. "You should sleep over!" she said. "Can you call your parents and ask if you can sleep over?"

I knew I couldn't do that, and I'm not sure what I said (certainly not "I'm not allowed to do anything"), but as I rode my bike down the hill, I felt hopeful. "I stayed at Clare's house until dinner time," I wrote in my diary that night. "I miss that family feeling that her house has. I love the way of their life. I could have moved in then and there. It was so nice and comfortable and I felt like there was really love out here somewhere."

On the trail this morning, I meandered, wanting to stay away as long as possible. But what was I going to do? I couldn't live in that house for another second. I'd long ago let go of getting away from this all and going back to Jessie. Ever since FP went to visit them and told me that no one even said my name, I'd cut off the part of me that believed I could still go back there. They didn't care about me anymore.

I'd shared a little bit with Clare a few months ago—just about the violence and how I wasn't allowed to do anything, and her response was an emphatic "You should go to the authorities." But who were "the authorities"? I'd imagined a scenario where I went to someone at the school—but who? The high school guidance counselor I'd met with about my future had given me a career survey to fill out and concluded from my answers that I should work in sanitation. I couldn't see confiding in her. I could go to a police station, but then where would I sleep that night, after I told them I couldn't go home? What if they made me go home anyway, until they figured out what to do? I could see cops arriving at the door and FP charming them somehow and then killing us all after they left.

I CAME TO A ROCK I knew well—slanted and flat and at a perfect angle to stretch out on, like a lounge chair. A beam of sunlight was shining through the trees onto it, and I lay down, face to the sky, feeling the warmth of the rock on my back.

I'd thought about telling one of my teachers what FP was doing to me. I'd been living with it for almost three years, and when I imagined talking about it to anyone, I thought about how they would probably say, "If it was so terrible, why didn't you leave?" Why didn't I leave? I didn't know the answer. I didn't know how. I didn't know if anyone would even believe me. I was fifteen—didn't that sound kind of old to just put up with it? If I'd tried to get out at fourteen, it would have sounded better. Fifteen sounded kind of like I didn't mind it that much.

I had that curse of seeming so cheerful and doing so well in school. I'd found a book in the library about "child abuse" and learned that I had none of the supposed signs of an "abused child." I wasn't aggressive or angry (oh, but I was so full of hate on the inside); I didn't have stomachaches or headaches that had no cause (I'd learned to live with the permanent knot in my stomach); I didn't cry for no obvious reason

(I cried all the time, but only when I was alone); and I had plenty of friends (who knew nothing about who I really was). I had nightmares—terrifying, suffocating nightmares—but I'd always had those. Annalee had them too. I thought they just ran in the family.

And besides, in my life I'd had two examples of what happened when you "told somebody." There was my mother's response, the memory carved into me like a jagged scar, especially because she still treated me like the Other Woman and, needless to say, had left me to fend for myself. The only other example was what happened to Frida the summer I was ten. One night on the Vineyard, she told me that one of the older boys was sneaking into our room in the very early morning and touching her over her panties while she slept. Or while she pretended to sleep. I was scared for her when she told me this—I was scared for myself. We both knew that accusing someone could get us into trouble, and we were on our own. The only thing I could think of was that she should sleep in bed with me; surely he wouldn't bother her if someone was sleeping next to her.

Even now, five years later, I remembered the next morning with a chill. She had climbed up to the top bunk to sleep with me, wrapping her arms tight around me and staying that way all night. It felt like I didn't sleep at all, waiting to see if he would come. Maybe I didn't believe her, maybe I didn't want to believe her, but as the first light of dawn peeked through the curtains, I heard the faint familiar jangle of the tag on his dog's collar and buried my head in the covers so that I could peek out and see the doorway. And there he was. He stood for a second, scanning the room, and I squeezed my eyes shut tight, afraid he would see that I was awake. I could hear him coming into the room and saw him stand over the bed where Frida usually slept.

It only now dawned on me that he could easily come to my bed next, since he wouldn't find Frida—why hadn't I thought about that? My heart was beating so loud in my chest that I was worried he would hear it. I turned my back to him, squeezing Frida tight and engulfing us in the covers. I could hear his footsteps coming toward us, then silence. A long silence. Was he just standing there? I could tell Frida was awake by her ragged breathing, and I prayed she wouldn't give us away.

After what seemed like forever, I heard his footsteps recede and then the screen door of the house squeak as it opened. "Is he gone?" Frida whispered, and I instinctively clamped my hand around her mouth and then took it away immediately, because it obviously scared her. I peered from under the covers and craned my neck enough to see out the window, where the path between the houses was visible. He and the dog were far off, headed down the road to one of the other houses.

We didn't say anything, because we both knew there was nothing we could do. I think she was just happy that I'd seen it with my own eyes and she wasn't alone in this. She slept in bed with me for the next few nights, and he showed up every morning. I didn't get a lot of sleep those nights. A few days later, she was gone. I heard that someone read about it in her diary and she was yelled at, slapped, accused of doing it all because she was in love with him, made to apologize to him for writing those lies, and sent away. First to Boston to be with George and then, when he tired of her, to the Farm. Back then, I wondered if that boy had orchestrated it all somehow—if the fact that she was suddenly sleeping with me made him angry, and, worried that she would tell, he'd planted a seed that she wasn't quite right, and someone had read her diary. Had I done the right thing? Frida's life had gone from bad to worse because of it.

This was what happened when you told the truth. I couldn't bear the idea of not being believed. I wondered what Mom would do if I told someone else. Would she act shocked and pretend she didn't know or claim that I was lying? Would she own up to the fact that she knew and not only did nothing about it but was angry at me for it? The first two options were horrifying, and I knew the third one would never happen. I was starting to realize that I simply had to get out. I didn't care if people knew, I didn't need anyone to be punished, I just wanted to get as far away from these people as I could. There was no way I was going to last until I graduated.

I thought about something my mother had said to me about a year earlier. "You have to be careful with men. You're like me—men are drawn to us. We have something about us that makes us very attractive to them, and it's not only about our looks." So later, when a friend's father exposed his erect penis to me at a sleepover, I simply left the room and didn't tell anyone. I figured he couldn't help himself and it was just my job to be careful, because men would be showing you their penises whenever they found a chance.

Eventually I ran into a man and a woman sitting on a log, eating granola bars. They had all the earmarks of people who'd been hiking for weeks—lean bodies, backpacks with metal plates hanging off the sides, dirty bandannas holding their hair back from their weathered faces. I stopped and chatted with them for a while—normal behavior in Appalachian Trail culture. They had come from Georgia and now they were in New York, and they were absolutely going to make it to Maine, where friends were waiting with hot showers and soft beds. But I noticed that their relationship seemed a bit strained and that the woman didn't speak much. I wondered if he hit her when they were alone, imagining how utterly unprotected she would be if he did, out here in the woods, mostly alone, for weeks on end. She would have no way to escape.

"But what are *you* doing out here?" the guy asked. I suddenly became aware of what I looked like—a teenage girl in non-hiking clothes at 7:00 A.M., deep on the trail, obviously having slept in the woods. It occurred to me that I could say, "I'm running away from home. I'm escaping from a horrible situation. Please help me." I was pretty sure I knew what would happen next. They would say, "Well, you should call the police," or offer to take me to a police station. But what if they didn't? After all, they were busy getting themselves to Maine. Or what if, like in *Invasion of the Body Snatchers*, I'd be seeking help from someone who I couldn't see was actually the enemy? What if they tricked me into going back home or the police brought me back to that house once I talked to them? I didn't trust this guy, and I wasn't sure what I wanted anyway. Was I even running away, or was I just making a statement? I told them I lived nearby and that I liked early-morning hikes. They finished their granola bars and hoisted their packs onto their backs. "Keep your food sealed away so the bears and coyotes don't start following you!" the guy said nonsensically, since I didn't even have a backpack or bag of any kind. I guess that was his way of saying goodbye.

"Good luck!" I said, waving as they walked off.

"You too!" the woman said, in that way that people do that doesn't really make sense. Or was she saying, "I see you, I can see you are in trouble. We can't help each other, but good luck"?

I sat on the log where they'd been sitting and thought about all the things that happen that people never talk about, that exist only between two people, that we will never know. Like that thirteen-year-old boy, when I was five. I'd been trying not to think about him, but when the hiker mentioned coyotes, I remembered something he once said to me: "Don't worry, if you get pregnant from this, we can just take the baby up into the woods and feed it to the coyotes."

He was one of the older boys in the Family. He was often disgraced and made fun of and was perpetually in trouble. Like me, he had only one parent in the Family, and perhaps because of that he was treated like a mistake, a non-person. I remembered how he would laugh, a kind of harsh and nervous laugh, and how he was often told that he had the devil inside him, and we all believed he did.

He'd come into the Bunk House in the middle of the night, as he often did, where I was sleeping alongside twenty other kids. The Bunk House then was half-built, the recently installed fiberglass insulation puffing out between the beams. The house smelled of new wood and the sawdust that covered the floor, and makeshift bunk beds had been built for us to sleep in. Knots in the beams looked like faces or flowers to us, and we'd drawn around them with markers and pencils, expanding on the knots to make monsters, or solar systems, or elaborate butterflies.

In the top bunk, where I usually slept, I'd started to pick at a part of the fiberglass that no one could really see, peeling away the brown paper to reveal the innards, which were fluffy and pink and looked like cotton candy. Each night I would pull off a tiny piece of it, the fibers so satisfying as they separated, the fluffy tendrils with their bits of glass twinkling in the low light. I would put the morsel in my mouth, willing it to be like the Turkish Delight from *The Lion, the Witch and the Wardrobe*. I thought reverently of the way it was described in the book:

"Each piece was sweet and light to the very center and Edmund had never tasted anything more delicious." It never was delicious, but I couldn't stop myself from going back night after night, in hopes that something wonderful I'd done had magically earned its transformation into a Delight.

On this night, while everyone else slept, I was playing with the fiberglass in the dark, rolling it between my fingers to make long pink spindles. Across the room, through the plastic-covered rectangle in the wall where a window would be one day, I could see a dainty sliver of moon. It was hard to sleep when I knew that boy might be coming. I heard the flimsy screen door to the house open and his cautious footsteps as he made his way across the echoey room. The floor creaked under his feet, and he stopped for a second. I closed my eyes tight, but not too tight, so I'd look like I was asleep. I'd noticed, though, that when you close your eyes to pretend to be asleep, your eyes still move under the lids, giving you away. I'd practiced hard to make my eyes still when they were closed, but I was nervous, so I don't think I was doing a very good job. I dared to peek out of one eye to see what he was doing. He was making his way around the room, hovering over Katie, then DeeDee, then Corrina. They were all sound asleep.

He started to turn toward my part of the room, and I slammed my eye shut. He was climbing up the ladder to my part of the bed. The whole structure moved with the weight of each of his feet progressing up the rungs. Now I could feel that his upper body was looming over me, but he just stayed that way for a while, doing nothing and saying nothing. I could hear the light snores of some of the kids and the rustle of the wind in the trees, outside in the dark. Finally he poked me gently and whispered, "Hey." It startled me, and my eyes flew open. "What are you doing?" he said nonsensically, like it was the middle of the day. "Come outside with me."

I sat up, making sure my nightgown was covering me, and climbed down that ladder, wishing it also went up to the sky, and I could climb the rungs until I reached that sliver of moon, which I still believed could possibly be made of cheese. I was praying someone would wake up but also being as quiet as I could. No one woke up, and he took my hand wordlessly and led me across the creaky floor and out into the warm night.

June bugs chirped loudly as I followed him down the steps, across the rocky yard, under the clothesline where hanging clothes swayed in the night breeze, and to the nearby toolshed. Once we were inside, he kneeled on the dirt floor in front of me so our heights matched and we were face-to-face, and he pulled out his penis, which was already erect. I knew from experience that this would be over pretty quickly, and I didn't say anything. I wasn't afraid of what was happening—it was familiar, though I didn't understand it—but I was afraid that we would be discovered and that I would somehow be in trouble because of it. I knew he had the devil inside him, and I wondered if what he was doing to me was because of that. Edging toward me on his knees now, he got very close, lifting my nightgown and then clamping his hands on the outside of each of my thighs, pushing them together tightly, and thrusting his penis between them over and over, faster and faster. His increasingly rapid breathing was always confusing to me. He made a noise of frustration suddenly and jumped up, scanning the room for something. His eyes landed on a horse blanket hanging on the wall, and he snatched it and spread it on the ground. I stood there, not really present at all, thinking about it being over, thinking about that corner in the bunk bed with my secretly torn fiberglass. He stared at me, momentarily perplexed. "Lie down on it!" he said, his voice an impatient whisper, as if I wasn't playing my part properly. I'd been here before, after all; I should know how things were going to happen. I lay down and he pushed my nightgown up over my waist, getting on top of me, situating his penis again between my thighs, squeezing them together, thrusting. The horse blanket was rough on my bare legs. Rougher still when he was finished and used it to wipe the semen off them. And that's when he said it, his voice a genuine effort to be reassuring: "Don't worry, if you get pregnant from this, we can just take the baby up into the hills and feed it to the coyotes."

I knew about pregnant but had never really thought about how it happened and never thought that this thing he did to me was something that could make a baby. I felt scared for my baby being fed to coyotes and wondered if he would bring me with him for this task or just take the baby and go up into the hills without me. I thought that if we had to do it, I would want to be there to say goodbye to her. She was suddenly real to me, and she was a girl. I didn't want her to die that way. I thought of the mournful words of a song we often sang called "Bury Me Not on the Lone Prairie":

> *Oh, bury me not on the lone prairie*
> *Where the coyotes howl and the wind blows free*
> *Where there's not a soul that will care for me*
> *Oh, bury me not on the lone prairie*

Just like the man in the song, my baby was going to be all alone when she was dead. Coyotes howling and cackling in the hills at night were a familiar soundtrack on the Farm, but forever after that night, when I heard them, I shuddered to think that maybe other people were feeding their babies to coyotes, and I wondered when my baby would come. Would I give birth to her in this shed and then he would take her? How long would that take? Wouldn't the adults notice?

Soon after this, he was just gone. Not to one of the other communities but kicked out of the Family. Erased. I never spoke of what he did to me, never asked the other girls, and really didn't think about it much. I remembered it, to be sure, but with a kind of confusion that went nowhere. I didn't feel guilt or shame—only relief that he was gone and that meant I would never get in trouble for it.

Here, sitting on this log in the woods, I thought about the coyotes and wondered how I would remember those nights if he hadn't said those words that were meant to comfort me. Is it possible I wouldn't have remembered at all?

But I couldn't stay on the Appalachian Trail forever, so I decided I would hike back to the road and walk to Clare's house. I didn't have a plan after that.

As I walked up Clare's driveway, dreading what would happen next, I saw her mother crouched in their flower bed, gloves up to her elbows, her face barely visible under a giant hat. The gravel crackled under my feet and she turned, then gasped, then raced toward me, hugging me tight. I wasn't used to being hugged and it startled me. "Oh, thank God!" she said, murmuring into my hair. "We thought you'd gone to the city and gotten into prostitution." I'd been gone for about fifteen hours.

After a long night in the woods, this household seemed like as good a place as any to get warm and figure out what I was going to do next.

CHAPTER 41

A FEW DAYS LATER, MY SUITCASE WAS LOADED IN THE BACK
of FP's Suburban and he was driving me to live at Granny's house.
Before I'd come home from Clare's, I steeled myself for the same old
hamster wheel of bullshit and even thought I might make some
demands—though I wasn't sure if I really would, because what could
those demands possibly be? I'd long ago stopped wanting things to
change. I knew they wouldn't, except maybe to get worse, and what
was "worse"? One or both of them going to prison sounded like an
improvement to me, so what was there to salvage? Clare's mother had
given me a ride home, and as I stared out the window of her car, I felt
the familiar numbness creep over me. "I scared them," I thought. "At
least I scared them." And then I didn't even care about that, because I
was just so tired.

I'd thanked Clare's mom and come inside the house and into the
kitchen, where my mother didn't say anything, only gave me a dramatic hug that made me feel nothing. FP stood nearby, arms calmly
folded, but something about the tension around his mouth told me he
was either furious or sad. Whatever. They both looked like they hadn't
slept all night, and I was happy about that.

Of course FP started in, at first saying, "Your mother and I talked
it over last night, and we think it's best if you go live with Granny." His
tone was so laughably earnest I almost missed what he was saying.
What after-school special was *he* in where he "talked over" things with

my mother? He blathered on, wandering in and out of wisdoms about how my mother and I clearly "weren't getting along," that it was obviously I wasn't happy, and I don't know what else he said, except it ended with him screaming, "You wanna get away from here so bad? Good. You're going. You got your wish! I hope you can live with yourself!" My mother was crying at this point, but neither of us had said a word for twenty minutes.

And now here we were in his car, on the way to my grandmother's house. FP was upbeat, smoking and babbling about how this was a good idea, and it was really his idea, and how Granny wasn't so happy about it at first, but he'd talked her into it. What the fuck had he said to her? I knew whatever he said couldn't possibly be the truth, which meant I'd probably been spun as a difficult teenager or some other nonsense, but I didn't care. My night on the Appalachian Trail, even if brief, had worked. I'd shaken something loose, finally. They weren't scared of me exactly, but I hoped it meant that they were starting to see there was no way they could keep me caged forever.

As he rambled on, I was in the familiar state of simply getting past him to the next thing, barely listening but nodding occasionally so he wouldn't explode out of nowhere, which was easy because the next thing was so unimaginably great. We were a half hour away from Dover, a knowable amount of time, at the end of which I would no longer have to hear his voice. I was reveling in the fact that he was inches from me in the driver's seat but would maybe never be that close to me again, and I was busy hating his smell, in my mind tolerating it for the last time. Coffee, from a Folgers can, which my mother made him every morning, ritualistically drinking a cup herself with her eyes full of fear. Lucky Strikes, but only because he wanted to be like the guys in the Family. Jeans that reeked of not being washed enough, the smell of dampness and paint wafting my way. It was nauseating because it was so familiar. But, I thought as I sat there in his passenger seat, he also smelled like Ivory soap, which was what we all smelled like because it was the only soap we had in that house. I never understood the commercial about it floating. "What floats? Ivory soap floats!" Who cared if soap could float? I knew that Granny had Dove soap in her bathroom, and once I got there, I would be happy not to have that particular smell in common with him anymore.

I was pulled out of this reverie about soap when he said, "But I promise to come visit you." Oh, there it was. Of course he wasn't going to leave me alone. He always had an angle. "We're not just going to abandon you with Granny," he chuckled. "Crazy old lady."

But he was speaking about some vague future, and this was now, where I had a new life. He dropped me off at Granny's, and after requisite pleasantries that chilled me, eventually he drove away. And there I was on her steps again with my suitcases, but, unlike last time, it felt like a safe place. "Thank God for Granny," I thought, as we walked up her steps together and Dennis took my bags. She did her usual grumbling—I'd learned she didn't like things to be different—but something about the way she looked at the car when FP drove away told me that she knew more than she would ever let on. Or maybe that she just didn't like him and had had her own experience with charmers who ended up being no good.

A week later I started school at Dover High. When I arrived at the office with Granny, she said, "Oh my, this school has changed a lot since your mother went here," and then promptly drove home. I was introduced to a woman named Linda. She was wearing a purple suit that strained at her breasts (something I had become newly self-conscious about when my own clothes did it). Her voice was comforting and welcoming, but she studied me with something I'd never seen before: She looked worried about me. I thought I'd finally figured out how to blend in, but her eyes told me differently. I could tell I stood out again. Dammit. She invited me to sit with her and her students at lunch—she was the beloved ESL teacher, and I discovered that a large part of the student body was new to the country and learning English for the first time. When a boy named Fernando offered me a ride home and I asked him why they called the town Doverico, he said there was a giant billboard at the San Juan airport that encouraged people to "Come to beautiful Dover, New Jersey," and that's why a lot of Puerto Ricans lived here. I took this to be true, though I didn't understand why this small town in New Jersey would be a desirable destination for someone from another country. He made sure to let me know he was from Venezuela.

I was called "the Princess from New York" and "La Blanca," and one day a girl walked me home and said, "I don't care what anyone says, I like your shoes." All that assimilation for nothing. New playing field. But Granny and Dennis both worked, and I could do whatever I wanted after school. I made friends; I dated boys; I called Clare and Brian almost daily, talking on the phone for as long as I wanted. I joked around with Uncle Dennis, made clothes for myself with Granny's expert help, and when I woke up in the morning, I felt so excited for life that I could barely control my joy. I worried about Annalee and baby Benjamin, but I couldn't allow myself to think about that too much.

FP or Mom would call every other night, either planning to visit or saying they would come get me and bring me to New York for the weekend. They'd somehow reframed the whole thing in a way that made me being at Granny's something they'd decided I "had" to do but we were all sad about.

At first I'd asked Granny to say I was in the shower when they called, but she laid down the law pretty quickly, saying, "I'm not getting in the middle of any of this—if you don't want to talk to them, tell them yourself." When the phone rang, she'd answer and then hold the receiver out to me with her version of a stern expression, which was wide-open eyes and raised eyebrows. She was never mean or a disciplinarian toward me, just grumpy. It wasn't easy to get her to say more than the stuff required to get through a day, but a few times we had long, lovely talks about her past, and I started to really admire her. She loved a tiny glass of sherry when she got home from work, accompanied by a sesame-seed-covered breadstick, and when she'd settled into her chair to enjoy these things, I would sit across from her on the couch and encourage her to talk.

While she was talking, I would try to envision the awkward young woman I'd seen in the few photos she had, her smile only present in the pictures taken before she got married. I also saw that she'd been a little overweight and forgave her for warning my mother against "having a fat teenager on her hands." She'd probably been speaking from some painful past experience. I was in the business of starving myself at the time and lusted after the breadstick she was taking tiny bites of as she talked. It was only forty calories, but still—there was no way I could afford to eat one of those every day.

I was beginning to understand that the life she was living had most definitely not been her dream. She had been a Marine in World War II and a "spinster" at thirty, eventually marrying the only taker at the insistence of her parents. I learned that my grandfather was a divorced man when she met him, a minor scandal in her world at the time, and that he was a semi-employed alcoholic with "a temper." She never spoke ill of him, but I was getting the feeling that he had not been a good man and she wasn't that sad when he died. She spoke wistfully of her daughter Nell but never about where Nell was now, and she did not speak of my mother's failures because there I was, exhibit A, a teenage girl living in her house.

Mom visited, FP visited, and I somehow avoided going back to that dreaded house in Garrison for most of the school year. I wrote letters to Clare, pined after baby Benjamin and how he was growing up without me, and didn't let on to FP and my mother that I was having a lot of fun at Dover High. There was a cosmetology school inside my new high school, and I was asked to be a model for their annual hair show. I never shared with them how magical it was when I sauntered across the auditorium stage in shiny maroon satin while Shannon's "Let the Music Play" blasted over the sound system. It seemed crucial to paint my life here as drab, as if it were some kind of punishment.

I dreaded FP's visits. He'd arrive by 10 A.M., wandering around Granny's like he owned the place, criticizing the clutter, waltzing into my bedroom and touching things. Just touching things, like he always did. I'd started to see him not as a calculated creature but an instinctive one: He wasn't smart enough to devise an evil scheme; he was just delusional and driven enough to make things go his way. He didn't know that his touching things in my room would make my skin crawl; he touched them like an animal would pee on things. I wasn't nearly as scared of him as I used to be, but there was still no relaxing in his presence.

When he visited, Granny would be polite and offer him coffee but then disappear into her bedroom. Dennis stayed in the basement. FP would take me to a nearby diner and, in between complaining about how expensive the food was or being rude to the waitress, say things like "Your mother has been crying and going through a lot of stuff, and I'm really surprised because I didn't think she cared about you that much" or "The shine has left your eyes." These words made me want to cry, but I did not. Instead, I'd count the minutes until he drove away, so relieved there was no way for us to be alone. When he was gone, I would erase him from my mind for days at a time, a new luxury.

But Brian was going to be home from college for a big football game, and I *had* to go back for that. While I didn't care about football in the slightest, I wanted to see all my friends, especially him. He'd been calling and writing; we definitely weren't dating, but I indulged myself in a little fantasizing about being his girlfriend.

I thought I might be in love with Brian. He was muscular but shy, popular without knowing it, said little, laughed often, and had a sly way about him that telegraphed that he did not care what people thought of him. He'd been the star quarterback of the football team in his senior year of high school, but he was dismissive of the status it brought him. Unlike his teammates, he had longish feathered hair, and his favorite shirt was from a Foghat concert he'd been to. His biggest passions were playing the drums and his band, Talon. He'd written me letters almost every other day since I'd been away, letters full of jokes and observations about people we knew, ruminations on life, and, every once in a while, a crumb of romance, but not directly stated.

FP wouldn't hear of me spending the weekend with Clare while I was in Garrison, and I needed him or my mother for the ride back and forth, so, as much as I didn't want to, I stayed in that house for two days. I did get to go to the game and see all my friends and goof around with Brian in the bleachers, but of course I had to come back when the game was over and not be a part of any of the fun stuff that people were doing afterward.

When I made it back to Dover, a day later than I'd wanted to, I wrote this letter to Clare:

OCTOBER 11, 1983

Dear Clare,

Wow—I had the most amazing weekend. (This is definitely an extremely sarcastic statement.) When I got home from your house, Mom was Mom, as usual, and I didn't do much. Lately I've felt very uncomfortable around her—which is really lousy. FP came home a few whiles later, all smiles and hum-de-dums, and I was thinking God! When is this family ever going to accomplish something? He brought home the movie "48 Hours" and after a lovely family dinner that was all smiles and laughter, we watched it. Somehow it wasn't funny at all. After the movie (about 10:30 on Saturday night) everything felt very weird. It's hard to describe but it seemed like everyone kind of realized "Well here we are and what the hell are we going to do about it." So I'm sitting in the living room reading and Mom and FP are sitting in the kitchen. I knew something strange was going on but I didn't really know what. Finally, FP said in this weird voice, "Guin, why don't you come in the kitchen?" So I did, and they were smoking pot. Yay! I just got really pissed—I guess because them smoking pot really just confused the issue at hand. And I don't think they've ever done it before—I mean since we've lived in Garrison. So I left, or tried to, but FP said "Stay here—can't you tell where you're supposed to be?"

So I sat in the middle of the kitchen floor. After a few minutes he offered me some and I said no. He said come on, you'll like it, don't be uptight, what's your problem, etc. etc. etc.—but I really didn't want to. I mean I'd love to smoke pot with you or someone like that. I don't know—just the right person and the right time. This was totally the wrong time. I feel enough at a disadvantage in that home without being high to boot. I was so annoyed with them!! Mom wasn't really into it—she said she didn't really want *to—but I guess she was trying to go with the flow. I said later to the flow, man! If that's the way it's flowing then I am going <u>against</u> the flow!!!*

So FP started getting nasty because I wouldn't smoke it. He was saying "Guinny does what Guinny wants when Guinny wants." He can really get offensive and mean and petty when he wants to. I don't think being high had anything to do with it. So then he starts going off on me and Mom. "When did you think we were going to talk about it? You think everything will just go away?" He starts shooting questions at me. "What are your feelings for me?" "Your mother?" Why this, why that, and he always asks questions that are impossible to answer, like "What kind of an idiot are you?" and then gets pissed when you don't answer. What am I supposed to say, "Class B, Section 5-DA idiot"?

So while FP is browbeating me, Mom is sitting there, and she looked like she was falling asleep or something. FP started talking to her, "Are you listening Bess?" "Do you have anything to say?" "Do you see what a little bitch your daughter is?" Anyway Mom said something that really pissed him off, and pretty soon he was screaming, and I mean at the top of his lungs. Red face, veins popping out of his neck and forehead—he really looked like a psychopath. He flipped over the table in our kitchen, (things went flying) punched the washing machine, and asked Mom something—I can't even remember what. He stood right in front of her, she was sitting down, and said "I'll give you ten seconds to answer me and then you're going through the fucking window." He was standing there hitting his fist into his other hand, right in front of her face, so hard it probably hurt <u>his</u> hand. Mom was so scared she couldn't even think straight—I could tell she was trying to answer him but she was so scared she couldn't get the words out, and after about three seconds he screamed "ANSWER ME!!" so loud I bet <u>you</u> could have heard it if you were quiet enough up at your house. I guess Mom finally said something because he never did hit her, but I bet he would have done some serious damage to her face if he hit her in that rage. Somewhere in the middle of that whole episode he came up to me and grabbed my face and shook me. *"Do you see what you're doing to me!!?"* he screamed. He didn't hit anyone, and what he did to me didn't even really hurt that much, so it's a lot better than he has been before. <u>But</u> I've never seen him in more of a total rage than on Saturday night. This dude was what you might call *pissed off!*

What we established with the lovely evening was this: All this time, Mom has been doing whatever she can to get FP and I away from each other, while maintaining that she was on FP's side. (You may ask why—it is because life is so much easier when you seem like you are on FP's side.) Mom has always favored Annalee, and as a matter of fact could give two craps about me—I am public enemy number one. FP told Mom he thought she was bad through and through, and that she didn't care what happened to me at all.

Then he came up to me (Mom walked out of the room—this was after he calmed down) and said *"I didn't hurt you, did I?"* and *"I'll do whatever you want."* (Side story—earlier in the evening when FP was trying to get me to smoke pot and I wouldn't he said he wouldn't drive me back to NJ unless I did—and he told Mom he'd take the engine out of her car if she tried to. I still refused the motherfucker—mostly because I just wanted to do whatever he didn't want me to. I figured if worse came to worse I'd hitchhike.)

Next morning, birds chirping—sun shining—god life is wonderful. Somehow the three of us end up in Benjamin's room discussing the situation and Mom says, *"Maybe everything he says is true—can you forgive me?"* We listen to FP lecture on how great he is, and how much we are scum bags. And then, god fucking dammit, everything was hunky dory. Everyone's fine, everything's nice—everyone acted like No Big Deal. Every single time something happens I think to myself—this is it. It's finally over. Thank god. I'm so thick! You'd think I'd learn by now that nothing, absolutely nothing, will ever happen that will make anyone do anything in my family!!! Oh GOD does it piss me off! Like when FP says *"I moved you to New Jersey because . . ."* Bullshit! I moved *myself to NJ because I am the only one in the family who has the least amount of guts or even brains to get the hell out! And I'm still not rid of them! We all went through holy hell and got absolutely nowhere.*

I told FP, flat to his face, that I consider our relationship a friendship—does it phase him? No! He's got an answer for all of it. So I got nothing out of it but a night of extreme terror that probably took about 10 years off of my life. And to boot—nobody felt like driving me home on Sunday night. On Monday FP took me out and bought me a pair of sweatpants so I can't really complain, because who really wants to go to school anyway. I was pissed at the time but thinking back on it, it was no big deal. So he drove me home last night and was pretty nice about it.

A thought just occurred to me—I'm going to leave this letter on my bed now while I am in the shower, and I know I'd never do that in a million years if I was in Garrison, because I know that never in a million years would Granny read it. It's weird because part of the reason is she doesn't care as much, but the weird thing is I like it when people don't care as much. I like it! Am I whacked or what? I guess I don't like it. What I don't like is FP. On the ride back here, I told him that I always get the feeling that he doesn't want me to have you, and he was annoyed with me. He said no, it's just that he feels I should deal with family before having fun with friends. But my friend is my family, and my family aren't even my friends! (Well put, wasn't that?)

Anyway, call me on Thursday night—after 9 but before 10 please. (9 is lower rates and 10 is Hill Street Blues). I pray you can come visit!

Love + kisses + slobber—Guin.

After that, I vowed to never *ever* be foolish enough to set foot in that house again. But FP kept coming to see me every weekend, staying later and later and sometimes just driving aimlessly around in his car in a way that made me scared he was going to kidnap me. He'd find lookout spots, like the kind in movies where teenagers go to make out, and then park and talk my ear off until the windows were completely fogged up and I wanted to scream. He would sometimes put his hand on my knee or find an excuse to touch me, and if he did I would jump out of the car and tell him I needed to go home, saying either that Granny would be worried or that I had homework to do before bed. He would grumble about it and talk some more but do as I asked. I had a little more power now, but not much.

Toward the end of the school year, he dropped the bomb on me: My mother was pregnant again and the baby was due in August. She was going to need me to help out after I was done with the school year. There was nothing I could say to get out of this. School would be over, and I would just be a selfish, lazy person if I refused to help out. In my final weeks at Dover High, I was so depressed I could barely get out of bed. It was hard to admit to myself that I was actually going back there, and though we all agreed I'd return to Dover for my last two years of high school, I knew that would be something I'd have to fight for when the time came. As I carried my suitcase up the driveway in late June, a wave of nausea came over me and I vomited in the bushes. No one noticed.

CHAPTER 42

IT WAS A TERRIBLY MUGGY, OPPRESSIVE SATURDAY AFTERNOON in August, and everyone was home but in different corners of the house. Mom was lying on the couch in the living room, nine months pregnant and incapacitated by the heat. Annalee was in her room. Well, it was my mother's room too now—since I'd been away living at Granny's, she had moved in with Annalee, something that was not explained to me. They'd set up a crib next to her bed in anticipation of the new baby. I now shared my very small bedroom with my brother, Benjamin, who was sixteen months old. He was a sweet baby, and I'd missed him, so I didn't mind at all. FP slept alone in the largest bedroom in the house. I wasn't allowed to see my friends or talk on the phone, although of course I talked on the phone all the time when FP wasn't home.

This afternoon FP was in his bedroom with Benjamin, and I could faintly hear him lecturing the baby about something as if he was talking to a teenager. He was so obsessed with having this boy, and it was painful to witness his intensity and how Benjamin was already trying so hard to please him. I had just hauled the vacuum cleaner into the dining room, robotically unwinding its cord as I counted down the days to my freedom. The baby was due in two weeks. That left only a week or so before school started, and I was going to have to figure out a way to get back to Granny's before then. I knew Granny was wise to FP now and would be happy to have me. I hoped. We hadn't ever talked about him openly, but the way she acted when he came to visit said it all.

I heard Benjamin whimper and then genuinely start to cry, and FP barked out, "You stop that whining right now!" and then everything was quiet again, and I kicked the vacuum cleaner's ON button as hard as I could, grateful for the sound of it to fill the void. All housekeeping that involved any physical exertion had become my job, and I'd dusted and vacuumed every room but this one. I hated this fucking room. I hated this fucking house. I hated vacuuming. I was seething about it all. "Fucking psycho," I said, since I knew no one could hear me over the din of the vacuum cleaner. Still, I said it under my breath.

It was damn hot, and when I turned off the vacuum a few minutes later to take a breath and pointlessly fan my face with my hand, I thought I heard a faint voice but wasn't sure. A lawn mower was buzzing in the distance. Then it came again—my mom, in a thin and desperate tone that I barely recognized. "Can someone come in here? You guys?" I was the closest and raced into the other room, where I found her lying on the camel-colored couch in a pool of blood that was as big as her body—and growing bigger by the second.

Just two days before, I'd found my mother sitting on the couch, hands resting protectively on her enormous pregnant stomach, staring anxiously out the window, the open copy of *Sophie's Choice* she'd been reading abandoned next to her. We'd seen the film the year before; Meryl Streep starred in a gut-wrenching tale of a woman forced to choose which of her two young children's lives would be spared during the Holocaust. My mother had been deeply moved by this film, as had I, and now she was reading the book, as if, I thought, the answers to her own problems might be inside the story.

Before I'd spent ten months away at my grandmother's house, I might have scoffed at her obsession with *Sophie's Choice*. She had, after all, effectively chosen between her children—she left the communities assuming she'd get Annalee and never see me again, and then she got saddled with me anyway, and we all knew how that was going. But in my time away, I'd gained a tiny sliver of perspective, and the seeds of seeing her as another trapped human rather than a failed protector had been planted. When I would start to feel this way, I ritualistically re-minded myself of all the terrible things she'd said and done, to stave off even a sliver of empathy, but that day something about how distraught she looked made me feel bad for her.

I sat down in a nearby chair and asked, genuinely meaning it, "What's wrong, Mom? You look upset." She gave one of her signature epic sighs and said nothing for a long time. "Mom—are you OK?" I finally asked, getting worried.

"There's something wrong with this baby," she'd said, still looking out the window. "Something doesn't feel right."

I stifled the urge to laugh. "Something doesn't feel right?" I thought. "There isn't a single right thing about you having this baby! Why are you even having another baby with this man, further tethering yourself to him and making sure we will all be prisoners forever? Who would bring another person into this house of horrors, and how the fuck am I back here again?"

But I'd learned that this was the kind of outburst that would only make her cry and would change nothing, and so it was pointless, and right now she seemed so freaked out that it just seemed mean. I fought the empathy again as it swelled up. Mean? Of course I was mean. She'd turned me into a mean person with the dog-eat-dog dynamic in this household, a never-ending cycle of betrayal and violence. Lately I'd noticed myself laughing like her sometimes—bitter, mirthless—and I hated that. I pretty much hated everything, living only for the distant, vague but bright light of finally escaping when I went to college.

What I said was "Come on, Mom, you've done this three times before. It's going to be fine." Indeed, a favorite expression of hers over the years had been "Oh please, after three kids, it's like Grand Central Station down there," one more nail in the coffin of me ever having kids.

But she sat up, one hand flailing in the air.

"Exactly. I've done this three times and so I know what it feels like when something is wrong." This time her tone was chilling, and I didn't feel like laughing at her anymore.

So now, two days later, when I found her lying in a giant pool of blood, I couldn't help seeing that she was right, that something *was* wrong with this baby, and it was terrifying. When I dashed in from the other room, she was weakly trying to prop herself up, blood running down her legs as she did. "FP!" I called out. "Help us!" He was there in a flash and scooped her up in his arms, carrying her out of the room, blood dripping off her onto the carpet as he kicked the front door open. "Clean up that mess!" he yelled over his shoulder, then hurried down the driveway to his truck, hoisting her into the passenger seat. Annalee had come out of her room, and as we heard the car peel out of the driveway, then looked at the bloody couch, we both burst into tears. From the other room, Benjamin started crying too. "You get him," I said to Annalee. "I'm going to get some paper towels." She nodded bravely, trying to control the little gasping sobs coming out of her, and walked out of the room.

In the living room a few minutes later, with Benjamin safely secured by Annalee in his playpen in the dining room, we pressed the paper towels into the couch and watched as blood seeped up onto our hands and engulfed our wrists. We didn't say anything, just cried and tried to soak up the blood. I was sixteen and she was nine, but for a moment we were both just scared kids.

A few hours later, the phone finally rang. I fled to the wall-mounted yellow phone in the kitchen and breathlessly grabbed it on the third ring. Annalee followed close at my heels, standing beside me and looking up anxiously as I answered.

It was FP, telling me that Mom was doing fine and that the baby was a girl, but they weren't sure if she was going to be OK because she'd gotten no oxygen to her brain from the time Mom started bleeding until they did an emergency C-section, which was about twenty minutes later. "But your mother is gonna be in bed for about three weeks until she heals," FP said, "so we're definitely gonna need you to stay around here." There was a smugness in his voice, I thought, because he knew it would be hard for me to say no to this. Still, Mom was alive and the baby was alive and it was a girl! I hung up the phone and said, "They're OK, it's going to be OK. We have a little sister, and they're naming her Julie. Julie Elizabeth!" Instinctively I hugged Annalee, then danced around with her a little, and she looked so surprised that I realized maybe I'd never hugged her before.

For the next few weeks, I was housekeeper and cook, my bedridden mother's caretaker, and in charge of the kids, including my newborn sister, who so far seemed just fine. It was easy to avoid FP during the day—he was usually working and there was so much to do, and when he came home even more to do—but nighttime was more of a challenge. After everyone was in bed, and my mother was convalescing in his bed (he'd made this concession while she recovered), I didn't have the excuse of homework to hide myself away, but I was not going backward. I was never going to be faced with his dick again.

I knew from experience that the only way to accomplish this was to antagonize him—a dangerous game, but not a difficult one. I knew his tricks. I deliberately overcooked his eggs; I folded his laundry in a haphazard way; I left the kids' toys scattered around. Yes, motherfucker, "Guinny does what Guinny wants."

At night I buried myself in books, and when he'd say, "Come watch 60 *Minutes* with me," I'd say, "I'm reading," and not look up. He'd say something like "Oh, don't we have attitude tonight?" and grab the book out of my hand, trying to be playful. I'd shrug and walk out of the room, holding my shoulders square, though I was terrified he would smash me in the back of the head as I walked out.

He'd make comments on what I was wearing: "That's new—really shows off your body." I'd say, "It's hot out," and vow to myself to never wear it again. Where I used to play along to save us all, I just didn't care anymore. He was going to hit Annalee no matter what I did, and Mom was safe for now; even he was above hitting a woman with a giant jagged wound across her abdomen—an emergency C-section, I'd learned, doesn't involve thoughtful cutting. Part of me wanted him to hurt me bad enough that he had to take me to the hospital. "Fucking break something," I would think. "I don't even care if I die."

I'd say that to myself, but I knew it was a lie. I did care. I wanted to live, if only to spite him. While it would be glorious if he *almost* killed me and went to jail for it, I knew him well enough to know that he wouldn't be that stupid. I didn't think he had romantic feelings toward me or even particularly sexual ones—I just knew that he couldn't stand the idea of me getting away.

In those weeks, I'd started to notice that as soon as I went to get ready for bed, he'd immediately go outside to walk our dog, Huey. This didn't register with me at first—time for bed, walk the dog one last time, brush our teeth, methodically turn out lights for fear of a big speech about the electric bill. Mom was in bed recovering, FP always had to get up early for work, and the babies would be up and needing things by 7:00 A.M. at the latest, if I was lucky.

I was getting ready for bed one night, as I usually did, in Annalee and Mom's room because that's where my clothes were. Baby Julie was asleep in her crib at last, and Annalee was somewhere under the lump in her covers. The house was nestled in the woods—you couldn't see any lights from other houses, so when it was dark, the windows were almost perfect mirrors if the light was on and you were inside. It was also very quiet at night—only crickets and summer wind.

I was studying my reflection in the window as I got undressed. As usual, I hated what I saw. Thighs too fat, head too big, and even though my breasts were the envy of most girls I knew, too big, too low, not like Brooke Shields's. And I was way too short, and my feet were too big for someone my size. Looking at my body in the mirror was a ritualistic act of self-criticism, but one I enjoyed in my own way, mesmerizing and private. "It's actually good that you weren't taller," my mother said to me once. "Then you'd just be a model, and your life would be over by the time you were nineteen." I'd made note of the fact that she thought I *could* be a model. But what did she know about being pretty? And even if she did think I was pretty, I knew she hated me for it. At least she couldn't call me fat now—I'd whittled myself down to ninety-nine pounds.

I mean, all the boys in Dover wanted to date me. Francisco had told me I was "hot"; Eddie Lopez had broken up with me because I wouldn't go to second base; Miche had asked me to the prom.

As I scrutinized my reflection, I thought of the time, at seven or eight years old, when I was visiting my mom in the New York community. She took me to Washington Square Park, where there was a fountain. I'd never seen a fountain and jumped into it without even asking, getting soaking wet and laughing as the water poured over me. It was impetuous, but I also knew back then that my mother wouldn't punish me for impetuous acts the way the adults I was usually with did. I came out from under the water, laughing and choking a little bit because I hadn't anticipated the force of the fountain. Breathless and elated, my thin summer dress clinging to my body, I shook myself off like I'd seen dogs do and sat on one of the steps that surrounded the fountain. As my mother laughed on a bench nearby, a man walked up to me with a camera that had a long lens and crouched down to ask, "Can I take your picture?" I remembered reveling in the request, happy that he thought I was worthy of a photograph but shy once his lens was pointed at me. After a few clicks, I couldn't take it anymore and ran back to my mother.

From then on, I would always think, "I'm going to be in a magazine!" I didn't see a lot of magazines as a kid, but when I did get ahold of one, I'd flip through it hoping to see a photo of me in the fountain. I hoped it meant I was as glamorous as the movie stars I admired. And then Jessie had said I should be Miss America, which meant I was pretty. But Jessie had said that before my body became this less-than-perfect thing I saw in my reflection.

Then I heard it—a jingling sound from outside, which startled me but was also familiar. It was the tags on Huey's collar, which meant FP was outside the window. I jumped out of view and behind the open closet door, heart beating, and wondered how long he'd been doing this. Putting the pieces together, I realized that it had been at least a week. I felt so stupid for not figuring out that he'd timed walking the dog so he could watch me undress. And then I felt angry. Hidden by the closet door, I quickly dressed and rushed to my room, eager to avoid him, not even brushing my teeth. I just got under the covers and turned off the light. Did he know I heard them outside? Had I looked startled? What would happen now?

It seemed like a really long time before I heard him come inside. He was usually back in the front door the minute I was done getting dressed—right, that made sense. In fact, since when did he even walk

Huey? We used to let him out for a few minutes on his own before bed and then call him in. But tonight FP was staying outside for much longer, and I wondered if he was also avoiding me, and if he was, I was glad for it.

The next night, I thought about just brushing my teeth while he walked the dog instead of getting changed, because what could he say? But I was in the business of pissing him off, and I wanted him to know that I knew what he was up to. So I still changed while he was out but behind the closet door so he couldn't see me. That first night he'd come back in the house before I was even finished, slamming the door and grumbling about there being "too much kids' crap on the front porch."

This went on for a few more nights, and the tension was mounting. On the third night he came in after walking the dog and I was already changed into my nightgown and rinsing out one of Benjamin's old bottles that I'd found under his crib. I heard FP come into the kitchen behind me, but I could tell from his footsteps that he'd stopped halfway across the room. "What are you doing?" he asked, and I knew he was trying to sound casual but didn't feel casual.

"Benjamin's really into throwing his bottle out of the crib lately," I said. "This one looks like it's been there for a few days." There was a long silence, and I focused on the sound of the water running and the hum of the refrigerator. I continued to scrub the glass bottle with a bottle brush, aware of his eyes on me.

"You want to tell me why you're hiding behind the closet door to get changed now?" I hadn't prepared myself for this question, and I didn't have an answer. I just shrugged, not turning around. "I asked you a question," he said. "Look at me when I'm talking to you." I turned around slowly, with the bottle still wet in my hands, daring myself to meet his gaze. "You think I'm spying on you, is that it?" he said. "You think the whole fucking world revolves around you?" The calmness of his voice was scary. I wanted to say something defiant, but I wasn't feeling very brave.

He walked over to the kitchen table and took a toothpick out of the small container that was always there. He leaned against the dryer, and I could tell I was about to get some huge speech. I imagined he'd been whipping this one up for a couple of days, justifying his behavior and trying to figure out how to put a spin on it. He chewed on the toothpick for a while, and it pissed me off to no end that I didn't have the nerve to walk away.

"Yeah, you only think about yourself," he finally said. "You've been walking around here like a selfish little bitch, like you're doing us some big favor. Do you even care about your mother? Do you think Jessie would be proud of how you're acting right now, all high and mighty like you have somewhere better to be? She'd be disgusted with you. This is where you belong, and this is where you're going to be staying. You have a lot of growing up to do, you know that? You think you know it all, but you don't know shit. You're still just a stupid kid. You manipulate everyone in this household, stir up shit, and cause problems for all of us."

My anger was mounting, but I was keeping it together.

"Did you go out with a lot of boys while you were in Dover? Huh? Sneaking around behind Granny's back? Thinking you're so smart because you can trick an old lady? Well, I have news for you—Granny doesn't care about you. She thinks you're a spoiled brat, just like we all do. She doesn't want you there—she's just doing what we tell her to do because she wants the money we give her."

He continued droning on and on and I wasn't listening anymore, feeling trapped by his voice. I was so sick of his voice. I was so angry at myself that I was back here, listening to his bullshit. Now he was going on about Jessie. "Don't think I forgot that she kicked you out," he said. "She doesn't care about you anymore. I mean, obviously you're never going back there—look at you. She wouldn't want you anyway. She wouldn't like what you've turned into."

And with that, I snapped. I screamed, "Shut up! Just shut the fuck up!" and before I knew what I was doing, I threw the bottle at him as hard as I could and was very surprised when it actually hit him in the shoulder. I watched his face go from shock to rage as he charged across the room at me. I instinctively put both my arms up and he grabbed them hard, hissing, "Who the fuck do you think you are?" inches from my face. I kicked him in the shin and managed to get one hand free, clawing at him like a wild animal. He got my arm in his grip again for a second, and we had an oddly quiet but intense struggle, just grunts and gasps, until he threw my arms back at me, leaving a long scratch on one of them. I was out of breath, looking down as blood oozed out of the scratch.

Down the hall, Julie started crying. FP shook his head. "You fucking woke up the baby." He started to walk away and then turned to say, "You're pathetic, you know that? I'm sending you back to Granny's. We don't want your bullshit here. You're beyond hope."

As he stormed out of the room, I looked at my arm, watching the blood trickle to my elbow, and then licked it off triumphantly. I'd definitely won this round.

Miraculously, he took me to Granny's the next day. This time he was not chatty and cheerful—in fact, he barely said a word. He didn't come in; he didn't even turn the car off. He got out to put my suitcase in Granny's driveway, then got in the car and drove off without saying goodbye. Good. He hadn't said he would come to visit or said anything about the future, and I dared to believe that I would never see his face again.

That was September, and he did completely leave me alone, but in October he kicked my mother out, and Mom, Annalee, Benjamin, and Julie all came to live at Granny's with me.

CHAPTER 43

BUT OF COURSE HE WASN'T GOING TO LET GO OF HIS SON, AND most weekends Mom would meet him in a motel somewhere near Granny's and take Julie and Benjamin with her, sometimes coming back with only Julie, and always looking exhausted and terrorized. I was sleeping over at a friend's house one night when apparently he showed up and got in a screaming fight with my mother, choking her in front of Granny and the kids. Horrified, Granny called the police and promptly got a restraining order against him. Now he wasn't allowed within fifty feet of her house or he'd be arrested and put in jail. Hooray for Granny! For the first time ever, I felt safe from him and happy that he was finally on record as a violent man. As horrible as it must have been for Granny to see it firsthand, now she knew the truth about what we'd all been living with. Well, enough of it to have her on our side, anyway. True to form, she never brought it up again, and I never knew if she thought that was the first time he was violent, but it didn't matter—he was away and the law said he had to stay away and that was enough for me.

The house was crowded, and Mom was constantly on edge, trying to find a job and figure out what was going to happen next. I helped with the kids as much as I could between school and the job I had at Brooks, a clothing store in the nearby Rockaway Mall. "I guess he made it pretty clear that it was only you he was interested in, didn't he?" she said to me once, and though that is certainly what it looked like, the resentful tone in her voice pissed me off, and after that I tried to avoid having any conversation with her that wasn't purely practical. In my mind, I'd saved us all. In her mind, I'd ruined her life. But I put my anger at her away, reminding myself that at least we were all safe now.

That lasted about six weeks.

I remember exactly what I was wearing that day, because in the scramble of the chaotic household that morning Granny had said, in her vaguely Victorian warble that sometimes cut to the bone, "Honestly, you look more like you're going to a party than going to high school." And though I knew this was pretty much her way of calling me a slut, I also thought, "I *do* look good, she's right." Because Granny's house was always full of notions—that is to say, buttons, snaps, zippers, and ribbons of all widths and textures—I'd recently become stylistically obsessed with a spool of very thin dark-pink velvet ribbon and wore a piece of it around my neck like a choker, tied with a tiny bow that took forever to get right. On this particular day I was wearing a skirt she'd help me make, and I'd gone so far as to put a tiny bow around my ankle too. I was wearing a fuzzy pink sweater, which I'd modified by cutting the cowl neck off, and delightfully high-heeled shoes. Being allowed to wear makeup and to dress pretty much however I wanted was so thrilling to me.

That afternoon I got home from school at the usual time and immediately turned on the TV to catch Martha Quinn on MTV, stepping over the kids' toys and flinging myself into Granny's chair, a stolen luxury since she was still at work. Julie was sitting on a blanket nearby, propped up between two pillows to keep her upright, and she waved a troll doll at me by way of a greeting. I got out of the chair and scooped her up, putting her in my lap, my eyes now glued to the screen to watch the video for "Do They Know It's Christmas" for the millionth time. Benjamin ambled into the room and presented me with what sounded like some very earnest questions, but they were in words only he understood. "Shhh!" I said, pointing to the screen. "It's the best part!" Boy George's mournful "oh, oh, oh," came just after Bono's questionable lyric "Tonight, thank God it's them instead of you," and the kids were transfixed. I sang along with each artist as they came on, and Benjamin clapped his hands.

Mom came into the room with her purse over one shoulder and keys in hand, briefly stopping to look at the TV. "I see we're watching *educational* TV," she said disdainfully, and then, "Watch the kids while I go to Pathmark—Annalee is across the street at the Bests' until dinnertime. Julie's probably in the market for a diaper change." She was out the door.

I waited until Martha Quinn's show was over before I picked up Julie and brought her into the bedroom to change her. "Come on Boolie Boo, you saggy butt," I said. "Come on, Anjin San," I said to Benjamin, and grabbed his hand. I dropped Julie down on the bed from slightly high up, which always made her giggle with glee as she landed. "But first we gotta hear my song!"

Julie sat up quizzically on the bed as I went over to my beloved boom box and rewound the well-worn recording I'd made of Billy Idol's "Eyes Without a Face." "It's so good," I murmured to myself, changing Julie as I sang to her. "It's easy to deceive, it's easy to tease, but hard to get release . . ." I dumped the dirty diaper into the diaper pail and scooped her up, dancing around to the song with her on my hip. Benjamin stood with his feet firmly planted on the ground, shaking his own diapered butt to the music. I cranked up the song as loud as it would go and sang at top volume into Julie's pudgy fist like a microphone.

"Turn that shit off," I heard over the din, and we all whipped our heads around to see FP standing in the doorway, appearing out of nowhere. My stomach dropped. He was supposed to be far away in New York; he wasn't allowed in this house, but there he was, his face tight with controlled rage.

Benjamin recovered from being startled and broke into a big goofy smile, raising his arms to be picked up. When his father scooped him up roughly and strode across the room to the boom box, Benjamin's smile faded as he felt the tension. A few days before, Benjamin had been eating gleefully in his high chair when he accidentally overturned his bowl of Cheerios and then burst into tears. I couldn't help thinking at the time, knowing his father, that this little guy had already come to fear FP's volatile nature, and nothing made his father more volatile than things not being just so.

FP jabbed at the STOP button, and the room was now stunningly silent.

"I don't want you rotting my kids' brains with this music," he snarled. My heart pounded. He sat down on the bed, shaking his head. "This bullshit has gone on long enough," he said. "It's time for you all to come home. For good this time."

Waves of panic washed over me. How long had he been standing there? Had he been lurking down the street, making sure there were no cars in the driveway, planning this ambush? "Where's your mother?" he asked. I barely got out the words "grocery store" before he said, "Well, start packing up your stuff. We're leaving as soon as she gets back, before Granny and Dennis get home. Where the fuck is Annalee?"

My mind raced. There was no way in *hell* I was going back, but how would I get out of this? Granny wouldn't be home for a couple more hours, and I knew if I could stall, he wouldn't dare still be in the house when she got here, because she would not miss a beat before she called the cops. I mustered all the normalcy I could, pretending not to be terrified, and said, "Well, I have to go to work at four," which was a lie.

"You're quitting that job," he said, "so there's no point in going. It's all over." Think fast, think fast.

"But today's the day I pick up my paycheck," I said. I didn't have a plan; I just needed to get away from him and think of one.

"What time are you done?" he asked. I told him I'd be done at seven, and he said, "OK, well, pack up now, and I will take you to the mall, come back here to get everyone loaded into the car, and we'll pick you up and drive to Garrison when you're done at work." All I could think was that I did *not* want to get into his car. He might drive straight to Garrison or, worse, leave Mom and Annalee behind and drive us to God knows where.

"Pack—everything?" I asked. He was already across the room,

yanking a dresser drawer open. He looked into the messy drawer of kids' clothes and recoiled slightly, putting Benjamin down, keeping his eyes on the disarray.

"Your mother is such a slob," he said, and gathered up all the clothes, putting them on the bed. He sat down and got to work folding them meticulously, deeply focused, making perfect piles. He picked up a yellow onesie. "Where did this come from?" he demanded. "Who gave her this?" It came as no surprise to me that he knew every item of the kids' clothing and that an unfamiliar onesie now threatened to be the thing that turned his controlled determination into violence. When I told him that it was a present from a neighbor, he nodded, taking this in, laying the onesie flat on the bed and smoothing it out before he started folding the tiny sleeves in. He looked up at me and smiled— relaxed, but not relaxed at all. "She's making friends with the neighbors, that's nice." I averted my eyes from his hands, with their chewed-to-the-quick nails and calluses from construction. They made me feel sick.

"You know, I've been thinking—it doesn't really make sense for you to go to college right after high school. The kids are still going to be really little, and we're going to need you to help out. You can wait a year or two, I think."

"Oh no oh no oh no" was all that ran through my head. But I stayed calm, reassuring myself that he couldn't do that to me, that I'd be eighteen when I graduated from high school and I could do whatever I wanted. Why was I even surprised? Still, I felt sickened by the idea that he was going to try to keep me stuck with them forever and angry that he thought I was weak enough to ever let that happen.

My thoughts were fracturing in so many directions; it felt like I was out of breath. Should I find a way to sneak to the bathroom and take off my makeup? It would be a matter of minutes before he noticed and it set him off. How long had Mom been gone? When she came back, would she go willingly? Fuck that. It didn't matter what she did, I wasn't going. Absolutely not. No matter what. I realized I was just standing there, frozen in place. But I couldn't show fear. He was distracted now, completely focused on the psychotic folding of clothes—

could I slip out the front door and go down the path through the woods to my friend Jennifer's? But it was a steep hill, and I wasn't sure I could do it quickly enough in these heels. What was I going to do when I got to the mall?

I could call the police—after all, he was breaking the law by coming to Granny's house. But Annalee had recently told me a story that made me less inclined to do that. She told me that sometime during the months after I'd been living at Granny's, one of her third-grade class-mates had reported seeing bruises on her, and Child Protective Ser-vices had come to the house. They'd called ahead to say they were coming, and FP had hissed instructions to her about what she needed to say to them. The social workers asked her a few questions and left, and the only thing that changed afterward was that he made sure the belt buckle didn't leave marks when he beat her. I didn't have a lot of faith in the cops. Granny had called them and gotten a restraining order, but it obviously meant nothing, because here he was, standing a few feet away from me.

I could call Brian. I would call Brian and he would come get me. But what if he wasn't home?

"Where does Bess keep the suitcases?" he asked, his voice almost cheery. I snapped out of it and opened the closet door, trying to reach the suitcases off a high shelf but not quite able to. He came up from behind me, grasping them over my head, forcing me to contort slightly to get out from under his arm. My skin crawled as I unwillingly brushed against him and smelled his Paco Rabanne cologne. Why was he wearing cologne? That was usually reserved for the rare times he and Mom went out to dinner or for some special occasion. I guess this was a special occasion to him.

I pulled my own suitcase from under the bed, knowing I would have to go through the motions of packing, buying myself time. I had one goal in mind: Get away from this man. Don't rile him up; don't show fear—in fact, don't show any emotions at all. I saw a pair of my sneakers and quickly slipped off my high heels, hiding them under the bed. I grabbed the sneakers and a pair of jeans. "I'm going to go change," I said, and headed toward the bathroom.

Behind the closed bathroom door, my hands were shaking as I turned on the faucet. I lathered my face and watched the mascara and eyeshadow form soapy dark circles around my eyes. "Ugh, I can't believe everyone in the mall is going to see me without makeup," I thought, for a moment letting this be the most distressing thing in my near future. I hoped Dani, the bitchy girl who worked at the Orange Julius across from Brooks and was always throwing dirty looks at me, wouldn't be working.

When I came out of the bathroom, FP was putting on the kids' coats. "We better hustle if you're going to be on time," he said. OK, so he was buying my lie, and the fact that he was taking the kids felt like an assurance that he wasn't going to kidnap me. I'd just realized there was a glaring hole in my fiction: If I was really about to leave for work, who was going to watch the babies? I was waiting for him to ask this, my mind racing with possible answers, but so far he hadn't put two and two together.

"I'm going to go across the street and tell Annalee where we're going," I said, hoping my voice didn't sound shaky. He cut me off with a scoff.

"No, you're not," he said calmly, not looking up as he roughly jammed a woolly hat over Benjamin's head. He might really be taking me to work, but he wasn't going to let me out of his sight before then. The mall was only a ten-minute drive away, and Annalee wasn't coming home until dinnertime, but it still seemed mean not to let her know. Plus, I wanted someone in the world to be aware that I was getting into his car. I was happy at least that she wasn't here to see this—she would have been as terrified as I was.

I felt nauseous climbing into his big blue Suburban. I didn't want to touch anything that he'd touched. I sat up as straight as possible so my back wouldn't touch the seat. It just made me feel better to do that.

"It's ten minutes," I told myself. "Just ten minutes, and then you will never be in this car again." I squashed the voice that wanted to remind me how many times I'd thought I'd seen the last of him. I nodded and smiled at whatever he was saying while he drove—I knew from experience that he could easily smash your face with his right hand while continuing to drive steadily with the left one.

As he pulled up to the entrance of the mall, I turned to the babies in the back seat and waved to them, saying, "Bye-bye. Bye-bye." They smiled and flailed their little arms around. I jumped out. "Be right here at seven," he said. I nodded and slammed the heavy door shut. I wanted to run toward the glass doors, but I walked calmly. I could hear that he hadn't driven away yet. I wanted to turn around and look at him one last time, because I'd promised myself this was really it. No matter what it took. Specifically, I'd promised myself if I ever had to be in the same room as him again, I would kill him or die trying.

Once I was safely inside, I ran to the escalator and took the moving stairs two at a time. I raced over to Brooks and found my manager, Colleen, standing at the entrance, looking very bored in her giant FRANKIE SAY RELAX T-shirt. "Colleen, hey—can I use the phone in the stockroom?" I asked, out of breath.

"Yeah, sure thing," she said, looking concerned for a millisecond and then going back to being bored. I rushed through the racks of oversized neon T-shirts as Wham!'s "Last Christmas" played over the sound system for the one millionth time. I heard Colleen call out, "Bettah not be long distance!" just as the door to the stockroom slammed shut.

Cramped among tall stacks of boxes, I called Brian, surprised that once I started talking, I began to cry hysterically. Brian had come to visit me a couple of times, and we'd kissed once on Granny's stoop, and now I guess he was my boyfriend, though we hadn't exactly said that yet. He knew some of what had been happening with my family—but not everything. I talked about the violence and how FP had "tried things," but I left that part vague, because it was just too hard to talk about and I didn't want Brian to judge me for putting up with it for as long as I had. "Call me back in half an hour," Brian said, his voice full of conviction. I called my friend Jennifer and asked if I could spend the night at her house, and could she get her older sister to come get me? I knew FP would be at the mall at seven, and I didn't want to be anywhere near here.

She said yes, and when I got to her house, I called Brian back. "I talked to my dad," he said, "and he said you can come stay with us. For as long as you want. I could come get you right now." I could hardly believe what he was saying.

"But—you're going back to college after the break—"

"Doesn't matter. You'll still be welcome to stay. I'll visit on weekends."

"OK, OK. Wow, that's amazing. That's totally amazing. I mean, your dad doesn't even know me."

"Well, he feels like he does because I talk about you all the time," Brian said, and I smiled to myself and thought I was the luckiest girl who ever lived. I told him I would call him later but that I wanted to say goodbye to everyone properly and get my stuff. FP was probably already waiting for me in the mall parking lot, because Granny would be home by now. Or was he? God, I hoped Mom and the kids weren't in the car with him. I called Granny's house and told her what had happened. "Oh, for heaven's sake!" she said when I told her FP had been in her house. That was Granny's way of saying, "Are you fucking kidding me?" Then she said, "I don't know when your mother was planning to tell me any of that, but she and the kids are here, and if they're going somewhere, it's news to me."

Mom had stood up to him? That was so hard to imagine. I wondered how long they'd waited in the mall parking lot, if there had been a fight, if they'd eventually come looking for me inside. Or maybe Mom had refused to get in the car in the first place? Whatever. None of it was my problem anymore. I was leaving! I was really and truly getting away from this family for good.

CHAPTER 44

"OK, WELL, CAN'T YOU JUST STAY FOR CHRISTMAS?" SHE SAID.
"It would mean so much to the kids." We were standing in Granny's
living room, and I glanced over at the giant Christmas tree stuffed
into one corner. I didn't mind Christmas—I didn't grow up with it,
but in the past five years I'd come to really like the whole tree ritual.
I liked the smell and stringing the sparkly lights, and now we had the
makings of actual "tradition," meaning there were ornaments that
were put away and carted out again for the tree. I'd made tiny red-
and-white felt stocking ornaments that said "Mommy," "Annalee,"
"Granny," "FP," and "Uncle Get Down," and I'd grown fond of a
delicate glass reindeer.

But I'd just told my mother that I was leaving. That Brian was coming to get me and I was leaving her, and all this bullshit, once and for
all. And she was bargaining with me about Christmas. I'd been down
this road before with her, and I wasn't falling for this shit again. Or was
I? I actually laughed—well, scoffed. The bitter, head-shaking scoff of a
middle-aged woman who has seen it all. "Don't be bitter," Jessie once
said to me. "You can't be bitter until you've experienced it all." These
days I could feel a part of me that had hardened, that was indeed bitter,
and I hoped it wasn't there for good.

I thought of that thing I'd been raised to believe about myself, that
I had something to learn and I was going to keep coming back to this

planet until I learned it. One thing I'd learned for sure: My mother was the duchess of denial, inaction, stasis, wait and see, and the path of least resistance. I would never never never be like her, and I would never again suffer because of who she was and the choices she made. She wasn't going to get me this time. I thought of this billboard we'd drive by all the time—an ad for a dentist, which showed a close-up of a mouth with many missing teeth, the remaining ones discolored and on their way out. It simply read, in a foreboding font, IGNORE YOUR TEETH AND THEY WILL GO AWAY. I thought this was very clever and pretty much summed up my mother's approach to life.

But, in a fit of perversity, I agreed to stay through Christmas, which was in a week. I think I wanted to give her a false sense of hope, to get back at her for the way she strung me along five years ago when I begged her to let me go home and cried myself to sleep every night and she said things like "Well, just let me know when you know . . ." She could trick eleven-year-old Guinevere, but sixteen-year-old Guinevere had learned how to play the game. And what was one more week anyway? I'd finally found a way out, a real and permanent way out, and I was experiencing a buoyancy I'd never felt before. I was the captain of my fate at last.

Besides, I had one more week of my job at the mall and was really enjoying how good I'd gotten at shoplifting. As much as I was excited for my new life, one that would not include violence, mindfuckery, or forced sexual contact, I felt worried for my mom and the fact that she had no money and three small kids and needed to get a new job. So I had begun to amass quite the professional wardrobe for her upcoming job interviews, and I was planning to give it all to her for Christmas. I genuinely wanted her to have it, yes, but I also wanted to watch her open present after present, because she'd know full well there was no way I could actually afford these clothes with my part-time minimum-wage job. I would take a perverse pleasure in watching her pretend there was nothing odd or of note about her teenage daughter giving her eight hundred dollars' worth of new clothes. We both knew she only saw what it served her to see.

By this point, I'd acknowledged to myself that the shoplifting wasn't just about having free stuff—the getting away with it had become quite the high. After working in the mall for three months, I'd learned how the security systems worked in most of the stores. Plus, the manual I'd been given when I started at Brooks had a small section on how to spot a shoplifter, so I'd developed several strategies based on what I learned there.

1. Have a shopping bag from another mall store, and have stuff in it. (I'd bring this bag from home.) This says, "I can afford things." 2. Put the things you steal into this bag. 3. If you feel like an employee has their eye on you, talk to them. I'd walk right up to that person who thought it wasn't obvious that they were lurking behind a coat rack and ask for the time. It somehow worked—they would inevitably get flustered, tell me the time, and then walk back to the register as if they were actually the guilty party. Sometimes I would engage them further, letting them know I worked at Brooks on Level 2, or holding a jacket up to my body and asking, "Do you think the blue one looks good on me?" 4. In 1984, almost every store's security system was simply an invisible laser/line at the entrance that would go off if you walked out with those bulky plastic tag things still on the clothes. It was always at about waist level. I'd pretend to yawn and stretch as I walked out, raising the bag over my head. Or, when I was feeling extra cheeky, I'd wave a cheerful "bye, thank you!" with the hand that was holding the bag full of ill-gotten booty. I'd stolen Brooks's machine that removed the security tag a few weeks ago. Part of me felt pleased too: "Look at me, with a shoplifting problem and a rapidly developing eating disorder." I was almost a normal teenager.

On Christmas morning, I felt a kind of happy I'd never felt before. Brian was coming the next day, and it was on to a new chapter. Granny was, as always, the first one up. Her waist-length silver hair, which was usually in a prim bun, was in a loose braid draped over one of her shoulders, and she was still wearing her nightgown. This felt like her saying, "I was a kid on Christmas morning once too," and she sat in her chair, watching us open presents with a twinkle in her eye.

Annalee was almost ten, Benjamin was one and a half, and Julie was four months old. Benjamin banged his new fire truck on the ground; Julie was busy chewing the eyes off a pink stuffed giraffe. "Mom," I asked as I watched them with their gifts, "do you have to give Benjamin such boy things and Julie such girl things? They're not even old enough to tell you what they want." Annalee played with a Spirograph set nearby.

"They are babies," said Mom. "I can't help if he likes boy stuff and she likes girl stuff. What do you want me to do, give them presents they will hate?" They did look happy. I felt a pang of how I would miss them and silently resolved to help Mom get away from FP once and for all, when I was situated safely at Brian's and back in school.

As she opened present after present from me—blouses, suit jackets, and scarves, all suitable for a professional setting—she went from thankful to surprised to alarmed. She was starting to look anxious when I handed her the tenth wrapped present, and she said, "Oh my, there's more?" The gift was a cream-colored silk blouse—I'd saved the fanciest for last—and she didn't even hold this one up to show everyone. She peered at the label on the neck and murmured, "How did you—" and glanced up at me. I was staring directly at her, hoping my expression said, "You know damn well how." Our eyes locked for a moment, and she looked pained. "Thank you," she said finally, and Annalee said, "My present for Mom next!" grabbing it from under the tree and scooting over to hand it to Mom.

The next morning I packed up everything I had at Granny's, which fit into two giant suitcases. I made a point of taking every single thing, even a pair of socks I didn't really like, to underline the fact that *I was not coming back*. I paced around in the living room, my suitcases by the door, looking out the bay window that faced Summer Avenue, pressing my face against the glass to see as far up the street as I could, waiting for Brian in his dad's white Ford Taurus. Mom was cleaning the kitchen, chatty and acting as if this was any other day.

My heart leapt a little when Brian finally pulled into the driveway. I mean, I *really* liked him, and we'd kissed, but I was about to move in with him and his family. And he was in college, so I was essentially about to move in with his father and his brother, two adult men I didn't know at all. After several years of choosing the devil I knew, I had decided to gamble on people who were potentially just new devils.

I'd told Brian on the phone the night before that I wanted him to just come get me—no hanging out, no long goodbyes. I had this instinct that if we faltered in any way, lost momentum at all, I'd be somehow sucked into a vortex or tricked into staying. I let him in the door, hugged him awkwardly because Mom was standing right there, and he politely said hello and then grabbed my suitcases to load them in the car. Mom was in the living room now, and her voice had gone a bit high and strained.

"Well," she said, "have fun." She gave me a hug then, stiffly and with a couple of pats on my back, which was totally strange. Did she know this was really it? When she pulled away, she put on a cheery smile and said, "I'll see you in two weeks." Remarkable. I didn't know if she was insane—like, did she hear when I said in no uncertain terms that I was never coming back—or if was she messing with me—like she knew something that I didn't. Or was she coping the only way she could think of in the moment, which was to pretend this wasn't happening? That sounded about right. But I said nothing, again fearing some kind of trap.

So all I said was "OK, Mom . . ." trying not to sound sarcastic. "She's not going to get it until it happens," I thought. "Just go go go go go."

"Call me when you get there," she said wistfully. I took satisfaction in knowing that I wouldn't. I hugged the kids and got in the car with Brian, and I was deliriously happy, if a little anxious.

In the car on the hour-long drive, Brian cranked up Steely Dan's *Gaucho*, drumming along to it on the steering wheel and occasionally using my knee as a hi-hat. "Fucking Purdie, man," he whispered reverently as the strains of "Babylon Sisters" began, referring to the drummer. Brian was always very attentive and thoughtful, unless a drummer he admired was playing, and then he'd get totally lost in the music. I didn't mind at all right now—he was avoiding the gravity of the moment, blasting the song, and I was free to watch the world go by out the window and really feel what was happening.

It had been five years of clawing my way out and away from these people, and I was finally free. I barely allowed myself to believe it.

CHAPTER 45

LLOYD SPEARS, BRIAN'S DAD, WAS A SIXTY-FIVE-YEAR-OLD retired Air Force guy who now drove the O'Neill High School bus. He was tall, round of belly from the whiskey he drank nightly, and hilarious. He had many dad jokes and loved to play David Bowie's "Golden Years" on the record player in the dining room, dramatically poking his head through the swinging door that connected to the kitchen to lip-synch to the "Come, b–b–b-baby" part. When you said goodbye to him, he'd say, "Abyssinia," with a casual send-off salute, and then pause, finger raised in the air, and ask, by way of quizzing you, "Which is now . . . ?" and you had to say, "Ethiopia." He had a way of being very serious but not serious at all. I soon realized that he didn't say much that wasn't a well-trod joke, and I found it delightful.

The afternoon when Brian and I arrived at his house, Lloyd was in the kitchen, wearing an apron that strained a bit over his belly, chopping vegetables, and organizing them around a piece of meat in a pan on the counter. He put out his substantial hand to shake mine and said, "Welcome. You stay as long as you want," then bowed to me as if I were some kind of duchess, sweeping one arm out, gesturing to his humble abode. He was a formidable man, quite tall and ruddy in the face, with close-cropped hair from his days in the military. But he had such a kind face, and though his words were brief, they felt sincere.

I was instantly in love with the house. It had a giant kitchen, grand dining room with a twelve-seat table, living room with a fireplace, and three bedrooms upstairs, plus a hangout room they called the family room, which is where the TV was. This was much closer to the houses I'd grown up in within the communities—enough space, beautiful things, an inviting front porch that looked out over a pond.

Brian took me upstairs to show me what would be my room—it was his sister Larraine's room, but she was in her twenties and lived with her boyfriend. As we walked down the hall, he pointed to a closed door, his voice lowered. "My brother Mike's in there. He's working nights, so we won't see him till dinner. You'll like him. He's a good egg." I followed him to Larraine's room, and he put my suitcases and banjo down and opened the closet door. "Dad made some space for you here—Larraine probably won't like it, but she's always mad about something. She's coming over for dinner tonight to get a look at you, but ignore her. She'll probably be annoying."

He opened a couple of dresser drawers to show me they were empty. I was nodding, taking it all in, and then we both stood there awkwardly. Did I just move in with my boyfriend at the ripe old age of sixteen? Were we kind of like brother and sister, or was it obvious that we would have sex now that I lived with him? I was a virgin, though I was pretty sure most virgins my age hadn't had the same experiences I'd had. Anyway, I wanted to have sex with him. I was in love with him for sure, but I also wanted to do it as a way of erasing everything that had happened before.

He opened his arms for a hug and told me he was going to hang with his dad and to come down whenever I felt like it.

I sat on the high twin four-poster bed with its elaborately carved posts and looked out the window. This small but lovely corner room also overlooked Roe Pond, with similar houses visible on the other side.

The room was still hers, however, and boasted the odd combination I'd become familiar with having gone to school with military kids. A black-light Lynyrd Skynyrd poster hung over an antique Austrian dresser, and a framed photograph of Lloyd as a young man in full Air Force uniform sat on top of it.

Was I really going to be a normal teenager now, who got to hang out with people and go to parties and do whatever she wanted? It was Christmas break, and I'd be back at my old high school in two weeks. I heaved a huge sigh of relief. FP probably knew that I was across the river from Garrison in Highland Falls, where Brian lived, but he didn't know exactly where the house was, and he wouldn't be able to get it out of Mom, because she didn't know the address either. Was it possible that I might never have to see his face again?

I heard someone coming up the stairs, and Lloyd appeared in the doorway, holding a stack of fresh towels. "Got these for ya," he said. "A lady should have her own towels, don't you think?" I smiled and nodded, overwhelmed by the sweetness of the gesture. "I'm putting them out here in the hall closet. They're the light-blue ones, and I won't let these grubby boys touch them. How do you like them apples?"

"Thank you," I managed to say. He gave a curt and comical nod of his head. "I hope you like overcooked pot roast, because that's what I'm overcooking," he said. "Dinner at five-thirty. Dress is casual." He winked at me and walked down the hall.

I spent the first week in Brian's house in utter bliss. Since Lloyd was a school-bus driver, he also had the time off. He cooked breakfast, lunch, and dinner for us and even fought us on doing the dishes. At night we'd hang out with Brian's friends in the basement of the house, which he'd set up as a kind of rec room—his drum set in one corner, a ratty couch, a record player. We drank beers, watched *Spinal Tap* over and over, and made out until the wee hours after his friends left. Brian's parents were divorced but good friends, and his mother, Hermine, came to visit from Austria. They had a family New Year's Eve tradition of making cheese fondue around the fire in the living room in an elaborate fondue set from Hermine's home country. We were even allowed to put Kahlúa in our hot cocoa. That night, Lloyd leaned in to me and, as an aside, said, "You should probably call me Dad. Everyone else around here does, so it's the best way to get my attention." Dad! I'd never called anyone Dad before. It was exciting.

But the next week Brian had to go back to college, and once it was just Lloyd and me in the house, with Mike asleep all day, I decided I should call my mother. The two weeks she'd pretended I'd be away were almost over, and as much as I wanted to scare her and not be in touch, I didn't want to scare Granny and Annalee and create more drama—I just wanted a smooth transition out. School was starting up again in a couple of days, and I was already planning the outfit I would wear for my triumphant return and daydreaming about what it would be like to be allowed to do whatever I wanted. It was the second half of my junior year of high school, and it was going to be glorious.

I pulled the phone over to the window seat in the family room and settled in, dialing Granny's number. Mom answered after the first ring, and when I said, "Hi, Mom," she said, "Hello, there you are. How's everything at Brian's?" I told her about the house and how I had my own room and how Lloyd was very nice.

"So Brian's gonna give you a ride back this weekend, or do you need me to come get you?" she asked. She was trying to sound very casual, but I could hear the strain in her voice.

"No, Mom, I'm staying here. Permanently. Like, until I go to college. I'm going back to school at O'Neill on Monday." There was a long pause on the other end before she sighed deeply.

"Actually, you can't."

"What? Yes, I can. Mom, I tried to tell you. I'm not coming back there. I'm never ever coming back there."

"In order for you to go to school in New York, I need to sign a piece of paper that gives you permission. It's across state lines, and that's the law. I'm your legal guardian and I live in New Jersey."

I tried to remain calm at this news, digging my fingernails into my palm to keep my voice steady. "OK, so can you do that, please?" It had never occurred to me that returning to my old high school would require anything but me showing up.

"No, I'm not going to do that. You belong here with your family, not with some strangers. Enough of this already. I need you to help out with the kids. I'm going to start work soon, and I can't afford to have them in daycare from morning to night."

Didn't she want at least one of us to be free? Or was she doing this because FP was somehow coercing her into it? Because I'm sure she

told him, and I'm sure it boiled his blood that there was simply nothing he could do about it—I'd finally be out of his reach.

But what my mother hadn't bargained for was that I was willing to
never go to school again if that's what it came to. I'd rather wait till I
was eighteen and go back to high school then, even though I'd be in
the same class as the kids who were freshmen now. So what. I'd figure
it out. I also knew my mother well enough to know she wouldn't be
able to live with the idea of having a daughter who was a high school
dropout, just for her own ego. It might make her look like a bad parent.

For three torturous weeks I didn't go to school, rattling around in
the house all day, restless, anxious, unable to focus on even reading a
book. I listened to Phil Collins's song "In the Air Tonight" over and
over, the perfect soundtrack for my rage-fueled determination. I'd
jump when the phone rang, hoping it was my mother finally giving in,
but she didn't call, and I didn't call her. "Just fucking let me go," I
seethed to myself. "I found a way out." And sometimes my thoughts
were more like prayer: "Please, I'm begging you, let me go." The afternoon my friends called to tell me that the induction ceremony for the
National Honor Society had happened, I ached with the loss. I'd been
working hard since freshman year to achieve excellence in "scholar-
ship, leadership, service, and character," and I knew I would have been
on that stage with them. The Honor Society gave out college scholar-
ships, and even if you didn't get one, it still looked great on your college
application. But you couldn't go to college if you didn't graduate from
high school, and that was starting to seem like a real possibility.

Then one Saturday morning, the phone rang and Lloyd answered
it. Brian was visiting from college, and we were upstairs in the family
room, listening to the latest record from his favorite band, Marillion,
sprawled on the foldout couch where we'd slept, still open and unmade
from the night before.

"Kids? Everyone? Come down to the kitchen right now, please,"
Lloyd called out. He sounded uncharacteristically serious. Mike was
still asleep, but Larraine had come over for breakfast, and when we all
gathered around the kitchen table, Lloyd said, "That was the police on
the phone. They are on their way over to take you back to your mother."

She fucking called the cops? What was her problem? All the times she should have called the cops, all the horrors we'd been through, and this was when she finally decided to make that move?

I looked at Brian. "What do I do? Should I hide?"

"No, kiddo," said Lloyd, his voice reassuring. "We'll get through this."

A few minutes later there was a knock on the door, and Lloyd let the two uniformed officers in. "Hiya, Ken, come on into the kitchen," I heard him say, and felt a little relief that he knew one of them.

The two men seemed uncomfortable as they came in, declining Lloyd's offer of coffee. The one named Ken looked at me and said, "Are you the minor in question?" He glanced down at his notebook. "You're Guinevere?" I nodded, gripping the side of my chair so hard it hurt my hand.

"You want to tell us why you ran away from home?" he asked. Lloyd was standing near me and put a comforting hand on my shoulder. I took a deep breath. This was it. I had to lay it all out in no uncertain terms or I'd be taken away. I'd never said any of it out loud before. I wasn't even sure I had the words. Somehow it had all come to this: I had to give what he did to me a name and say it out loud to strangers if I wanted to be free of him.

"There is a man—not my mother's husband, but they have two kids together—and he beats my mother and my sister." I had to say the rest. I didn't want to make it real by saying it out loud, but I had to. "And me too," I continued, my voice barely above a whisper. "He beats me too, but only if I don't do sexual things with him. It's been like this since I was twelve."

The officer's eyes widened, and he shifted his weight from one foot to the other, glancing over at his partner. He had a pained expression on his face as he put his notebook in his back pocket and said, "Well, OK. I'm very sorry to hear that. It doesn't sound like home is a safe place for you."

I was staring down at the knots in the wood of the kitchen table, tracing the swirls around and around with my eyes, barely able to process what he was saying. Everyone around me was completely still. The officer cleared his throat.

"But I'm sorry to tell you the law says you have to be with your legal guardian until you either go through the process of emancipating yourself, which takes some time, or you turn eighteen, so you're going to have to come with us."

"I'm going to be her legal guardian," Lloyd said, out of nowhere. "I'm working on that right now." This was the first I was hearing of it. "Just give the kid a break and let her stay here until I sort that out, won't you? It'll probably only take a couple more days." My eyes welled up with tears of gratitude as I anxiously studied the officer's face.

"All right, Lloyd, yeah, we can do that." He shook Lloyd's hand, saying, "You folks have a good rest of your day," and Lloyd walked them to the door.

I jumped up and hugged Brian, tears streaming down my face. Lloyd came in then and I hugged him too, resting my head on his barrel chest, at a loss for words.

"I kinda made up the legal-guardian thing on the spot," he said, deadpan, and after we all laughed about it for a long time, he said, "But I will do that. I won't let them take you back there."

Later that day, my mother called to say she would sign the document that would allow me to go to school in Highland Falls, and I was finally, finally free.

On Monday morning when I got on the school bus, Lloyd swung the doors open for me. As I climbed the stairs, he simply gave me a small nod and I nodded back, barely restraining a smile, and walked past him to take my seat.

CHAPTER 46

A YEAR LATER I WAS SITTING ON THE STAGE OF THE HIGH
school auditorium, posing for the Honor Society group photo. I had
everything I'd dreamed of now that I lived with Lloyd. I was the editor
of the school newspaper, had performed in three plays, and had been
on a trip to Europe with Brian over the summer, which I paid for with
my two jobs and the help of his mother, who we visited in Wiesbaden,
Germany.

One of my jobs was at the new McDonald's (big news in the small
town of Highland Falls), and the other one was at the Thayer Hotel on
West Point, famous because five years earlier it was where the Iran
hostages had stayed when they were released after 444 days in captiv-
ity. I liked that it had this history, but I also liked that, though we were
under legal drinking age, my friend Brigid and I were allowed to serve
bottomless champagne, and we sauntered out to the parking lot every
Sunday afternoon with several bottles of André in the large purses we
brought to work just for this purpose.

At Lloyd's house, when I came downstairs every morning, there
would be the breakfast he'd made for me before he went to work: an
omelet, half a grapefruit, and a glass of orange juice. Either I'd see him
an hour later when I got on the bus, or I'd get a ride to school from one
of my friends. I'd call if I wasn't going to be home for dinner, and other
than that he asked nothing of me. I could stay out as late as I wanted,
but I knew if I was home he'd always be upstairs in the family room,

slowly sipping his drink of choice—a tall glass of Slice soda spiked with Wild Turkey, the neon green of the soda made muddy by the dark whiskey. When I got home—from play rehearsal, from dinner at a friend's house, from an evening McDonald's shift—I'd make sure to come in to where he was and say hello. The conversation would usually go something like "Hi, Dad, just want you to know I'm home." He'd look up from the TV, eyes a little glassy, and say, "The kids are all right?"

"We are all right," I'd say back, and we'd smile at each other and return to our respective evenings. It was like living alone, but not in a lonely way. I knew he was there if I needed him. There was that time I brought two bottles of André to a high school dance, and when the security man at the entrance asked to look at the contents of my bag, I challenged, "Do you have a search warrant?" The man got a bit flustered and confessed that he did not, but my triumph was interrupted by the sound of a cork popping and bubbly spewing through the bottom of my wicker bag onto the paved entryway. I'd taken off the foil for quick access, not realizing that de-foiled corks have only a few minutes before they make their way into the great outdoors. Undaunted by the fact that I wasn't going to be allowed in, I got a bunch of my friends to party in someone's van in the parking lot. The cops came, but with a drunk Lloyd in the back seat of their squad car. He told me the call came in to an officer who was with him at a party, and the cop said, "Hey—isn't this your kid?" When I poured myself into the police car next to him, he put his arm around me, patting my shoulder as we headed home, chuckling to himself. I came down for breakfast the next morning to find an open bottle of Budweiser next to my orange juice and eggs. When I looked up at him, he raised his eyebrows and said, "How ya doing, Car 34?" Car 34 became his nickname for me—the number of the cop car we'd shared.

We never spoke of that day in the kitchen when I had to say all those horrible details out loud to the police. One day Lloyd just took me to an office on West Point where I got my photo taken for a military ID that said LEGAL GUARDIAN: LLOYD SPEARS on it, and that was the end of that.

I wore high heels to school and as much makeup as I wanted, and I charmed the gym teacher out of making me change for gym—he was also the cheerleading coach and Clare was a cheerleader, and that connection meant I was an exception too. I refused to say the Pledge of Allegiance in homeroom (very controversial in a school full of military kids), pretended to be bisexual with my friend Carson (but was pretty sure that only one of us thought it was a joke), and sometimes spent the day slowly sipping peach schnapps out of a McDonald's cup my friends and I had bought at the drive-thru that morning. I discovered T. S. Eliot and Virginia Woolf in my AP English class and wrote impassioned essays for the school paper about important things like the indignity of a new utensil called a spork. I saw the Kinks in concert at West Point and had my first lesson in the price of all those fresh-faced cadets letting you get that great spot in front of them at the show: their hands all over you. I felt very deep when I played the cassette of a new artist named Suzanne Vega on my Walkman. I was voted Most Sophisticated of my senior class. I ate only ice cream at lunch, because it was the easiest thing to puke up a few minutes later. When people asked which character I was from *The Breakfast Club*, I'd say Molly Ringwald, but the truth was I felt like Judd Nelson in a Molly Ringwald costume.

When people in school asked what happened—why had I been away?—I told them my mother had to relocate for work and I wasn't happy there, so she let me come back here to my old high school. I'm pretty sure no one believed this, but by this point I'd learned that people usually didn't want to hear the elaborate, complicated, and uncomfortable truth—they wanted a simple and knowable answer to their question so we could all move on.

For myself, I put the recent past away. To engage with it was to let it ruin how great my life was now. There was a power in its erasure. Being someone else was second nature by now, and I fully inhabited the carefree and busy high school girl I was pretending to be, so much so that I believed she was really who I was. The other girl remained dutifully contained, but some pieces of her seeped through here and there. In the spring of my senior year, the theater at West Point showed the film *E.T.* daily for at least a month. My friend Judie and I would sit in the rear of the mostly empty theater every day after school, crying our eyes out from the minute E.T. is taken away from Elliott until the end of the movie, when E.T. finally has to say goodbye and get onto the spaceship with his people, and we know that he and Elliott will never see each other again. Judie and I never asked each other what we were really sobbing about—the way we went back day after day said it all.

I had been out in the World for nearly seven years, and I had effectively erased any external signs of my "unusual" childhood. I never talked about it at all, which made life so much simpler. I'd learned not to stare, though there were vestiges of the socially unacceptable eye contact: People often thought I was flirting, because I still hadn't quite mastered the Art of Looking Away like a native. Too much eye contact is creepy; just a tiny bit too much eye contact is an invitation, especially if you are a teenage girl. I'd long since stopped bragging about playing the banjo or loving Bing Crosby and the Andrews Sisters, and I'd learned to pretend I'd seen the *Brady Bunch* episode that everyone else was reminiscing about. I'd done it: I was passing as a World Person.

The most important thing to me during this time was the essay I needed to write to apply to college. Guidance counselors advised us that getting into college was now more competitive than ever and said we should highlight our extracurricular activities, goals achieved, obstacles overcome, and what made us stand out.

What made me stand out? I had zero athletic achievements; my extracurricular activities were sparse because I'd been in a prison for half my high school experience. My verbal SAT score was nearly perfect, but my math score was embarrassingly low, which amounted to an unspectacular total number. I wasn't surprised when I got the scores back, because I'd panicked so much on the math section that, halfway through, I asked the fates to tell me if I should fill in the tiny circles next to A, B, or C. The fates, I learned a few weeks later, were also not so good at math.

"What is unique about me?" I thought. "I'm good at word games, and getting good grades, and men always tell me I'm pretty when I walk down the street, which feels like something I'm good at. I'm good at adjusting, I'm good at making new friends, I'm good at being the person I need to be when I meet people—I'm pretty much good at everything but sports and math. Debate team. Essays. Participation. Lemon squares. Turkey tetrazzini. Bargello. Finding four-leaf clovers. Ways of being. Hiding the truth. Making up lies on the spot. Acting like I am perfectly fine when I am crumbling inside."

I'd buried Jessie, Daria, Clotilde, and the fields, houses, and beaches of my childhood deep—I'd had to pretend to be too many other people since then. But it was dawning on me that absolutely no other person applying to college would have my story. Because I was so unaccustomed to talking about my real life, the prospect of writing about it was exceptionally daunting. I hardly knew what it was to me anymore. It was hard to believe that the thing I'd learned to carefully shut away could now be an asset.

I sat at the dining room table in Lloyd's house, compulsively sweeping my hand back and forth over its gleaming varnish, thinking, and what I came up with was that if I didn't talk about the Lyman Family and maybe hint at my struggles to escape my mother and FP, I was just a boring girl who had a vague interest in journalism because I thought Barbara Walters was cool.

Brian was away as always, and I could hear Lloyd upstairs chuckling at the show *Night Court*. I really wanted someone to talk to about this, but I'd barely told either of them anything about the first eleven years of my life, so it didn't seem like an option. I'd pined for the Lyman Family for all these years—why was I hesitating now, when I knew that talking about them might be the thing that got me into college? The answer was that when I pictured the people at colleges reading my essay and being scandalized, or fascinated, it made me cringe. It felt cheap to use my story that way.

In the end, I chose to write about growing up in the Lyman Family, calling it a "commune" (knowing they would only ever call themselves that to World People) and glossing over what happened to me after I left. "It was a challenge to come from being home schooled and enter the sixth grade," I wrote, "but through perseverance and hard work, I am able to be where I am today."

As I anxiously handed the manila envelopes with my applications inside to the mailman a few days later, I had the irrational thought that somehow Jessie or someone in the Family would read what I'd written and think I was a sellout.

Despite my mediocre SAT scores, I was accepted to all four schools I applied to. I assumed I'd made myself stand out with that essay. Before I applied, my mother said she would take me to visit the campuses of Vassar, NYU, and Barnard, with one caveat: I had to apply to Sarah Lawrence. "It was the place I really wanted to go when I was your age," she said, "but Granny wouldn't hear of it. She wanted me to have a practical skill, so I went to Northeastern in Boston to study nursing." When she said this, I realized I'd never thought of my mother having dreams, and for the first time I was seeing how horribly they'd been thwarted. She'd chosen to go to Northeastern University in 1967, where she met some strangers on the street hawking a free alternative newspaper called *The Avatar* around the same time she realized she was pregnant with me, and she had decided to devote herself to a group of people because of it. And that's why I was who I was. The randomness of it truly unnerved me.

Once it was time to decide on a school, I was on the phone with her, sitting in the same place I was when she'd informed me she wasn't going to let me finish high school. When she asked, "So come on, which one are you going to choose?" we'd already been talking about it for over an hour. Vassar was where the women in *The Group* had gone; Barnard just sounded classy; my visit to NYU had scared me a bit— I didn't think I was ready to live in a city in that way. "I feel like I will always wonder what it would have been like if I don't go to Sarah Lawrence," I finally said.

I'd kept the letter Jessie sent me when I was thirteen, reading it and rereading it over the years. "We work at it, striving for inner consciousness, self development on the inside instead of on the outside. This life we live is not for everyone, only if you have Mel inside of you." I didn't know if I "had Mel inside of me"—on the one hand, I did, because life with the Family was who I was, where I was from, an inseparable part of me. On the other hand, I'd gone so far astray and so much time had passed—was I one of them anymore? One thing for sure was that my longing for them never went away, and I kept these words she'd written close to my heart: "I want you to know that you are always welcome here and that everyone misses you."

After I'd decided where I was going to school, I was suddenly consumed with the need to go back and see everyone before I went. I was eighteen now, and for some reason it was very important to me that they knew I'd turned out OK, and that I still cared about them. I wrote to Jessie and her response came a week later, inviting me to visit the Vineyard that summer. I was thrilled and nervous, realizing that part of me hadn't been sure she'd even remember who I was.

CHAPTER 47

When I got to the vineyard, there were hugs, questions, and exclamations about how much I'd grown, but soon I was integrated into the mechanics of the day, helping to prepare for an afternoon at Windy Gates, packing a cooler full of sandwiches and then folding a pile of beach towels still warm from the dryer. I liked that nothing came to a grand halt because I was visiting—it told me that it felt perfectly natural to everyone that I was there. It was fascinating to see everyone: Normalynn and Jackie looked like real grown-up ladies, and babies I once bathed had morphed into raucous little kids. Daria was a bit shy with me at first but warmed up later, saying, "I just didn't know what to expect," and we were soon catching up and laughing as we wandered through some of our favorite spots in the woods. Jessie asked me, "How does it feel to be here?" and the answer was that it felt like an incredible relief. Missing them had been so constant and painful that it had become a part of me, and now that I was here I felt a tight coil inside me relax. I knew I'd never felt like this in Garrison, at Granny's house, at Lloyd's house. I was truly home. These people really knew me. They looked into my eyes and didn't feel the need to look away.

In Jessie's House, a framed photo of their old softball team hung over the kitchen table. As I sat there drinking wine one night with Daria, I noticed something. FP was in the photo, but his face was crudely scratched out. When I asked Daria about it, she laughed. "I was sitting right here when he saw it," she said, "and he just stopped talking and looked away and didn't say a word for a while after." I asked her about his visit all those years ago, and she said, "Oh, it was so awful and weird. No one knew what the fuck he was doing here—he just kind of invited himself and Mommy said yes, but once he got here, she immediately regretted it." I told her how much anguish it had caused me and how he'd made me believe he was welcome here and I wasn't, and she simply said, "What an asshole." I thought about how long I'd been holding on to that pain and how disconcerting it was that a few words from Daria had the power to erase it in a heartbeat.

I was sad when I realized Clotilde wasn't on the Vineyard, and I wondered where she was—if she was even still in the Family—but I was treading lightly, careful not to poke my nose where it wasn't welcome. In fact, I didn't even know if some people still believed that Melvin was alive, and when I was alone with Daria and thought to ask, it felt like a dangerous question, even to her. I hadn't heard anyone speak of him in the present tense, as they did before I left, but I hadn't been here for very long and knew I wouldn't be privy to the important conversations.

One morning after breakfast, I was standing under the plush arch of grapevines near Jessie's House, admiring how grand they had become. I was plucking grapes off the vine and eating them, enjoying how they made my lips itch slightly, just as they had when I was a kid. Jackie came out and said hello with her radiant smile, then asked if I would brush her hair, which still fell luxuriously down to her waist. "I'm trying to wear it down more these days," she said, settling into a wrought-iron chair. "George got pissed at me because he says he loves my hair down and why can't I wear it that way for him?"

As I brushed, she talked about her life and how happy she was, and then we fell silent and there was only the sound of the brush as I pulled it through her wavy locks. After a while, she asked me what I wanted to study in college, and I said I didn't really know yet—something to do with writing, maybe journalism. "You shouldn't go," she said. "You can write here. This is your home; this is where you belong." The soothing way she said it—so calm and sure it was the clear truth—made me want to believe her, and I allowed myself to imagine it.

"Think about it," she said. "If you just come home, you can write whenever you want! You won't have to worry about a job and supporting yourself—you'll never have to work a day in your life again." I gazed across the expanse of lawn that gave way to a hill I'd giddily rolled my body down many times as a kid and over to the shed that I'd rushed toward every time people came back from a fishing trip, eager to collect the perfect scale from each fish so I could glue it into my diary. If I did stay, would I be invited to live here, in the place that held the memories of the happiest I'd ever been?

Jackie wasn't the only person who'd brought up the idea of me staying in the last few days. Someone asked me why I would go to college if I wasn't even sure what I wanted to study, and someone else said, "Just come back for a year—what's the rush? Everybody wants you to be here."

It was hard to sleep that night. I had two more days here, and with every passing minute, the pull to stay grew stronger. Restless, I got out of bed and wandered to the familiar window in the upstairs bedroom where I was sleeping. I remembered that, long, long ago, I'd woken up like this in the middle of the night and looked out this window to see little creatures, smaller than me, made completely of light and glowing as they danced around in a circle. In the moment I'd opened my mouth to speak and wake up some other kids to marvel at what I was seeing, but I was afraid any noise would scare the little creatures away, so I just stood and watched them in awe, closing my eyes and opening them again several times to make sure it wasn't a dream. I still believed I really saw those creatures. This place was magic; of course I did.

I sat down on the ten-foot circular rug in the middle of the room, studying it and noticing how worn it had become. All the girls had started hooking this rug when I was nine, and it took years to finish. At the center, a giant blazing sun of yellows and oranges; around the sun, blue sky with birds and butterflies in it; then green vines crawling all the way around the outer edge. We never had a planned design for the rug—you just made a cloud if you felt like making a cloud and

made a flower on the vine if that's what moved you. That speckled but-
terfly was Samantha's work; Corrina made this patch of dark sky one
night when we were very sad together. We spent hours talking and
laughing around this rug or quietly focused on our little section of it.
There was nothing like this in the rest of my life—objects that told a
long story, objects that would stay in the same place for always.

I had to stay here, didn't I?

I wanted to tell Jessie first, but when I woke up the next morning
she'd been out fishing since dawn. That was OK; she was always back
by dinner. I desperately wanted to tell Daria, but I knew it was important to tell Jessie first—to ask her, really, even though I felt certain she
would say yes. So I went through the hours with a happy secret, amazed
at how much can change in a few days and how important college had
seemed to me and now not at all. I'd been through the trial that was
the world, and I'd found my way home. I laughed at myself for not
seeing this all sooner.

That night after dinner, everyone sat in the living room, drinking
wine and talking, as they usually did. I'd decided I would talk to Jessie
later, when there weren't so many people around, and right now I was
sitting on the floor, looking around the room, feeling a surge of love
and belonging.

At that moment, George, who was seated in a nearby armchair, put
his empty glass in front of me as he was talking. He didn't look at me
or turn my way, just dangled his empty wineglass in front of my face,
the unspoken command being "Get me more wine."

Dutifully, I took the glass and got up to refill it. As I entered the
kitchen, it struck me that most of the women were doing dishes, floating around to refill glasses, or getting the kids ready for bed. Women
served men here. I had been raised that way, of course—but now I was
really seeing it, and panic started to expand inside me, and then sadness. This was exactly the way my mother and FP lived. In fact, this
was the dynamic they had been emulating, and I couldn't return to
anything that felt remotely like the life I'd fought so hard to get away
from. There was no way I could stay.

I suspect that I latched on to the problem of the rigid gender hierarchy because it was easier than facing up to some of the other disturbing truths about them. I didn't think I was better than them, but I knew I could never be happy here. Letting go of that sense of belonging was hard, and I cried when I said my goodbyes. There was no talk of "keep in touch" or "come back soon." We all knew you were either in or out, and I'd chosen people I hadn't even met yet over the family that raised me.

As the melancholy horn of the ferry signaled its departure, I rushed to the top deck, eager to disguise my tears with wind and sea spray. I let my hair whip around my face as I watched a young family pose against the dazzling blue sky, joyously shouting, "Cheese!" in unison. The ferry lurched in the choppy waters, and as I grabbed the railing to steady myself, I wondered who I would choose to be when I started Sarah Lawrence College in two weeks—would I simply close this part of me off forever? I knew I loved those people and would always be devoted to them in some way. They were the family that raised me, and if I'd imagined them into something perfect so I could survive the last seven years, I was forever grateful for that. As I watched the Vineyard shrink on the horizon, I desperately hoped I'd made the right choice.

ACKNOWLEDGMENTS

THANK YOU TO THE PEOPLE WHO SAID THE THINGS THAT fueled me forward:

My literary agent, **Bill Clegg,** for encouraging me to "Stay in scene." These simple words had a profound impact on my approach to telling this story. I also liked it when you said, "Holy fucking shit," after reading an early chapter. I feel fortunate to have an agent with a writer's heart.

My editor, **Gillian Blake,** who said, "The thing about writing a book is it kind of has to be the only thing you are doing." I know that now! Thank you for your patience and unflinching insights. You taught me a lot.

James Marcus, who's been saying "You should really write a book" to me since the day we met. And then, "No, really, you should write a book" a million times after that. What would this process have been without your friendship, hilarity, and generous counsel? You are the glue.

Sam Green, you've been jabbing a finger at me for years—every time I told a good story—saying, "You gotta put that in the book, T!" It worked and I did.

And **José Muñoz,** who had been whisper-chanting "Tell about the Moonies" in my ear since 1986. I wish you were here to read this. I can't stand it when big things happen and you're not here.

Thank you to **Clare Burke,** who came back into my life just in time to say, "Hey—I saved all the letters and audiotapes you sent me in 1983 and 1984. Do you think they might be useful for your book?" The answer is yes, incredibly useful. What a gift.

Thank you to the people who read chapters or listened to me read them aloud:

Mary Harron, John Walsh, and **Ruby and Ella Walsh:** Amazingly, I have an entire family of people who each have their own sharp insights and have been willing to read and advise every step of the way.

Uba Akpom, Jane Clark, Mia Donovan, Clement Goldberg, B Peru, Kevin Shulman: Thank you for listening, reading, asking questions, especially the dreaded one: "How's the book going?" It made a world of difference to know you were with me.

Thank you to the people who provided all the spaces in which I wrote this book:

Jane Clark and Bob Tourtellotte, Emmett McCarthy, Sandi Dubowski, Matthew Kunzman, and the breathtaking High Rock studio at **Yaddo** and the sheer magic of Mixter studio at **MacDowell,** where I was invited to write.

Thank you to the people who took care of **Marbles the Dog** for me while I wrote: **Jane Clark, Isabelle Mecattaf, Kristina Feliciano, Mia Donovan, Nay Tabbara,** and **Clara Dubau.** I love Marbles more than anything but it is hard to write when she is staring at me.

Thank you to the communities that make me who I am: the one I grew up in, the LGBTQIA+ community that I belong to, the students I've taught, the artist residencies I've delighted in, the production teams I've worked with on many films. You remind me that I'm at my best when I am part of a bigger picture.

The hugest gratitude to my sister **Annalee Lanier** for spending countless hours on the phone, cheering me on, making me laugh, and knowing sometimes I just needed to talk about something else. I can't imagine my life without you in it.

Isabelle Mecattaf, my love, you were with me every second of this process and did everything and anything to support me as I went from sad to elated to overwhelmed to determined. When I had big ideas for projects or adventures for us, you gently said, "But, Bébé, don't you have a book to write?" Thank you for always making it the most important thing. I am a lucky lady.

ABOUT THE AUTHOR

GUINEVERE TURNER is an acclaimed screenwriter and director. She has written such films as *American Psycho*, *The Notorious Bettie Page*, and, most recently, *Charlie Says*, among others, and she wrote for and played a recurring role on Showtime's *The L Word*. An essay she wrote for *The New Yorker* is the inspiration for this memoir. She lives in Los Angeles.

ABOUT THE TYPE

This book was set in Caslon, a typeface first designed in 1722 by William Caslon (1692–1766). Its widespread use by most English printers in the early eighteenth century soon supplanted the Dutch typefaces that had formerly prevailed. The roman is considered a "workhorse" typeface due to its pleasant, open appearance, while the italic is exceedingly decorative.